Media, Journalism, and "Fake News"

Recent Titles in the
CONTEMPORARY WORLD ISSUES
Series

Books in the **Contemporary World Issues** series address vital issues in today's society such as genetic engineering, pollution, and biodiversity. Written by professional writers, scholars, and nonacademic experts, these books are authoritative, clearly written, up-to-date, and objective. They provide a good starting point for research by high school and college students, scholars, and general readers as well as by legislators, businesspeople, activists, and others.

Each book, carefully organized and easy to use, contains an overview of the subject, a detailed chronology, biographical sketches, facts and data and/or documents and other primary source material, a forum of authoritative perspective essays, annotated lists of print and nonprint resources, and an index.

Readers of books in the Contemporary World Issues series will find the information they need in order to have a better understanding of the social, political, environmental, and economic issues facing the world today.

Media, Journalism, and "Fake News"

A REFERENCE HANDBOOK

Amy M. Damico

ABC-CLIO®

An Imprint of ABC-CLIO, LLC
Santa Barbara, California • Denver, Colorado

Library of Congress Cataloging-in-Publication Data

Names: Damico, Amy M., author.
Title: Media, journalism, and "fake news" : a reference handbook / Amy M. Damico.
Description: Santa Barbara, CA : ABC-CLIO, 2019. | Series: Contemporary world issues | Includes bibliographical references and index.
Identifiers: LCCN 2019028640 (print) | LCCN 2019028641 (ebook) | ISBN 9781440864063 (hardback) | ISBN 9781440864070 (ebook)
Subjects: LCSH: Journalism—Technological innovations—United States. | Journalism—United States—History. | Broadcast journalism—United States—History.
Classification: LCC PN4784.T34 D44 2019 (print) | LCC PN4784.T34 (ebook) | DDC 071/.3—dc23
LC record available at https://lccn.loc.gov/2019028640
LC ebook record available at https://lccn.loc.gov/2019028641

ISBN: 978-1-4408-6406-3 (print)
978-1-4408-6407-0 (ebook)

23 22 21 20 19   1 2 3 4 5

This book is also available as an eBook.

ABC-CLIO
An Imprint of ABC-CLIO, LLC

ABC-CLIO, LLC
147 Castilian Drive
Santa Barbara, California 93117
www.abc-clio.com

This book is printed on acid-free paper (∞)

Manufactured in the United States of America

The amount of news and information in the United States is overwhelming. Newspapers, television shows, radio programs, blogs, and digital news sites provide news reports, investigative journalism, commentary, and opinion on a regular basis. Popular television talk shows discuss information of interest to viewers, while political talk radio presents perspectives on current happenings in government. Facebook news feeds, a variety of news aggregators, Twitter, and YouTube steadily recommend content to users, and some on social media and web platforms share their own ideas, perspectives, and reporting. In this information landscape, one must be skeptical. Accompanying the sheer amount of quality news is information that is sensationalized, misleading, or outright false. Heightened awareness of problematic information has, in part, contributed to perceptions among some that the news can't be trusted and that news reporting may be too partisan or otherwise biased. Additionally, while legacy and digital media provide more content than one can realistically engage with, quality reporting in communities across the United States is decreasing as more and more local newspapers close their doors or make other cutbacks. Some larger news organizations are also struggling to find sustainable business models that keep their news organizations running at a time when the subscription- and advertising-generated business model for news has been disrupted in the digital age that has marked changes in news production, distribution, and consumption as a result of the internet.

These specific challenges might be contemporary ones, but the news industry has always faced challenges and dealt with change. As the news and information industries in the United States developed, new technologies threatened, and ultimately disrupted, aspects of previously held status quos of news production and distribution. Different forms of reporting evolved. Problems of financially challenged news organizations, unreliable information, partisan news, and less-than-perfect reporting are part of the industry's history.

News and information that is reliable and verifiable is central to a functioning democracy. In the United States, journalists and others are relied on to report the news, share worthy information, investigate relevant issues, provide context for current events, and uncover truths those in power may want hidden. High-quality journalism provides people with the information needed to help understand the world, the nation, and regional and local communities. Those informed by a variety of reputable news sources are positioned to make informed choices that impact aspects of their lives. The system, however, is not perfect. News consumers, and particularly those who are in the early stages of integrating news as a part of their media diet, would benefit from cultivating a set of news and media literacy skills that empower them to critically assess content. An understanding of the basic history of news media and an awareness of contemporary issues in the production, distribution, and consumption of news and information in the United States can assist news consumers in better navigating the immense amount of information that is available every day.

The topic of media, journalism, and "fake news" in the United States covers a lot of ground. This book provides readers with a starting point in understanding aspects of this complex and ever-evolving topic. The following summaries of chapter content provide guidance on where to find particular information.

- *Chapter 1, Background and History*, offers a broad overview of the development of the news and information industries in the United States. Beginning with American newspapers and ending with the cultural integration of the internet, this chapter discusses key moments in the history of print journalism, broadcast radio and television, cable television, online news, and social media.

- *Chapter 2, Problems, Controversies, and Solutions*, presents some of the contemporary challenges and problems present in the current news and information environment. At a time when online news is pervasive, newspapers are closing, and large media companies are acquiring more power, new concerns about news as a key component of democracy are being articulated. The chapter also describes what research suggests about connections between a politically polarized culture and people's perceptions of, and use of, news media. The spread of various forms of unreliable information, aided by developing technologies, presents unique challenges to news consumers who are looking for accurate material; this chapter also describes different forms of what is sometimes broadly called "fake news." Finally, Chapter 2 summarizes some of the solutions experts are hoping will address the problems.

- *Chapter 3, Perspectives*, is comprised of nine essays written by professionals and scholars who offer their perspectives on specific components of this broad topic. Journalists provide their viewpoint on aspects of the news industry, offering readers a perspective that comes from their professional experiences, while scholars share their ideas informed by research on such topics as news media representation, social media bots, and the need for media and news literacy.

- *Chapter 4, Profiles*, focuses on highlighting some of the many individuals and organizations that provided and currently provide news and information to citizens. Many of these figures and organizations changed the direction of, or contributed to, the development of various forms of news reporting or information dissemination in the United States. Others are notable for the nature of their work—work that consumers engage with to learn about issues in their communities, politics, areas of human interest, and national and international news.

- *Chapter 5, Data and Documents*, provides additional material that supports some of the topics discussed elsewhere in the book. The Data section of the chapter presents summaries of relevant research findings, while the Documents section compiles excerpts of relevant primary texts that provide the reader with further information on the topic.

- *Chapter 6, Resources*, offers an annotated list of sources that may help those interested in finding out more about aspects of this topic. This chapter also includes a list of tools one can use to evaluate information.

- *Chapter 7, Chronology*, presents a short chronological list of some dates and events that inform the history of news and information in the United States.

The book concludes with a succinct glossary of relevant terms for reader reference as well as a comprehensive index.

Media, Journalism, and "Fake News"

Introduction: What Is News?

Where do you get your news and information? Do you look online? Listen to the radio? Read a newspaper? Watch television? Do you consult multiple sources? How do you evaluate the accuracy of information? What is news anyway?

For a story to be newsworthy, it needs to provide new information that is of interest to an audience. There are several news "values" that journalists and scholars consider when evaluating whether a story is news. Edd Applegate (2011) states that news addresses conflict, reports on progress and disasters in society, summarizes consequences of actions or events, focuses on prominent people, identifies novel or unusual events, often reports on sex scandals, and considers the proximity of the news content to its audience (47–48). W. Lance Bennett (2016) defines news as "*(a) the reporting of actions and events (b) over a growing variety of publicly accessible media (c) by journalism organizations and an expanding spectrum of other content providers, including ordinary citizens*" (25; italics in original). The American Press Institute (2018a) defines journalism as "the activity of gathering, assessing, creating, and presenting news and information"

This political cartoon highlights the trend of "yellow journalism," sensationalized and often false reporting, that was present during the late 1800s as a tactic to sell newspapers. The newspaper owner depicted in the image is possibly newspaper owner Joseph Pulitzer. Pulitzer competed with William Randolph Hearst, another newspaper baron, to sell the most papers. (Library of Congress) and stipulates that journalism is different from other forms of information because its "value flows from its purpose, to provide people with verified information they can use to make better decisions, and its practices, the most important of which is a systematic process—a discipline of verification—that journalists use to find not just the facts, but also the 'truth about the facts.'" Another definition of journalism reads: "Journalism is the activity of collecting, presenting, interpreting or commenting on the news for some portion of the public" (Stephens 2014, xiii).

Though there are some shared general understandings of what news and journalism are, the way information is shared is not uniform. Different news outlets may prioritize different stories or report on similar events using different angles. News gatekeepers, people who make decisions around what stories are published or produced, also determine how much prominence a report gets. Different news outlets cater to different audiences and adjust their reporting accordingly. The internet has provided opportunities for the expansion of news reporting and has raised new versions of challenges that have always been present, such as citizens' need to identify information that may not be appropriately researched or accurate.

Why is high-quality news important? One of the fundamental ideologies in the United States is that an independent free press functions as a mechanism that holds people and institutions in power accountable. In a democracy, as the ideology suggests, access to high-quality, accurate information empowers citizens to understand local, national, and international issues and events. High-quality news provides people with the information needed to inform their vote and engage as citizens. Independent reporting helps explain complicated topics and events to the public using understandable language while providing appropriate context. While the idea that a democracy is best supported by embracing a free press is clear, the system is not perfect. News reports are influential, and it is especially important for news consumers to critically think about the information they are presented with.

The history of news and information in the United States is a story of the development of the various media forms that bring news to others. It's also a story of the evolution of journalism as a profession, various genres of news media, and the shifting nature of the audience from consumers of news to consumers and creators of news. This history is complicated and rich with detail, often revealing issues that are similar to contemporary concerns. As Brooke Gladstone (2011) states, "Everything we hate about the media today was present at its creation: its corrupt or craven practitioners, its easy manipulation by the powerful, its capacity for propagating lies, its penchant for amplifying rage. Also present was everything we admire—and require—from the media: factual information, penetrating analysis, probing investigation, truth spoken to power" (20).

This chapter provides a broad overview of the history of news and information in the United States. It describes some key moments in the history of American journalism and describes the development of some popular media that, while are not necessarily considered traditional forms of journalism, provide information to consumers. It also briefly summarizes how elements of the information landscape have been informed by changes in technology, reporting, and challenges to the status quo.

The Development of the Press and the American Revolution

Historian Frank Luther Mott (1962) explains that although the first printing press was set up in the colonies in 1638 in Cambridge, Massachusetts, newspapers did not become part of colonial culture, a culture initially preoccupied with establishing life in the New World, for more than fifty years. Before newspapers, the colonists got their news from personal letters, newsletters written by professional writers that were systematically circulated through the colonies, and English newspapers brought over by ship. Eventually, the colonist press began to print bits of news in the form of broadsides—notices printed on a single sheet of paper that were sold on the street. The early governmental view of the printing press in many countries was that it was "dangerous" because the ability to share information via distributed papers was perceived as a threat to current autocratic government control (6). As a result, publishers had to adhere to strict licensing and censorship rules and were also cognizant of their potential loss of business if they offended government or other officials who were sensitive to any printed criticism.

The first American newspaper, *Publick Occurrences Both Forreign and Domestick*, was launched by Benjamin Harris on September 25, 1690, but only lasted one issue. Four days after it was published, officials banned the paper because they claimed that Harris did not have a license and were upset with the paper's critique of Indians and reporting on the personal life of the king of France (Stephens 1988). The next attempt at publishing a newspaper, however, was successful; the *Boston News-Letter* lasted seventy-two years. The weekly paper reported on the politics found in London newspapers and "also included news of the arrival of ships, and even reports on fires, accidents, court cases and acts of piracy" (Stephens 1988, 184).

Over time, other colonial newspapers developed, and writers, to the dismay of officials, began to use the press as a vehicle for expressing discontent. One key court case resulted in a shift in the function of the press. In 1735, John Peter Zenger of the *New-York Weekly Journal* was arrested and jailed for printing criticism of the corrupt governor William Cosby. During his trial for seditious libel, Zenger's lawyer helped persuade the jury that newspapers could criticize government leaders, provided the criticism was true. This landmark case resulted in newspaper publishers feeling more freedom to print honest criticism of those in power (Stephens 1988).

It became evident that newspaper content could shape public opinion. During this political period in colonial journalism, articles in newspapers challenged governmental actions, coinciding with the colonists' growing discontent with English rule (Mott 1962). The division among those living in the colonies was reflected in numerous newspapers. On the one hand, there were newspapers that reflected the views of the colonists who were resistant to the English government, called Patriots. For example, the *Gazette*, a high-circulating Boston, Massachusetts, paper, continually published "the kind of political articles which eventually prepared the minds of the people for the ideas of independence" (Mott 1962, 75). Other papers presented the Tory point of view, the view of the English government, or tried to remain neutral. As momentum was gaining toward the American Revolution, those living in the colonies gravitated toward the press that reflected their point of view. Colonial newspapers featured essays by writer activists such as John Adams, Samuel Adams, and John Hancock—essays that helped shape public opinion in support of the eventual American Revolution (Hillstrom 2010). Not all of these writers adhered to what today would be considered ethical journalistic practices; they would sometimes exaggerate viewpoints and lie. For example, revolutionary leaders wrote fake accounts of British military actions in order to solidify support for the revolution (Gladstone 2011; Soll 2016). Mitchell Stephens (1988) points out that "the true power of this press was its ability to enfranchise and unify the Americans. . . . The role of the news in the American Revolution is best understood not as an uncharacteristic anti-authoritarian outburst but as an entirely characteristic exercise in animating and binding a new society, in producing 'a junction' of a majority of the American people" (190).

After the revolution, the new government recognized how important it was, in a democracy, for the press to operate free of political interference. The Bill of Rights, passed on December 15, 1791, contains the first ten amendments to the U.S. Constitution. The First Amendment reads, "Congress shall make no law respecting an establishment of religion, or prohibiting the free exercise thereof; or abridging the freedom of speech, or of the press; or the right of the people peaceably to assemble, and to petition the Government for a redress of grievances." Journalist and historian Christopher Daly (2012) summarizes what this law means in regard to democracy by stating, "The press is empowered by the First Amendment to discover facts and to articulate arguments not for its own benefit but for the benefit of the public as a whole. In order for them to govern themselves, the people must have reliable information. The press freedom asserted in the First Amendment is therefore a trust placed in the press on behalf of the broader society. The rights expressed in it belong to all Americans" (46).

After the passage of the Bill of Rights, newspaper content continued to be produced along political lines. Different political parties would financially support newspapers, and newspaper reporting reflected the owners' political positions, a fact readers were aware of (Bennett 2016). These various practices could inspire debate, but there was also an element of corruption in the news business, and personal attacks on individuals were common (Bennett 2016; Mott 1962). Even when newspaper content was not inflammatory, the press remained partisan. When looking at these texts through today's ideas about journalism and news reporting, scholars Robert McChesney and John Nichols (2005) suggest that although there were problems with partisan press–oriented reporting, such news could "draw people into public life" because it tended to "contextualize political issues so that citizens could recognize seemingly random events as part of a coherent pattern."

Changes in News Reporting

In the early 1800s, cultural changes resulted in a shift in the newspaper business. An increase in literacy and the new ability for papers to be mass produced on cheaper paper changed both the interest in, and production of, newspapers. The invention of the cylinder press allowed for fifteen hundred newspapers to be printed per hour, a huge increase over the ability to print a few hundred papers overnight (Hillstrom 2010). Prior to these developments, people subscribed to newspapers, paying ten to twelve dollars a year for a six-cent paper (Schudson 1978). The new technology prompted the establishment of what is called the penny press, where large numbers of papers were printed and sold on the street for a penny each. The amount of newspapers increased; there were one thousand papers being published in 1830; three thousand were published by 1860 (Hillstrom 2010). Additionally, newspaper editors incorporated a new type of news reporting, an attention-grabbing style inclusive of local and human interest stories that prompted readers to buy a paper every day (Daly 2012). Some of these stories were fake, including stories of life on the moon in the "Great Moon Hoax" of 1835, a story that was written as satire but believed to be true, and reports of slave uprisings that resulted in violent actions against African Americans ("The Great Moon Hoax" n.d.; Soll 2016).

According to Michael Schudson (1978), the emergence of the penny press in 1833 was significant for several reasons. The circulation of the papers was high because newsboys sold papers on the streets, resulting in more egalitarian news consumption. The penny press also had a hand in establishing the modern concept that news could be relevant to all readers. For example, the *New York Herald*, founded by James Bennett, included reporting on sports, the arts, finance, city life, crime, high society, and foreign affairs, ultimately influencing the direction journalistic reporting would take (Mott 1962). The popularity of penny papers resulted in a shift in the industry. Schudson (1978) observes that "until the 1830s, a newspaper provided a service to political parties and men of commerce; with the penny press a newspaper sold a product to general readership and sold the readership to advertisers" (25). The penny press's philosophy was to maintain political independence by not associating with political parties and to let the reader decide how to evaluate newspaper content. Whereas the partisan press discussed issues from their sponsors' political perspective, the penny papers "began laying the groundwork for the claim that would become the hallmark of the American mass media, the principle that eventually came to be known as objectivity" (Daly 2012, 64).

In addition to the penny press, other developments during the mid-1800s contributed to the evolution of news production and distribution. In 1846, as a response to a country that was growing in population and in territory expansion, the Associated Press was formed by a group of reporters who agreed to share stories with its members in order to more economically and efficiently report on and distribute news to the nation. The development of this news agency inherently prompted writers to remove political perspectives from their reporting so that all stories would be printed in any newspaper, regardless of the paper's political affiliation (Bennett 2016). By 1861, telegraph technology was being used to connect the nation through a series of wires, allowing for real-time communication throughout the country, a transformative practice that informed the development of the telephone, fax machine, and internet (Associated Press 2011). The process of sending news reports over the wires contributed to the development of the who, what, when, where, and why of journalism reporting because the telegraph technology required the simple transmission of ideas; after these essentials were telegraphed, receivers could transform content into news reports (Bennett 2016). Historians trace the "inverted pyramid" style of reporting to this time period as well. In this story structure, the news report begins by sharing the most important story elements and ends with information that is not as essential. Although this style of reporting is still used today, it is controversial given the emphasis on a brief summary of facts rather than a story that places the facts in a necessary context (Scanlon 2003). Though journalism has evolved to encompass different reporting styles, such as interpretive journalism, literary journalism, and advocacy journalism, news wire services, such as the Associated Press and Reuters, remain a central component in news dissemination.

Although historically the dominant audience for mainstream newspapers was typically the colonists' descendants, early newspapers also targeted other demographic groups. Many black press publications, such as *Freedom's Journal* and *North Star* (later named *Frederick Douglass' Paper*), addressed issues related to black rights while also condemning slavery, lynching, and the Ku Klux Klan (Mott 1962). The first Native American newspaper, the *Cherokee Phoenix*, was founded to keep the tribe informed and united as they faced pressure to move west (Pulley 2017). Other newspapers were produced by and for other demographic groups. Several hundred papers were published in different languages, offering content of specific interest to their reader. Numerous groups who immigrated to the United States founded, produced, and distributed newspapers, referred to now as the "ethnic press," for their respective ethnic groups. Thousands of papers were started after the Civil War; the peak of the ethnic press was around 1907, when over one thousand presses were operating (Rhodes 2010). These papers addressed aspects of immigration and reported on news from the readers' home country and current local community (Miller 1987). Papers also "expressed a group's values, heritage and changing sense of identity" and "socialized its readers to the United States as it educated them and became itself a tool of adjustment" (Miller 1987, xiv). Today newspapers that target black Americans, Latinos, Asians, Native Americans, and many other ethnic groups focus on stories that the mainstream media does not prioritize while also offering alternative narratives to dominant news reporting.

In addition to newspapers, citizens gathered information from magazines, periodicals that were distributed throughout the country, rather than within a specific region like newspapers. Magazines had an unsuccessful beginning in the mid-1700s, but by the mid-nineteenth century, the production of magazines increased and publications such as the *Saturday Evening Post, Godey's Lady's Book, Harper's Weekly*, and many others became popular. Magazines were created to appeal to particular interest groups—some publications focused on agriculture, others on science, and others on morality (Peterson 1964). As the magazine industry expanded, so did the foci of the different publications. While magazines before the Civil War, which took place between 1861 and 1865, did not typically report the news, they are credited with the discussion of social issues such as the abolition of slavery, women's right to vote, and labor issues (Daly 2012; Peterson 1964).

Shaping Public Opinion

As the newspaper business expanded, so did its influence on the public. Though newspaper reporting was less likely to be politically partisan than it was in earlier times, editorial pages featured powerfully written perspectives that played a role in shaping public opinion. For example, in his high-quality newspaper the *New York Tribune*, which began in 1841, influential publisher Horace Greeley penned numerous editorials about nutrition, pollution, and the elimination of slavery (Hillstrom 2010). News reporting on the Civil War (1861–1865), combined with images distributed by Civil War photographers, informed the public of the gruesome nature of the conflict and prompted calls to end the war (Trescott 2010). After the war, new types of reporting continued to develop. Joseph Pulitzer hired Nellie Bly, an undercover reporter who pretended to be insane to research and document what was revealed to be horrible treatment at New York City mental hospitals (Hillstrom 2010). Pulitzer focused his paper, the *New York World*, on political reporting as well; he assigned journalists to exclusively cover politicians in Washington, DC, and also advanced a "story model" of journalism, reporting that emerged from human experiences and drama (Daly 2012; Hillstrom 2010). Pulitzer also transformed the *New York World* to be comprised of sensational news, "crusading, progressive politics," "attention grabbing campaigns," and "aggressive, intelligent news coverage" (Stephens 1988, 209). This style, called "new journalism," was financially successful and was soon imitated by other publications. Most notably, William Randolph Hearst purchased the *New York Morning Journal* in 1892 to compete with Pulitzer and transformed it into a sensational newspaper that emphasized shocking and scandalous stories (Hillstrom 2010).

This sensational reporting became known as "yellow journalism," a name derived from a popular comic character dressed in yellow called "The Yellow Kid" that appeared in papers that published sensational news stories, referred to as the yellow press. Although some yellow journalism is credited with exposing problems in society, the methods used in this kind of reporting are criticized for the advancement of sensationalized and often inaccurate information that may have unfairly influenced the public (Gladstone 2011). The power of yellow journalism is pointed to analyses of reporting that preceded the Spanish-American War, a war that historians call the first press-driven war because, while the extent of it is hard to measure, the pervasive nature of yellow journalism and the ongoing competition between Pulitzer and Hearst to publish stories that implicitly called for military intervention may have contributed to the public support of the Spanish-American War in 1898 (Great Projects Film Company 1999). Hearst, in particular, understood that a war would increase sales of his newspapers, and he employed numerous reporters to cover the situation (Daly 2012). Some say he published fabricated inflammatory drawings of Cuban officials (Soll 2016). At the same time, Hearst was reportedly appalled by the terrible living conditions Cuban citizens were enduring, so his choice to focus reporting on these events highlights how the lines between journalism's quest for profit and providing information as a public service are blurred (Gladstone 2011).

The Establishment of Professional Journalism

Given the pervasiveness of sensational newspapers, critics of this type of reporting increased. It had become clear that such reporting was often distorted, prejudicial, partisan, and extreme, and journalists were worried about their reputations considering their beliefs in the role high-quality news plays in a democracy (McChesney and Nichols 2005; Winfield 2008). The yellow press was marketed toward a working-class demographic who engaged with the sensationalism as a form of "escape," while the more educated "affluent middle class" was receptive to news that was framed as "objective, nonpartisan and tasteful" (Bennett 2016, 160). These distinctions in news audiences prompted some publications to establish themselves as providing an alternative to sensational reporting. For example, the *New York Times* advanced an "information model" of news that stood in contrast to the factual Associated Press reporting and the yellow press and appealed to the economically advantaged and educated New York readers (Schudson 1978). Mary Baker Eddy started an alternative paper, the *Christian Science Monitor*, which soon became respected for its high-quality reporting (Winfield 2008). A shift toward professionalizing journalism also occurred. Joseph Pulitzer called for the establishment of professional schools of journalism, an explicit acknowledgment that some of his paper's yellow journalism was problematic, and by 1908, the University of Missouri established the first school of journalism in the United States (Winfield 2008).

In practice, lines between newspaper writers and editors and newspaper owners were drawn to avoid reporting that was influenced by the owners' interests. This allowed editors and reporters to independently report the news (McChesney and Nichols 2005). Reporting adhered to a set of ethical standards that asked journalists to responsibly engage in accurate, fair, and honest reporting that provided a public service (Winfield 2008). One of the key standards that emerged in the process of professionalizing journalism was the prioritization of the ideal of objectivity in news reporting.

Schudson (1978) traces the history of the embrace of objectivity to the early 1900s when the integration of public relations into news reporting and the World War I propaganda campaign impacted news writers and consumers. First, the development of the public relations profession resulted in press agents' writing informing and inspiring news stories, making it difficult for readers to determine the difference between agents' information and reporters' information. Second, as many journalists were part of the World War I propaganda campaign, they, and their readers, eventually reflected on how information about the war was constructed to achieve a favorable response. One result of this, writes Schudson, was the establishment of "specialization," whereby reporters knowledgeable on various topics became more critical of press agents' information and wrote stories accordingly. Another result was the popularization of newspaper column writing, an approach taken by, for example, the influential journalist Walter Lippmann, where aspects of the news that occurred in an increasingly more complicated world were put in context, explained, and analyzed (Whitman 1974). Because interpretive reporting and column writing were not available vehicles for all journalists to use as a way to present information, the profession needed a framework that would demonstrate the seriousness and reliability of the journalistic work being done. According to Schudson, "This is what the notion of 'objectivity,' as it was elaborated in the twenties and thirties, tried to provide" (151).

As journalism as a profession developed, the principle of objectivity became a fundamental part of its practice. There are general guidelines many journalists are given in order to achieve objectivity. Journalists are often required to remain politically neutral when examining all sides of an issue, adhere to ideals of decency, engage in truthful reporting by focusing on facts attributed to reputable sources or observations, avoid any suggestion of bias, and submit work to an editor who will confirm that these standards are met (Bennett 2016, 161–162).

While few disagree that journalists should adhere to a set of professional principles, the concept of objectivity has a long history of being met with skepticism. Some journalists believe that attaining objectivity is an impossible task and attempting to write objectively can strip reporting of important context (Applegate 2011). Others submit that journalism can never reach the ideal of objectivity because the entire process of putting together a news report relies on making choices about what angle to use and what sources to rely on (Bennett 2016). Journalism professor Jay Rosen (2010) dismisses the idea of objectivity—what he calls "The View from Nowhere," a phrase used by a philosopher who claims people are able to step back from their current position to gain an "enlarged understanding" of a situation. Rosen argues that journalists cannot, and should not, dismiss their own positions given that they come from "digging, reporting, verification and mastering a beat" but should be transparent in disclosing where information is coming from. Additionally, as so-called objective reporting relies on official sources, and official sources offer information that presents a topic in the way they want the public to understand it, the outcome may result in reporting that favors the "official" view on the story, which may or may not be accurate (Bennett 2016; Schudson 1978). Finally, sometimes when journalists feel pressured to ensure that their reporting is objective, they may include perspectives from groups or spokespeople who are advancing information that is widely disputed, leading to what is called "false balance" (Bennett 2016, 178). The Society of Professional Journalists (SPJ), a prominent national organization, advances a code of ethics that addresses guidelines for professional practice under categories such as "seek truth and report it," "minimize harm," "act independently," and "be accountable and transparent" (SPJ 2014). In the latest revision of the code of ethics, the word "objectivity" is no longer present, an implicit acknowledgment of the difficulties in achieving such a principle (Bennett 2016).

Investigative Journalism

The investigative journalism tradition includes work that exposes hidden truths or identifies "social conditions or patterns of institutional conduct" (Shapiro 2003, xv). Examples of investigative journalism date back to before the American Revolution and include reports on such topics as the slave trade and political corruption (Shapiro 2003). The early twentieth-century "muckraking era" is a touch point in investigative journalism history. The muckraking movement began as a response to the poor working and living conditions many working-class Americans and immigrants endured after the Industrial Revolution.

During this time, journalists, now called "muckrakers," a reference to a literary character who rakes dirt, wrote well-researched stories about such societal problems as poor working conditions, child labor, political corruption, and the cutthroat business practices employed by wealthy business owners. *McClure's Magazine* is considered the "flagship magazine of the muckraking movement," largely because of the January 1903 issue's publication of "three explosive investigative reports" that many consider a key moment in American journalism history (Hillstrom 2010, 121). The articles exposed ruthless business practices at Standard Oil (John D. Rockefeller's oil company), government corruption in six U.S. cities, and illegal behavior in the Pennsylvania coalfields (Hume 2008). The detailed facts investigative journalists exposed through their work helped to increase public support for government intervention in reforming these problematic institutional practices (Hillstrom 2010).

This era of journalism lasted from the end of the nineteenth century to about 1914. Though the muckraking era "ended" in historical terms, journalism historians acknowledge muckrakers' significant contributions to the investigative journalism tradition because their rich, detailed reports relied heavily on facts, often prompting advocacy for social reform (Hume 2008). Seen as the "antidote" to yellow journalism, many note the influence of the early twentieth-century muckrakers on contemporary investigative reporting (Hume 2008, 274).

Investigative journalism remains central to journalism practice today, and investigative stories are authored by journalists working in print, radio, television, and digital environments. Throughout the twentieth century, journalists exposed horrific conditions on Indian reservations, in juvenile jails, and in meat-packing facilities and had reported on mining disasters and aspects of war and suffering (Shapiro 2003). Some writers employed investigative techniques to publish books and articles that raised citizen awareness about potentially devastating situations ranging from Rachel Carson's reports on pesticides' impact on the environment to Ralph Nader's examinations of car safety. Other notable works of investigative journalism include Seymour Hersh's documentation of the Vietnam War's My Lai massacre, an attack U.S. soldiers carried out on an estimated five hundred Vietnamese civilians, and the *New York Times*' reporting on the presence of the Pentagon Papers, secret military documents that revealed that the American people had been misled about the Vietnam War. A series of investigative reports by Bob Woodward and Carl Bernstein, now known simply as "Watergate," exposed connections between a break-in at the Democratic National Committee headquarters at the Watergate Hotel and President Nixon's administration. Investigative journalism has continued to inform the public and raise awareness on a range of topics including the tobacco industry, the dangers of drugs and chemicals, examinations of sexual misconduct in Congress, reports on the growth of the intelligence community after the September 11, 2001, terrorist attacks, the exposure of the National Security Agency's (NSA) surveillance program that targeted American citizens and international officials, and many, many others (Dews and Young 2014; Lewis 2017).

Newsmagazines

Another landmark in the history of journalism was the establishment of the weekly newsmagazine. Newsmagazines were being published in the nineteenth century. For example, the weekly magazine *Pathfinder* consisted of rewritten news articles from other publications and a number of entertainment feature articles (Peterson 1964). However, it is *Time Magazine* that is credited with having the most cultural influence (Daly 2012; Peterson 1964). *Time*, a weekly magazine that compiled the news of the week and, similar to *Pathfinder*, included stories about art and culture, was first published on March 3, 1923, by creators Henry (Harry) Luce and Briton Hadden (Peterson 1964). Initially *Time* provided concise summaries of the news, largely taken from daily newspapers, but as the publication developed, a narrative form was used to report the news, a departure from the current style of newspaper writing (Peterson 1964).

Time writers did not initially adhere to the principles of balanced reporting and interpreted the news from their own purview, a choice that did not impact their success (Daly 2012). Readers enjoyed the way the weekly publication presented and packaged the news, and competitors such as *U.S. News* (later *U.S. News and World Report*) and *Newsweek* emerged in 1933. All of these newsmagazines addressed the challenge of keeping up with the proliferation of daily news available in the newspapers (Peterson 1964). Though critics of the newsmagazines pointed out that news was framed as entertainment, that there was a conservative bias in reporting, and that magazines did not always distinguish between facts and perspectives, these publications prospered (Peterson 1964). Time, Inc. as a company grew, launching other successful magazines such as *Fortune* in 1930 and *Life* magazine in 1936. *Life* was known for its "pictorial journalism" and used high-quality photographs to convey feelings of the accompanying articles (Peterson 1964, 348). Through pictures and accompanying text, *Life* covered World War II, presented topical features, and profiled both famous and average people, showing readers what "life" looked like (Peterson 1964).

Initially smaller in scale, but also influential as a newsmagazine, was the *New Yorker*, launched in 1925 and described by its founder Harold Ross as a magazine "published for a metropolitan audience" that was "sophisticated" and "interpretive" and whose "integrity will be above suspicion" (Peterson 1964, 248). The *New Yorker's* high reporting standards, sometimes provocative content, and biographies influenced journalistic reporting despite its localized, smaller circulation (Peterson 1964). The *New Yorker* contributed to the development of journalism by extending the focus of in-depth reporting "far beyond standard categories of crime and courts, politics and sports" (Daly 2012, 202).

While *Time, Life,* and the *New Yorker* prompted the eventual launch of other journalistic publications because of their success, Peterson (1964) points out that several magazines and their publishers were also leaders in the mass dissemination of information in American culture. Though it did not deal with current news, the popular *Reader's Digest* succeeded by condensing and sharing articles of interest in an easy-to-read format. McFadden Publications produced magazines that provided information about healthy living and created popular magazines featuring sensational content. The magazine industry demonstrated that if information was packaged appropriately, the industry could appeal to different types of consumers via a variety of publications.

As was the case with newspapers, the magazine industry featured publications that targeted different demographic groups of readers. One of the most successful black American publishers was John H. Johnson, the founder of Johnson Publishing. He launched three successful publications for black readers: *Negro Digest* in 1942 (a magazine similar to *Reader's Digest*), *Ebony* in 1945 (similar to *Life*), and *Jet* in 1951, a magazine that reported news about black Americans in politics, sports, and entertainment. These magazines presented a more complete picture of black experiences and culture in the United States, inherently challenging dominant narratives present in "white" publications (Daly 2012; Martin 2005). Today, multiple news and general-interest magazines—some national, others regional—are published for the variety of racial and ethnic demographic groups living in the United States.

Radio News Broadcasting

At the beginning of the twentieth century, Americans began to get their news from another developing medium: radio. The discovery of electromagnetic waves and eventual development of radio technology had a profound effect on the development of broadcast journalism, as well as on the culture as a whole. In its early days, a mix of companies, nonprofit entities, and individuals were operating radio stations, but the popularity of this practice led to problems with reception because station signals were interfering with one another (Daly 2012). To address these issues, the U.S. government intervened and eventually passed the Radio Act of 1927, legislation that ultimately shaped future broadcast policy. The act stipulated that airwaves were a public resource and therefore publicly owned, but the government, through its newly established Federal Radio Commission (FRC), could grant station licenses (Barkin 2003). The act also established that while radio content was protected by the First Amendment, obscene language was banned and stations had to operate in the "public interest, convenience and necessity," two stipulations that were not clearly defined (Barkin 2003; Daly 2012).

Journalism historian Daly (2012) points out that the government catered to the commercial radio operators who lobbied the government to craft rules that favored them. Under the Radio Act, radio operators had to periodically reapply for their licenses, and the FRC prioritized giving licenses to those who could generate the clearest signals, operate the most hours, and be easily trained in Washington, DC, on the newest rules. Given that companies had the resources to buy the best equipment, hire staff, and pay for travel, the rules favored granting licenses to commercial stations. Three years after the act was passed, nonprofit radio stations decreased from two hundred to sixty-five (Daly 2012, 211).

The American decision to promote the commercialization of radio differed from other countries where a governmental oversight of radio development prioritized public service, as was the case with the British Broadcasting Company, or BBC (McChesney 1999). In the United States, radio became primarily a commercial medium financed by program sponsorship and advertising (Barkin 2003). A few years later, the Communications Act of 1934 replicated the legislative template established by the Radio Act of 1927, resulting in further support of the commercialization of other developing media forms (Daly 2012). This act established the Federal Communications Commission (FCC), which remains in place today, as a replacement for the FRC. The FCC was founded as a bipartisan group of commissioners who would act as regulators of phone, television, and other electronic media (Barkin 2003).

As radio sales increased, radio news and other programming became part of many American lives. Individual radio stations connected with one another to form networks, eventually leading to the establishment of the National Broadcasting Company (NBC), the Columbia Broadcasting System (CBS), and the American Broadcasting Company (ABC) (Barkin 2003). Unlike printed news, radio had the ability to immediately report news as soon as it happened. Before radio, newspapers would produce "extras"—newspaper supplements that covered breaking news after the official newspaper had been printed. Radio altered the consumer's reliance on these news sources; "people didn't run out to the street for the news, they tuned their dials and they listened" (Douglas 2004, 161). Initially radio news reporters relied on newspapers and newsroom wire services for broadcast content often using, with their permission, their copy (Stephens 1988, 277). Eventually, some newspaper journalists transitioned to become radio journalists, and the formally complex language used to deliver the news shifted to accommodate for a listening, rather than reading, audience. As Stephens (1988) points out, "The modern newswriting style—short sentences, simple, clear, concise wordings—was honed on the radio" (277).

Susan Douglas (2004) points out that broadcast journalism was "invented" during this time. She documents that several, now familiar and potentially problematic, broadcasting characteristics emerged as the form developed: radio news coverage could be sensational, news commentators could be controversial and/or excessively partisan in their opinions, the lines between news and entertainment were often blurred, and some radio commentators advanced information that was made up or incorrect. Additionally, concerns about news monopolies began to emerge; by 1940, one-third of radio stations were owned by newspapers despite a current FCC investigation into such monopolies. Radio news organizations wrestled with the concept of reporting objectively, especially given the somewhat informal, and personal, type of communication the broadcast allowed for. Radio news reporters were warned against providing their own opinions or expressing emotion when reporting, guidelines that were not always adhered to (Douglas 2004).

But the main development of broadcast journalism was, perhaps, connected to the coverage of the events that preceded World War II and World War II itself. Although the public attended movie shows each week where elements of World War II were shown via newsreels, and although newspapers and magazines published articles and multiple war photographs, Douglas (2004) argues that the public's daily engagement with news about World War II was through listening to it on the radio and suggests the fact that World War II was a "radio war" is not represented well enough in history. During World War II, radio journalists reported on the war, bringing the conflict into American homes by sharing audio from the reporting scenes and using sound effects to increase engagement (Douglas 2004; Stephens 1988). Additionally, radio news reporters explained content to the listening audience, often acting as educators and analysts. One popular voice belonged to Edward R. Murrow, now an iconic figure in journalism. Murrow was a CBS reporter who reported on World War II from Europe. His voice and style of reporting were embraced by listeners, and as a result of his strong work and popularity, Murrow was permitted to hire a team of foreign correspondents who contributed to expansive war reporting (Barkin 2003). Central to Murrow's style was his ability to engage the public in understanding the war's trajectory (Daly 2012). Radio news reporting continued after the war, but ultimately the development of television broadcasting changed the dominance news radio had in the culture.

Network Television News Programming

Technological developments that informed the eventual achievement of television broadcasting were taking place as early as the 1920s, and by 1941, CBS was airing two short newscasts a day (Stephens 1988). World War II stalled television development, but the radio networks continued to develop television technology after the war, and by the 1950s, television as a medium and television news as a source of information became part of the American culture. Television news began as a mash-up of a radio news–oriented style of reporting delivered by newscasters—later called "talking heads"—and previously captured newsreel footage (Stephens 1988). Viewers responded positively to the ability to view events, actions, and places; newsreels were soon replaced by "film reports," and the power of the visual medium became established (Stephens 1988, 282). Edward Murrow and Fred Friendly's *See It Now* documentary series is an early example of television journalism; Murrow and Friendly effectively used the medium of television to captivate audiences' interests in a range of stories from how soldiers were faring during the Korean War to the lives of coal miners in the United States (Barkin 2003). Regularly scheduled television news programs developed in the 1950s and 1960s, and the daily national network newscast became a staple in television programming. Many notable television journalists began their long-running careers during this time, including Walter Cronkite, Chet Huntley, and David Brinkley. During the "network era" of television, when the three television net-works were dominant, television news anchors were seen as authority figures. Barbara Walters became the first woman to coanchor the network news in 1976, but by and large, network anchors were men. Other network news anchors who took on the role through the twentieth century include John Chancel-lor, Harry Reasoner, Tom Brokaw, Peter Jennings, Dan Rather, and Connie Chung.

During the network era, television news consistently dem-onstrated the power of the visual image. Many point to the Richard Nixon and John F. Kennedy presidential candidate debate in 1960 as early evidence of the persuasive impact of the television visual, as viewers were reportedly swayed by Ken-nedy's telegenic presence during the debate (Daly 2012). Tele-vision also possesses the power to unify Americans; constant, commercial-free television news coverage of President Ken-nedy's assassination and aftermath in 1963 is often noted as an early example of how television was perceived as a medium that could bring the country together (Barkin 2003). Since then many, many televised events, from the moon landing to the collapse of the Berlin Wall to the September 11 terrorist attacks, have facilitated shared national viewing experiences.

Whereas World War II was central to the development of radio news broadcasting, the Vietnam War, referred to as the first television war, illustrated the power of television report-ing. In one often-cited example, reporter Morley Safer's 1965 on-the-ground reporting in Cam Ne, Vietnam, showed the viewing audience actions taken by the U.S. Marines to destroy local homes despite a lack of resistance by the Vietnam people (Stephens 1988). President Johnson complained about the news report, CBS executives were unhappy, and, as a result, the station aired more stories about the war that were positive (Stephens 1988). At other times, television brought grim war footage into American homes. In general, though, images from the Vietnam War were not inflammatory, and it wasn't until the late 1960s that the television reporting on the war shifted in tone, reflecting some of the cultural opposition to a conflict that was not perceived as winnable (Hallin 2004).

Stephens (1988) points out that although television news brought information and often captivating images into the homes of Americans, news content was distilled and packaged in ways that favored sound bites and attractive, articulate people over in-depth reporting. Although in recent years, local television news has engaged in more investigative reporting, local newscasts often focus on crime and allocate large portions of the newscast to weather, sports, and entertainment (Rundlet and Gill 2018). As a result, newspaper content developed to provide more analysis, depth, and additional features that television news didn't always offer (Stephens 1988). Over time, however, the metropolitan newspaper industry struggled economically as they lost advertising revenue to television (Downie and Schudson 2009). At the same time, the packaged television newscast also influenced the newspaper form, most notably with the development of *USA Today*, a newspaper known for its color and visual style that evoke the look and feel of television news. *USA Today* became successful and influenced the aesthetic of many smaller papers (Daly 2012).

The FCC requirement that broadcasters serve the public interest applies to television broadcasting as well as radio. Television executives viewed their news programming as fulfilling this mandate, and they did not initially expect their news programming to make a profit for the station (Daly 2012). This changed when the CBS weekly newsmagazine program *60 Minutes* debuted in 1968. The program appealed to a broad audience and was popular, entertaining, and profitable (Barkin 2003). The show "made newsworthy topics entertaining and entertaining issues newsworthy, eventually contributing to a blurring of the line that had traditionally separated the two" (Barkin 2003, 51). *60 Minutes* invented a new genre of news reporting and was soon followed by the debuts of NBC's *Dateline* and ABC's *20/20*, programs that were also profitable for their respective networks, solidifying the establishment of news as a business opportunity rather than a public service (Barkin 2003; Daly 2012).

Public Broadcasting

One exception to the commercialized, profit-driven radio and television news markets is public broadcasting. Prompted by a report about noncommercial educational television by the New York Carnegie Corporation, President Lyndon Johnson signed the Public Broadcasting Act in 1967, legislation that established public broadcasting in the United States. As a result of the act, the Corporation for Public Broadcasting (CPB) began funding the Public Broadcasting Service (PBS) to distribute programming to public television stations. On the radio side, National Public Radio (NPR) was established in 1970 to both produce and distribute news and other programming. NPR drew from the success of Murrow to engage in as much on location reporting as they could, using the sounds of the location to convey atmosphere and depth and using background music and sound effects to enhance the listening experience (Douglas 2004). In 1971, NPR debuted *All Things Considered*, a newsmagazine program that both reported and provided commentary on news that extended beyond Washington, DC, and in 1979, NPR launched their morning news program *Morning Edition*. The organization's first news talk program, *Talk of the Nation*, began in 1991, a show the organization credits with establishing public broadcasting's news talk radio format (NPR n.d.). From its beginnings in the early 1970s until the mid-1990s, NPR witnessed a large growth in audience as their programs increased from airing on 104 to 520 stations nationwide (Douglas 2004).

In 1974, the National Public Affairs Center for television was established to develop broadcast news content. Over the decades, the CPB allocated public money to fund many public radio and television initiatives such as the National Minority Consortia, a group that supports the production and distribution of public television programs about black Americans, Latinos, Asian Americans, and Pacific Islanders, and the Native American Satellite radio network, an initiative supporting the distribution of radio in rural areas. The long-running television programs *Frontline*, an award-winning documentary news series, and *NewsHour*, an evening national newscast, debuted in 1983 (CPB n.d.).

Today, in addition to *NewsHour*, public affairs–oriented programming airs on public broadcasting stations, and PBS *NewsHour* also produces digital content. There are three main audio organizations: NPR, American Public Media (APM), and Public Radio International (PRI). These organizations produce and distribute news and other radio programming and also produce such digital content as written articles and podcasts. Some individual public radio stations also produce and distribute news stories. Audience-funded news programs like the long-running *Democracy Now!* may air on public media stations. Though government funding of public broadcasting has been debated over the years, with some public broadcasting outlets having to adjust to budget cuts, public broadcasting organizations serve millions of viewers and listeners and obtain large amounts of their funding from corporate donors, foundations, and audience members (Stockwell 2017). Currently, public broadcasting is expected to continue. Pew Research reports that both in regard to audiences and economic stability, the public broadcasting services that provide news are performing well, with money allocated to news budgets on the rise (Grieco 2018).

Talk Radio

Coinciding with the development of NPR news programming was the development of a larger audience for political talk radio, a genre of radio programming that previously garnered small audiences in regions throughout the country. Though the substance of political talk radio and NPR were quite different at the time, and remain so today, Douglas (2004) argues that the two radio forms were "mirror-image twins, each speaking to a profound sense of public exclusion from and increasing disgust with the mainstream media in general and TV news in particular. They both became electronic surrogates for the town common, the village square, the general store, the meeting hall, the coffeehouse, the beer garden, the part, where people imagined their grandparents—even their parents for that matter—might have gathered with others to chat, however briefly, about the state of the town, the country, the world" (284–285). People tuned into talk radio and NPR to hear a more complete discussion of the issues than what was being offered on television news. Both NPR and political talk radio producers wanted to reengage the public in listening, participating, and experiencing information through the radio format, and in this, both approaches were successful.

Historians mark the establishment of the political radio talk show genre as taking place in the 1980s when radio stations featuring all talk show programming, or a combination of news and talk show programming, increased fourfold over a decade (Douglas 2004). The growth of the political talk show genre can be attributed in part to the repeal of the Fairness Doctrine, the FCC policy in place from 1949 to 1987 that required broadcasters to air balanced points of view when discussing controversial subjects. It was understood, under the doctrine, that it was in the public interest that equal time be given to different positions on issues, and when this requirement was eliminated, radio personalities, largely conservative, could advance one point of view on their programs (Clogston 2016). While, perhaps ironically, many Republicans opposed the elimination of the Fairness Doctrine, it was the conservatives who emerged as the dominant talk show hosts after the repeal and remain in this position today (Clogston 2016).

Talk radio engages listeners with the news and often prompts them to take action. The early power of talk radio was demonstrated by talk radio hosts protesting a 51 percent congressional proposed pay raise in 1988, resulting in citizen protests and the eventual halt of the increase (Douglas 2004). Political talk shows also share similar characteristics such as the reliance on provocative, "shock-jock"–oriented discourse that is often offensive. Programs also rely on what is termed "tabloid-hot news monsters," stories that are delivered angrily and "stoke rage" in listeners (Brown 2017, 499). Sound effects, vocal impersonations and studio laughter, paper shuffling, or desk pounding also set the stage for their programming (Douglas 2004). Talk radio hosts invite listeners to call in and join the conversation. Political talk radio's popularity rose as more Americans participated in discussions about the news with their new cell phones and audiences for programs expanded as satellite technology increased. The conservative engagement with the talk show hosts' discussion of issues is enhanced by the call-in format. While conservative television has its share of influential voices, "talk radio exerts arguably a broader continuous daily agenda-setting influence with its two-way, interactive, call—and—response format" (Brown 2017, 500).

One of the most influential political talk radio hosts is Rush Limbaugh. According to his website, Limbaugh launched his nationally syndicated show in 1988 on fifty-six stations and since then has grown his reach to six hundred stations reaching twenty-seven million people each week. In his challenges to mainstream reporting, which he views as elitist and liberal, Limbaugh offers his own point of view about the news, telling listeners how to interpret it. Limbaugh's commentary is well researched, and he found an audience with conservatives— mostly white men—who did not align themselves with the point of view of mainstream media (Daly 2012). Many, especially those who agree with this politics, find Limbaugh to be funny, provocative, and entertaining as a radio host. The impact of Limbaugh's work is difficult to dismiss; a 2002 Gallup poll characterized their finding that about 20 percent of Americans get their news from talk radio as *The Rush Limbaugh Effect* (Carlson 2002). Pew Research reports that talk radio is the most listened-to radio format (Shearer 2017). According to *Talkers Magazine*, in 2018, such talk show hosts as Limbaugh, Sean Hannity, Dave Ramsey, Michael Savage, and Glen Beck, regularly commanded over ten million listeners ("Top Talk Audiences" 2018). Political talk radio remains a part of the media landscape today, and it is a frequent talking point in discussions around the impact of partisan news media.

Cable Television and 24-Hour News Networks

The development of cable television ended the network era where broadcast television stations commanded the television audience and drove the market. Cable provided specialized programs to niche, fragmented audiences, introducing the idea of narrowcasting. Ted Turner created a new model of journalism with the debut of his 24-hour news network called CNN (Cable News Network). The network debuted on June 1, 1980, and within a year, it had reached ten million households (Daly 2012). CNN's business model relied on profits generated from cable subscriptions and advertising, the choice to hire few highly paid well-known news professionals, and a commitment to only produce news (Daly 2012). Initially the organization did not have the respect of the traditional news networks, which referred to CNN as "Chicken Noodle Network," but Turner eventually prevailed as he continued to invest in his idea of providing ongoing news coverage every day to the public within a cablecasting model that easily allowed for any cuts to breaking news reporting (Barkin 2003).

CNN continued to establish itself as a credible network with its reporting on the 1990–1991 conflict in the Persian Gulf, offering 24-hour news coverage of the situation (Daly 2012). CNN covered the conflict in real time—utilizing a team of reporters they sent to the region—and viewers could watch or hear the events unfolding. CNN's dominance as a source of news became apparent when Vice President Dick Cheney stated that he was watching CNN to keep informed on the Persian Gulf situation, and other networks interviewed CNN reporters for information or opted to use their footage (Carter 1991). When the twenty-first century started, CNN had six cable networks, including CNN International, resulting in CNN being present in 212 countries and territories (Barkin 2003).

Although CNN remained without a competitor for years, this changed in 1996 when Australian media mogul, Rupert Murdoch, who owned media throughout the world through his company News Corp, established Fox News. Fox News was initially positioned as a conservative news alternative to CNN and the broadcast television networks that had developed a reputation for being liberal in their news report framing (Barkin 2003; Daly 2012). Fox News advanced two slogans: "fair and balanced," which suggested that other news was not, and "We report. You decide," which implied that their news reports were factual while other news contained too much opinion (Daly 2012). The opinion and talk shows that Fox News featured were conservative in nature, featuring weak, liberal counterpoints (Barkin 2003). While there has been debate whether the news division's reporting is absent partisan bias, scholars have stipulated that the network is overtly conservative in both its talk show and news programming. Examples cited to support this view include Fox's internal memos on how to cover conservatives when they hold powerful positions, Fox News' coverage of the 2000 election that squarely favored a win by George Bush over Al Gore, and its reporting on the Iraq War (Barkin 2003; Daly 2012). Today, Fox is widely known as a conservative organization.

A more liberal news outlet, MSNBC, a collaboration between NBC News and Microsoft, also began in 1996. The partnership included the development of MSNBC.com, an innovative news website that was often the first to integrate technical advances such as live video, video streaming, and news feeds (NBC News 2010). MSNBC also launched a 24-hour cable news channel. As it developed and gained viewers, the cable news channel followed the same structure as Fox News but aired a number of politically opinion-oriented shows that are more liberal, rather than conservative, in their focus. Some nationwide research has demonstrated that more partisan media channels, specifically Fox News and MSNBC, negatively impact people's knowledge and understanding of current events (Cassino, Woolley, and Jenkins 2012).

News Satire and "Fake News" Television Shows

While news satire has historically accompanied traditional journalism in the form of written pieces, cartoons and comics, and news parody texts such as *The Onion* and *Saturday Night Live*'s "Weekend Update," the broadening of this genre occurred with the debut of *The Daily Show*, a comedic, "fake news" television satire program on the cable network Comedy Central. Mimicking the style of cable news and cable news–oriented talk shows, *The Daily Show* began in 1996, but its rise in popularity occurred after Jon Stewart took over as host in 1999 (he hosted until 2015). Stewart shifted the focus of *The Daily Show* to satirizing news and politics in ways that challenged some of the information disseminated by mainstream television and cable news programs, a focus that remains in place today with current host Trevor Noah. The program's popularity prompted the development of other "fake news" TV programming, most notably *The Colbert Report*, which aired from 2005 to 2014, staring *The Daily Show* alum Stephen Colbert as a version of a cable news television pundit. The popularity of these award-winning programs may have resulted from the frustration citizens had with mainstream reporting that allowed for officials to spin versions of events that didn't line up with known evidence; these "fake news" programs made it their business to highlight and critique misleading spin in entertaining and provocative ways (Bennett 2016). Fake news programs also suggested that the press is not doing its job in "making independent corrections" of information advanced by officials and other spokespeople to position their messages in ways that support a particular agenda (Bennett 2016, 19).

Research demonstrates that some viewers looked to *The Daily Show* and *The Colbert Report* for news and have trust in them as news sources (Gottfried and Anderson 2014). This inclination is not without merit. A Pew Research study on *The Daily Show*'s content revealed that while Stewart consistently stated that his program is not a real news show, the satiric content of the program is journalistic in nature, similar to cable and radio talk shows where hosts discuss and provide informed commentary on news stories (Pew Research Center 2008). Additionally, a highly publicized research report from Fairleigh Dickenson University demonstrated that viewers who only tuned into *The Daily Show* were more informed on current events than those who only tuned into Fox News (Cassino, Woolley, and Jenkins 2012). By 2013, *The Daily Show* and *The Colbert Report* were the most watched late night television programs by adults (TV by the Numbers 2013).

Over the years, critics have discussed the journalistic aspects of this genre of "fake news"–oriented programming, now more commonly referred to as news satire, when considering such programs as *Last Week Tonight* hosted by John Oliver, formerly of *The Daily Show*. Oliver structures his program like a news report and, using comedy to punctuate his delivery of information, provides well-researched feature stories on a range of relevant topics. Like his predecessors in the genre, Oliver dismisses the idea that he is a journalist, but as many have pointed out, significant research, fact-checking, and analysis of information inform his "reporting," suggesting that some journalistic components inform his work (Poniewozik 2014; Suebaeng 2014). Others reiterate the value satire, especially news satire, plays in the culture. Programs such as *The Daily Show*, *Full Frontal with Samantha Bee*, *Last Week Tonight*, and late night comedy segments such as "A Closer Look" on *Late Night with Seth Meyers* encourage audiences to think critically while also pointing out false information in a comedic way (Maza 2017).

Tabloid Television News

From the late 1980s through the turn of the century, another prominent form of television influenced mainstream television reporting. Called "tabloid television," these programs were described as a mix of "news about crime, sex, scandal and celebrity—with an emphasis on any combination of the four" (Barkin 2003, 64). People's enduring interests in tabloid news stories have been documented as far back as the 1500s, and news reports in all forms have historically included tabloid reports (Stephens 1988), so it is not a surprise that tabloid television would establish itself as part of the television news landscape. Tabloid television encompasses three styles of programming: reality TV, where recorded instances of policing, rescues, and other dramatic action are edited with supplemental reenactments to tell a story; issue-driven talk shows, where guests, audiences, and hosts engage in confrontational discussions about the topic at hand; and news shows, where the television newscast format is imitated but the delineation of content differs from mainstream news reports (Glynn 2004).

One of the programs that launched the development of newscast tabloid television was *A Current Affair*, a program that infused tabloid reporting with techniques used in a standard newscast format. The program fused fact, gossip, and drama in an entertaining, sensationalized format, and its popularity prompted the development of similar types of tabloid shows such as *Inside Edition* and *Hard Copy* (Barkin 2003). Media scholars point out that tabloid news often gives voice to members of the population who oppose the "truths" reported by those in power via traditional journalism, and while tabloid approaches can be criticized, their popularity demonstrates a level of acceptance for the form by many (Glynn 2004). Despite traditional journalism's critique of this method of storytelling, tabloid television shows had an impact on the production of mainstream news; television newscasts, newspapers, and news-magazines spent time and space covering sensational news stories that would not previously have been given as much, or any, attention (Barkin 2003). Some elements of courtroom trials were televised, and this shift in the content and nature of news coverage set the stage for the around-the-clock news reporting on the O.J. Simpson story—an arrest and criminal trial that emerged after the brutal murder of Simpson's former wife, Nicole Simpson, and her friend, Ronald Goldman (Barkin 2003).

Media Consolidation

Concerns about consolidated media ownership and its potential impact on news production are not new. In the 1930s, for example, newspapers owned numerous radio stations, and because many newspaper editorial pages were critical of the then current president, Franklin Delano Roosevelt, the president warned broadcasters through his press secretary that the government would be on the lookout for "false news," a term news executives interpreted as "news critical of the administration's policies" (Douglas 2004, 182). While this example points to concerns about potential partisan reporting, other articulated concerns about consolidated media ownership suggest that in a consolidated news environment, there is less competition, a lack of diversity, and a proliferation of homogenous reporting that is not representative of all public concerns. At the beginning of the twentieth century, regulations were enacted to ensure diverse ownership of media outlets and to prevent one company from monopolizing a particular media market.

In the latter part of the twentieth century, however, this changed. As media systems developed and became more profitable, companies that owned or had holdings in media outlets continued to acquire more radio, television, and newspaper companies, leading to what is referred to as "big media" or media consolidation. The growth of media conglomerates was aided by a number of deregulatory policies over the decades that relaxed previous standards that limited the number of media outlets one entity could own (Douglas 2004). Toward the end of the century, the Telecommunications Act of 1996, which allowed for integration across different parts of the communication industry in an attempt to increase competition as new technology was being developed, also lifted rules that prevented cross-ownership of media outlets and eliminated many ownership limits (Messere 2004.). The elimination of these ownership caps has allowed for a media landscape that is controlled by a handful of media conglomerates.

The presence of pervasive media consolidation has raised questions around whether quality news reporting practices can exist within a corporate structure that is focused on profit. Media consolidation also presents an inherent conflict of interest since it is uncertain whether journalists can honestly report on the industries, topics, or issues connected to their corporate owners (Daly 2012). Often referenced writers Ben Bagdikian and Robert McChesney provide detailed accounts of the corporate ownership of mainstream media and the influence of advertisers on news production. In *The Media Monopoly*, a book that has been updated numerous times to reflect ownership changes, Bagdikian (1997) describes how a handful of large corporations came to own the majority of media outlets in the country. Bagdikian argues that the structure of concentrated corporate ownership limits democratic expression and results in news reporting that favors corporate interests, decreases competition in regional markets, and does not provide sufficient information for American citizens to be informed about the complexities of regional, national, and international topics. Similarly, in *Rich Media, Poor Democracy*, McChesney (1999) echoes many of Bagdikian's points and discusses how the deregulatory results of the Telecommunications Act of 1996 supported additional growth of global oligopolies that produce the majority of news and entertainment content in the United States. McChesney argues that this corporate media structure has severely compromised democracy by producing homogenized news content, embracing advertising, and elevating entertainment programming. McChesney points to the value of public broadcasting and proposes detailed suggestions for media reform.

Media consolidation has made it difficult for smaller media companies and minorities to participate in the news business. A series of FCC research reports published in 2000 highlighted some of the outcomes of the Telecommunications Act of 1996, including the difficulty women and minorities faced in trying to obtain broadcast licenses, and the discriminatory practices that women and minorities faced when trying to establish themselves in the broadcast industry. The report's executive summary states, "Small telecommunications businesses generally, and those owned by women and minorities in particular, report that the market consolidation permitted by the relaxation of the FCC's ownership rules has created nearly insurmountable obstacles to those seeking to enter, or even survive as a small player, in the broadcast industry" (FCC 2000, 35). Other aspects of this report demonstrate that minority-owned broadcast stations are more likely to air diverse programming and hire diverse talent on radio programing and that there are few women owners of broadcast stations.

Although the digital revolution has since changed the media landscape by providing many alternatives for news online, the debate about media consolidation as it relates to news production and distribution remains today. Some proponents of consolidation point to the success of internet streaming sources as worthy competitors to "big media" and dismiss antitrust concerns (Molla and Kafka 2018; Stewart 2014). However, in contrast to the fifty companies that owned 90 percent of American media in 1983, six companies controlled that 90 percent in 2012 (Stewart 2014). Additionally, large technology companies such as Google, Apple, and Facebook have become powerful players in the media landscape, ensuring that debates about big media and news production will persist.

Digital News and Information

It is often stated that the internet drastically changed the news industry, and while this is true, the news industry faced challenges before the digital revolution. Radio, television, cable television, and around-the-clock news programming all functioned as alternative sources of news and as sources of entertainment that audiences spent time with instead of reading the newspaper, thus playing a role in declining newspaper sales, the elimination of the evening paper, and eventual newspaper closings (Stephens 2014). Media consolidation practices and a focus on news' lack of profitability played a role in shrinking budgets allocated for television news departments (Gunther 1999). Although newspapers, news radio programming, and television news remain key components of the current news media landscape, their future is uncertain. A 2016 Pew Research report revealed that 57 percent of news consumers report that they often watch television news, while 25 percent report obtaining news from the radio, and 20 percent report often getting news from newspapers. This same study indicated that 38 percent often obtained news online, a number that study authors suggest might grow given younger respondents' preferences for online platforms over older respondents' preferences for newspapers and television (Mitchell et al. 2016). Subsequent research indicates that 93 percent of adults access some news online and that digital native news outlets, news organizations that have only existed online, attract more than twenty million unique visitors a month (Stocking 2018).

There is little disagreement that the internet disrupted traditional newsgathering, production, and distribution practices. The change is so significant in the news industry that the news outlets that were the dominant voices in the dissemination of news and information in the United States are sometimes referred to as the "legacy media" (Bennett 2012). The digital revolution that brought to the culture a networked environment where news and information can be easily posted online, distributed, and commented on did not happen all at once. As internet technology evolved, so did its presence in American life; the shift in the practices of news and information can be understood in this context.

In their introduction to their book on "participatory culture," a term that refers to the public's easy involvement as creators and distributors of content, Aaron Delwiche and Jennifer Jacobs Henderson (2013) provide a summary of the four phases of the technological developments that led to the current, connected, digital sphere. In the first phase, which they call "emergence" (1985–1993), everyday consumers began to use personal computers for a range of activities, some institutions began to network their computers, and the World Wide Web was established as a digital space. Phase two, "waking up to the web" (1994–1998), is described as a time when the public began to engage with the internet, using new graphic, rather than text-based, web browsers. People began to create their own web pages, link to other websites, and use newly formed sites such as Yahoo!, Amazon. com, Craigslist, and Google. In phase three, "push button publishing" (1999–2004), web publishing systems became easy to use and prompted even more people to "share, annotate, publish and remix digital information" (6). Finally, Delwiche and Henderson call phase four "ubiquitous connections" (2005–2011), a period where video sharing and digital publishing expanded due to the development and integration of powerful internet broadband. At the same time, smart mobile devices emerged and became integrated into the culture. Since 2011, technological advances have continued, and computers, smartphones, and tablets continue to increase their capabilities. Additionally, social media platforms such as blogs and the microblog Twitter, wiki sites (e.g., Wikipedia), content-oriented sites (e.g., YouTube), and social networking sites (e.g., Facebook) have proved to be powerful players in the news and information landscape, while the more traditional forms of media, such as newspapers, news radio, and television newscasts continue to adapt and adjust to the ever-changing convergence culture.

News Goes Online

While everyday citizens were engaging with the use of developing technology, so too were established news organizations. At first, websites run by news organizations delivered news content to consumers, often for free, while other sites such as Digg, the Huffington Post, and the Drudge Report initially functioned as news aggregates, providing links to news stories found on the web. As the internet allowed for traditional media to be accessible online, "it was also subtly changing those media in the process" (Cullen 2013, 254). In comparison to traditional printed news and scheduled radio and television broadcasts, news stories can be easily and very quickly shared online. Online news stories can be frequently updated by the author and easily shared and commented on by the consumer. According to scholar Stuart Allan (2006), one early "test case" of the power of online reporting was the Oklahoma City bombing in 1995. The online reporting of this tragedy was comprehensive and included eyewitness reports, maps of the area, discussion forums, information about disaster relief, and traditional news reports—information that was continuously updated. At the same time, not all of the reporting was accurate, and some posts were later determined to be pranks. This example, as well as many others, demonstrates the powerful capability of online platforms while also pointing to issues around credibility and fact-checking in an environment where content is easily and quickly posted and distributed.

As the legacy media established reporting on web platforms, they adopted media convergence–oriented practices— radio news programs developed websites with audio and written reports, newspaper websites integrated short video reports, television news websites included written articles, and some news companies established a presence on YouTube. News outlets eventually developed their own applications for smart TVs and mobile devices. The emergence of the podcast, content in a downloadable or streaming audio file, allowed for news outlets and others to provide a range of news and informational programming.

While print, broadcast, and cable news organizations were developing their online presence, digital-only news sites developed, producing content in ways that differed from traditional media formats. The online magazine *Salon*, which debuted in 1995, began by publishing issues every two weeks but evolved to publishing content on a less structured schedule (Kamiya 2005). The online magazine *Slate* debuted in 1996, and its founder noted his shift in thinking about magazines when considering the online format, pointing out that an online magazine didn't have to adhere to the traditional format of publishing "issues" periodically (Kinsley 2006). Over the years, other news-oriented companies emerged. News aggregators such as the Drudge Report, which began as an email newsletter in 1995 before migrating to the web, and Google News, which began in 2002, remain influential today. Other news aggregators such as Yahoo! News, which began in 2001, curated links to online news stories on their web pages and later began supplementing this work with original reporting. Debuting in 2005, the Huffington Post curated information and published a range of original content. The Breitbart News website launched in 2007. New types of information providers also emerged. Digital fact-checkers such as Snopes, which began in 1994, and Politifact, which began in 2007, provided assessments of information and are just two of many websites that provide similar services. Reddit began in 2005 and allows users to submit, vote on, and discuss content found online, inherently directing readers to chosen news, and other, stories. The controversial website WikiLeaks, a publisher of news leaks and secret information, began in 2006. BuzzFeed also launched in 2006 and publishes a mix of serious news, celebrity news, quizzes, and lists. More recently, Vox, known for its use of explanatory journalism, debuted in 2014.

The establishment of so many digital news outlets has impacted news departments industrywide. While larger newspapers have begun to figure out how to maintain operations via digital subscriptions and other sources of revenue, mid- to small-sized papers are struggling. Since the 1800s, news was financially supported from money gathered from selling the publication (in-person sales or subscriptions) and from money paid by those buying ads in the publication (Stephens 2014). When many news-oriented websites began posting their content, the previous funding structure of news disintegrated since consumers did not want to pay for something they could obtain for free online. Subscriptions and sales of printed publications decreased, and many who previously bought printed advertising space have since moved their business to the web, advertising in online environments or posting for free on sites like Craigslist (Daly 2012). Traditional, or legacy, media has developed an online presence, ultimately taking advantage of the benefits of media convergence but, in many cases, not generating enough revenue to support previously larger news departments. The printed newspaper industry has declined—newspaper staffs have been cut, and many newspapers have reduced their news coverage or folded (Downie and Schudson 2009).

In their report on the state of journalism after the digital revolution, Leonard Downie and Michael Schudson (2009) document that local reporting, in particular, was hit hard as "fewer newspaper journalists were reporting on city halls, schools, social welfare, life in the suburbs, local business, culture, the arts, science or the environment, and fewer were assigned to investigative reporting" (5). Additionally, many papers decreased or eliminated the number of correspondents who covered international news, news from the state capitals, and news from Washington, DC. The authors write, "A large share of newspaper reporting of government, economic activity and quality of life simply disappeared" (5). The lack of demand for printed material extends beyond newspapers. Some newsmagazines, such as *Newsweek* and *U.S. News and World Report*, have stopped producing print versions of their work and are available through an online subscription only. Currently the news industry is continuing to figure out how to support comprehensive journalism in a competitive digital market while remaining economically stable.

Shifts in News Producers and Audiences

The internet, however, did not just offer another way of accessing traditional news and information. As the participatory nature of this online culture emerged, the power dynamics between producers of information and consumers of information changed. Whereas the barriers one has to cross to publish a magazine or newspaper or broadcast in the mainstream television and radio arenas are prohibitive for the average citizen, this is not the case with creating and sharing information online. Because of this, the internet set the stage for incredibly powerful shifts in the production, distribution, and consumption of news and information in the United States. Adrienne Russell (2011) describes this as a "networked era of journalism," where the public "create, investigate, react, (re)make, and (re)distribute news" and where all media, regardless of their status, "intersect in new ways" (1).

Some news-oriented online content diverged from the traditional approach to reporting. Blogs (formerly called "web logs") are frequently updated posts that share information on a particular topic and often include links to other content on the web, images, and clips. A key characteristic of blogs is that posts are seen in reverse chronological order, with the newest entries posted at the top of the blogging website. Early news-oriented blogs added to, and sometimes challenged, traditional news coverage on particular topics: "most bloggers were pulling together their resources from a diverse array of other sites, often in a way that resituated a given news event within a larger context so as to illuminate multiple angles" (Allan 2006, 49). While initially traditional journalists did not see bloggers as central to the news and information landscape, this perspective has shifted as it has become clear that bloggers have demonstrated their capabilities in shaping the news agenda and challenging mainstream news narratives.

One early, often-cited example of this blogger influence centered on the reporting of thinly veiled racist comments made by Senator Trent Lott in 2002 at a birthday party for retiring senator Strom Thurmond. The traditional media did not report on these comments until they were written about in two blogs, *Talking Points Memo* and *Tapped* (Russell 2011). Other bloggers culled together Lott's previous comments from other events and speeches to show that his words were part of a pattern of remarks with racial overtones (Allan 2006). While there is debate around the bloggers' role versus the mainstream media's role in advancing this story, which ultimately resulted in Lott stepping down, bloggers were recognized for keeping the story alive, putting pressure on the mainstream media to cover the story, and, in the end, raising the profile of blogging as a powerful force in the news media sphere (Allan 2006). Some bloggers "developed their own personal news brand, picking up tips, building sources, and breaking stories" (Russell 2011, 77). Professor and media professional Jeff Jarvis was an early supporter of blogging and blogs as a valid source of information, arguing at the time that the new media form of blogging provides an opportunity for any news event to be reported in ways that keep "the public constantly informed" (Spanogle 2011, 16). Jarvis argues for what he calls a "digital first" philosophy where news is positioned as a public service and not "broken up by medium, such as print, web and mobile, but by readers' needs, depending on their interest and how much time they have available" (Edge 2015).

Mainstream journalists were slow to acknowledge bloggers as journalists and credible sources of information because of the nature of blog writing, which is often subjective or opinion oriented. However, bloggers challenge the assumption that traditional news is always objective or accurate and make the point that the sources used in blogs are often embedded in the work (Allan 2006). The increasing presence of popular bloggers resulted in a shift in deference to the traditional model of news reporting where professional journalists produce and disseminate news to an audience; bloggers were using their research skills to provide informed commentary on news and advance their own stories (Daly 2012; Stephens 2014). As the popularity of blogging increased, so did traditional media's integration of blogs into their offered news organization content (Allan 2006).

Other aspects of the online news culture emerged. Citizen journalists are people who, though not trained as or employed as journalists, document events as they happen or report on news that comes out of their own research. Using mobile devices to upload or stream content, citizen journalists have reported on natural disasters like the tsunami that hit Indonesia in 2004 and the Arab uprisings that began at the end of 2010. Journalism crowdsourcing, "the act of specifically inviting a group of people to participate in a reporting task—such as newsgathering, data collection, or analysis—through a targeted, open call for input; personal experiences; documents; or other contributions," became a component of online journalism (Onuoha, Pinder, and Schaffer 2015). Live blogging, when writers post content as an event is happening, emerged as a journalism practice. The increase in public participation in researching and reporting on the news has resulted in challenges to mainstream media's "monopoly over information—not just the reporting of it, but also the framing of what's important for the public to know" (MacKinnon 2005, para. 1). This power shift is significant because it dismisses the previous construct of media gatekeepers and allows for almost anyone to break a story, a story whose reception by an audience will determine whether or not it is shared and discussed widely. It also has raised discussions about who is a journalist, the credibility of information produced by those who are not professional journalists, and a shifting understanding of news audiences (MacKinnon 2005).

In her discussion of the networked era journalism, which she marks as taking place between 1990 and 2010, digital media studies professor Russell (2011) argues for an expanded under-standing of journalism:

> Journalism here refers to the wealth of news-related information, opinion, in various styles and from various producers, which together shape the meaning of news event [*sic*] and issues. Journalism has extended far beyond stories created for television broadcast outlets or for publication in traditional commercial newspapers and magazines. Journalism can be a conversation that takes place in the blogosphere, an interactive media-rich interface on a mainstream or alternative news site that provides context to a breaking story; the work of any number of fact-check sites; a tweeted camera-phone photo of a breaking news event; a comment or comment thread on a news site; a video game created to convey a particular news narrative, and so on. (22)

Whether or not one agrees with this definition of journal-ism, the presence and popularity of the digital forms of news-oriented content Russell points to have dramatically altered the state of the news industry.

Additionally, social media networking sites have emerged as entities that play a powerful role in sharing news with users. Facebook, YouTube, and Twitter, in particular, are popular pro-viders of shared news stories, and social network users share and repost news stories, some posting original news content themselves. Research shows that in 2013, 30 percent of adults in the United States obtained news from Facebook, 10 per-cent obtained news from YouTube, and 8 percent obtained news from Twitter (Anderson and Caumont 2014). In 2018, 43 percent of adults obtained news from Facebook, 21 per-cent obtained news from YouTube, and 12 percent obtained news from Twitter (Matsa and Shearer 2018). Social media has been credited with raising awareness of stories that might not have been covered and engaging citizens in responding to local, national, and international stories. It also has been credited with spreading false information easily and quickly, inherently demanding that an informed public takes steps necessary to evaluate information that comes across their screens.

Finally, other technologies may become part of the mainstream news experience. The *New York Times* and the *Washington Post*, for example, now incorporate augmented reality (AR) as a newspaper feature available to those with a smartphone or tablet as a means of engaging readers with their content. Virtual reality (VR) is also being used by journalists. Pioneered by Nonny de la Peña, immersive journalism engages viewers in experiencing virtual constructions of real-world events through a VR gaming platform. Several news organizations, such as the *New York Times*, VICE, PBS's *Frontline*, and the *Wall Street Journal*, are creating news-driven VR content, and while the form is still being developed as a journalistic vehicle, projects to date demonstrate how it assists in viewers' understanding of events (Goldman 2018). Like all forms of media, the digitally driven VR is easily altered, potentially raising more issues around potential misuse of the medium because it "feels real" (Bailenson 2018).

Conclusion

Americans need reliable information to make informed decisions and understand local, regional, national, and international events. The ways of obtaining this information have tremendously expanded since the first newspaper was published in 1690. The evolution of the print, radio, and television news industries provided new outlets for journalists to work in and develop and establish new types of reporting. The integration of the internet and digital technologies has continued this trend while also dismantling long-held ideas about journalists and audiences. Each newly integrated technological change has resulted in alterations to the nature of the production and distribution of news and information; the full impact of the current digital information age on the news industry and journalism itself has yet to be realized. Finally, the news culture keeps changing as news providers continue to develop and experiment with new forms of reporting and new technologies that assist them in sharing important information about the world.

Bibliography

Allan, Stuart. 2006. *Online News: Journalism and the Internet.* Maidenhead, England: Open University Press.

American Press Institute. 2018a. "What Is Journalism?" Accessed June 7, 2018. https://www.americanpressinstitute .org/journalism-essentials/what-is-journalism/.

American Press Institute. 2018b. "What Makes Journalism Different from Other Forms of Communication?" Accessed June 7, 2018. https://www.americanpressinstitute.org/ journalism-essentials/what-is-journalism/makes-journalism-different-forms-communication/.

"America's Anchorman." n.d. RushLimbaugh.com. Accessed May 29, 2018. https://www.rushlimbaugh.com/ americas-anchorman/.

Anderson, Monica, and Andrea Caumont. 2014. "How Social Media Is Reshaping News." Pew Research Center Journalism and Media, September 14. Accessed June 19, 2018. http://www.pewresearch.org/fact-tank/2014/09/24/ how-social-media-is-reshaping-news/.

Applegate, Edd. 2011. *Journalism in the United States.* Lanham, MD: Scarecrow Press.

Associated Press. 2011. "America's Original Wire: The Telegraph at 150." CBSNews.com, October 24. Accessed June 7, 2018. https://www.cbsnews.com/news/ americas-original-wire-the-telegraph-at-150/.

Bagdikian, Ben. 1997. *The Media Monopoly.* 5th ed. Boston, MA: Beacon Press.

Bailenson, Jeremy. 2018. "How Virtual Reality Could Change the Journalism Industry." PBS.org, January 15. https://www.pbs.org/newshour/economy/making-sense/ how-virtual-reality-could-change-the-journalism-industry.

Barkin, Steve. 2003. *American Television News: The Media Marketplace and the Public Interest.* Armonk, NY: M.E. Sharpe.

Bennett, W. Lance. 2016. *News: The Politics of Illusion.* 10th ed. Chicago, IL: University of Chicago Press.

Brown, Robert. 2017. "The President of Talk Radio: The Crystallization of a Social Movement." *American Behavioral Scientist* 61, no. 5: 493–508. doi:10.1177/00027642.

Carlson, Darren. 2002. "How Americans Get Their News." Gallup.com, December 31. Accessed June 26, 2018. https://news.gallup.com/poll/7495/how-americans-get-their-news.aspx.

Carter, Bill. 1991. "CNN Takes an Early Lead in Coverage of the Gulf War." *New York Times*, January 17. Accessed from the *New York Times* Archives, May 15, 2018. https://www .nytimes.com/1991/01/17/business/the-media-business-cnn-takes-an-early-lead-in-coverage-of-the-gulf-war.html.

Cassino, Dan, Peter Woolley, and Krista Jenkins. 2012. "What You Know Depends on What You Watch: Current Events Knowledge across Popular News Sources." Public Mind Poll Study, Fairleigh Dickenson University, May 3. Accessed June 28, 2018. http://publicmind.fdu.edu/2012/confirmed/.

Clogston, Juanita "Frankie." 2016. "The Repeal of the Fairness Doctrine and the Irony of Talk Radio: A Story of Political Entrepreneurship, Risk and Cover." *Journal of Policy History* 28, no. 2: 375–395. doi:10.1017/ s0898030616000105.

Corporation for Public Broadcasting. n.d. "History Timeline." Accessed June 25, 2018. https://www.cpb.org/aboutcpb/ history-timeline.

Cullen, Jim. 2013. *A Short History of Modern Media.* Hoboken, NJ: Wiley Blackwell.

Daly, Christopher. 2012. *Covering America: A Narrative History of a Nation's Journalism.* Amherst: University of Massachusetts Press.

Delwiche, Aaron, and Jennifer J. Henderson. 2013. "Introduction: What Is Participatory Culture?" In *The Participatory Culture Handbook,* edited by Aaron Delwiche and Jennifer J. Henderson, 3–9. New York: Routledge.

Dews, Fred, and Thomas Young. 2014. "Ten Noteworthy Moments in U.S. Investigative Journalism." The Brookings Institution, October 20. Accessed June 1, 2018. https://www.brookings.edu/blog/brookings-now/2014/10/20/ten-noteworthy-moments-in-u-s-investigative-journalism/.

Douglas, Susan. 2004. *Listening In: Radio and the American Imagination.* Minneapolis: University of Minnesota Press.

Downie, Leonard, and Michael Schudson. 2009. *The Reconstruction of American Journalism.* Columbia Journalism Review Archives. Accessed July 1, 2018. https://archives.cjr.org/reconstruction/the_reconstruction_of_american.php.

Edge, Abigail. 2015. "Jeff Jarvis: Rethink Journalism towards Being a Service." Journalism.co.uk, June 4. https://www.journalism.co.uk/news/jeff-jarvis-rethink-journalism-away-from-being-a-content-service-/s2/a565365/.

Ehrlich, Matthew C. 1996. "The Journalism of Outrageousness: Tabloid Television News vs. Investigative News." *Journalism & Mass Communication Monographs* 155: 1–24.

The Federal Communications Commission. 2000. "FCC Creating Opportunity: Policy Forum on Market Entry Barriers: Staff Executive Summary." Accessed June 8, 2018. https://www.fcc.gov/fcc-creating-opportunity-policy-forum-market-entry-barriers-december-12-2000.

Gladstone, Brooke. 2011. *The Influencing Machine*. New York: W.W. Norton & Company.

Glynn, Kevin. 2004. "Tabloid Television." In *The Encyclopedia of Television*, edited by Horace Newcomb, 2nd ed., 2249–2252. New York: Routledge.

Goldman, Naomi. 2018. "Nonny de la Peña: Pioneering VR and Immersive Journalism." VFX Voice, April 3. http://vfxvoice.com/nonny-de-la-pena-pioneering-vr-and-immersive-journalism/.

Gottfried, Jeffery, and Monica Anderson. 2014. "For Some the Satiric 'Colbert Report' Is a Trusted Source of Political News." Pew Research Center. Accessed December 12, 2014. https://www.pewresearch.org/fact-tank/2014/12/12/for-some-the-satiric-colbert-report-is-a-trusted-source-of-political-news/.

"The Great Moon Hoax." n.d. History.com. Accessed June 7, 2018. https://www.history.com/this-day-in-history/the-great-moon-hoax.

Great Projects Film Company. 1999. "Crucible of Empire, The Spanish-American War. Yellow Journalism." PBS.org. Accessed July 1, 2018. http://www.pbs.org/crucible/frames/_journalism.html.

Grieco, Elizabeth. 2018. "Public Broadcasting Fact Sheet." Pew Research Center Journalism and Media, June 6. Accessed June 25, 2018. http://www.journalism.org/fact-sheet/public-broadcasting/.

Gunther, Marc. 1999. "The Transformation of Network News." *Nieman Reports*, June 15. http://niemanreports.org/articles/the-transformation-of-network-news/.

Hallin, David. 2004. "Vietnam on Television." In *The Encyclopedia of Television*, edited by Horace Newcomb, 2nd ed., 2446–2448. New York: Routledge.

Hemmer, Nicole. 2016. "How Conservative Media Learned to Play Politics." *Politico*, August 30. https://www.politico

.com/magazine/story/2016/08/conservative-media-history-steve-bannon-clarence-manion-214199.

Hillstrom, Laurie Collier. 2010. *Defining Moments: The Muckrakers and the Progressive Era*. Detroit, MI: Omnigraphics, Inc.

Hume, Janice. 2008. "Reform, Consume: Social Tumult on the Pages of Progressive Era Magazines." In *Journalism 1908: Birth of a Profession*, edited by Betty H. Winfield, 265–282. Columbia: University of Missouri Press.

Kamiya, Gary. 2005. "Ten Years of Salon." Salon.com, November 14. https://www.salon.com/2005/11/14/salon_history/.

Killelea, Eric. 2017. "Alex Jones' Mis-Infowars: 7 Bat-Sh*t Conspiracy Theories." *Rolling Stone*, February 21. https://www.rollingstone.com/culture/lists/alex-jones-mis-infowars-7-bat-sht-conspiracy-theories-w467509.

Kinsley, Michael. 2006. "My History of Slate." Slate.com, June 8. http://www.slate.com/articles/news_and_politics/slates_10th_anniversary/2006/06/my_history_of_slate.html.

Lewis, Charles. 2017. "Investigating Power." Investigatingpower.org. Accessed June 1, 2018. https://investigatingpower.org/.

MacKinnon, Rebecca. 2005. "Blogging, Journalism and Credibility." *Nation*, March 17. https://www.thenation.com/article/blogging-journalism-and-credibility/?print=1.

Martin, Douglas. 2005. "John H. Johnson, 87, Founder of Ebony, Dies." *New York Times*, August 9. https://www.nytimes.com/2005/08/09/business/media/john-h-johnson-87-founder-of-ebony-dies.html.

Matsa, Katerina E., and Elisa, Shearer. 2018. "News Use across Social Media Platforms 2018." Pew Research Center Journalism and Media, September 10. http://www.journalism.org/2018/09/10/news-use-across-social-media-platforms-2018/.

Maza, Carlos. 2017. "Comedians Have Figured Out the Trick to Covering Trump." Vox.com, April 3. https://www.vox.com/2017/4/3/15163170/strikethrough-comedians-satire-trump-misinformation.

Messere, Fritz. 2004. "U.S. Policy: Telecommunications Act of 1996." In *The Encyclopedia of Television*, 2nd ed., edited by Horace Newcomb, 2285–2288. New York: Routledge.

McChesney, Robert. 1999. *Rich Media, Poor Democracy*. New York: The New Press.

McChesney, Robert and John Nichols. 2005. "The Rise of Professional Journalism." *These Times*, December 7. http://inthesetimes.com/article/2427/the_rise_of_professional_journalism.

Miller, Sally M., ed. 1987. *The Ethnic Press in the United States: A Historical Analysis and Handbook*. Westport, CT: Greenwood Press.

Mitchell, Amy, Jeffrey Gottfried, Michael Barthel, and Elisa Shearer. 2016. "The Modern News Consumer: News Attitudes and Practices in the Digital Era." Pew Research Center Journalism and Media, July 7. Accessed June 16, 2018. http://www.journalism.org/2016/07/07/the-modern-news-consumer/.

Molla, Rani, and Peter Kafka. 2018. "Here's Who Owns Everything in Big Media Today." Recode, June 11. Accessed June 14, 2018. https://www.recode.net/2018/1/23/16905844/media-landscape-verizon-amazon-comcast-disney-fox-relationships-chart.

Mott, Frank L. 1962. *American Journalism: A History, 1690–1960*. New York: The Macmillan Company.

National Archives. n.d. "The Bill of Rights: A Transcription." Archives.gov. Accessed July 15, 2018. https://www.archives.gov/founding-docs/bill-of-rights-transcript#toc-amendment-i.

National Public Radio. n.d. "Overview and History." Accessed June 26, 2018. https://www.npr.org/about-npr/192827079/overview-and-history.

NBC News. 2010. "MSNBC.com's History." NBCNews
.com, March 26. Accessed June 28, 2018. https://www
.nbcnews.com/slideshow/msnbc-coms-history-35541370.

Onuoha, Mimi, Jeanne Pinder, and Jan Schaffer. 2015. *Guide
to Crowdsourcing*. TOW Center for Digital Journalism,
November 20. Accessed July 16, 2018. https://www.cjr.org/
tow_center_reports/guide_to_crowdsourcing.php.

Peterson, Theodore. 1964. *Magazines in the Twentieth
Century*. 2nd ed. Urbana: University of Illinois Press.

Pew Research Center. 2008. "Journalism, Satire or Just
Laughs: 'The Daily Show with Jon Stewart,' Examined."
Pew Research Center Journalism and Media, May 8. http://
www.journalism.org/2008/05/08/journalism-satire-or-just-
laughs-the-daily-show-with-jon-stewart-examined/.

Poniewozik, James. 2014. "Unfortunately, John Oliver, You
Are a Journalist." Time.com, November 17. http://time.com/
3589285/unfortunately-john-oliver-you-are-a-journalist/.

Pulley, Angela. 2017. "Cherokee Phoenix." *The New Georgia
Encyclopedia*, April 25. https://www.georgiaencyclopedia
.org/articles/history-archaeology/cherokee-phoenix.

Rhodes, Leara. 2010. *The Ethnic Press: Shaping the American
Dream*. New York: International Academic Publishers,
Peter Lang, Inc.

Rosen, Jay. 2010. "The View from Nowhere: Questions and
Answers." PressThink, November 10. http://pressthink.org/
2010/11/the-view-from-nowhere-questions-and-answers/.

Rundlet, Karen, and Sam Gill. 2018. "Beyond 'Live at Five':
What's Next for Local News?" Medium, April 5. Accessed
July 23, 2018. https://medium.com/informed-and-
engaged/beyond-live-at-five-whats-next-for-local-tv-news-
d72a15b427a.

Russell, Adrienne. 2011. *Networked: A Contemporary History
of News in Transition*. Malden, MA: Polity Press.

Scanlon, Chip. 2003. "Writing from the Top Down: Pros
and Cons of the Inverted Pyramid." Poynter, June 20.

Accessed June 7, 2018. https://www.poynter.org/news/ writing-top-down-pros-and-cons-inverted-pyramid.

Schudson, Michael. 1978. *Discovering the News: A Social History of Newspapers*. New York: Basic Books.

Shapiro, Bruce, ed. 2003. *Shaking the Foundations: 20 Years of Investigative Journalism in America*. New York: Thunder's Mouth Press.

Shearer, Elisa. 2017. "Audio and Podcasting Fact Sheet." Pew Research Center Journalism and Media, June 16. Accessed June 28, 2018. http://www.journalism.org/fact-sheet/ audio-and-podcasting/.

Society for Professional Journalists. 2014. "SPJ Code of Ethics." Last modified September 6, 2014. Accessed June 7, 2018. https://www.spj.org/ethicscode.asp.

Soll, Jacob. 2016. "The Long and Brutal History of Fake News." *Politico*, December 18. https://www.politico.com/ magazine/story/2016/12/fake-news-history-long- violent-214535.

Spadora, Brian. 2008. "The Future of News: A Case for Literary Journalism." Poynter.org, January 29. https://www .poynter.org/news/future-news-case-literary-journalism.

Spanogle, Howard. 2011. "Social Media Provide Editors with Opportunities and Challenges." *Communication: Journalism Education Today* 45, no. 2: 14–16.

Stephens, Mitchell. 1988. *A History of News: From the Drum to the Satellite*. New York: Viking Penguin, Inc.

Stephens, Mitchell. 2014. *Beyond News: The Future of Journalism*. New York: Columbia University Press.

Stewart, James. 2014. "When Media Mergers Limit More Than Competition." *New York Times*, July 25. https:// www.nytimes.com/2014/07/26/business/a-21st-century- fox-time-warner-merger-would-narrow-already-dwindling- competition.html.

Stocking, Galen. 2018. "Digital News Fact Sheet." Pew Research Center Journalism and Media, June 6. http://www.journalism.org/fact-sheet/digital-news/.

Stockwell, Norman. 2017. "Public Broadcasting at Fifty: From a Proud Beginning to an Uncertain Future." *Progressive*, November 6. http://progressive.org/magazine/public-broadcasting-at-fifty-from-a-proud-beginning-to-an-un/.

Suebaeng, Asawin. 2014. " 'Last Week Tonight' Does Real Journalism, No Matter What John Oliver Says." The Daily Beast, September 29. https://www.thedailybeast.com/last-week-tonight-does-real-journalism-no-matter-what-john-oliver-says.

"Top Talk Audiences." 2018. *Talkers Magazine*, May. Accessed June 26, 2018. http://www.talkers.com/top-talk-audiences/.

Trescott, Jacqueline. 2010. "Mathew Brady's Photographs Made a President, Captured Reality of Civil War." *Washington Post*, November 7. http://www.washingtonpost.com/wp-dyn/content/article/2010/11/03/AR2010110304140.html.

TV by the Numbers. 2013. " 'The Daily Show' and 'the Colbert Report' Finish First Quarter 2013 as Number 1 and Number 2 among Adults 18–49." TVbythenumberszap2it.com, April 4. https://tvbythenumbers.zap2it.com/network-press-releases/the-daily-show-and-the-colbert-report-finish-first-quarter-2013-as-number-1-and-number-2-among-adults-18-49/176487/.

University Library, University of Illinois at Urbana-Champaign. "American Newspapers, 1800–1860: City Newspapers." Accessed May 15, 2018. https://www.library.illinois.edu/hpnl/tutorials/antebellum-newspapers-city/.

Whitman, Alden. 1974. "Walter Lippmann, Political Analyst, Dead at 85." *New York Times*, December 15. https://www.nytimes.com/1974/12/15/archives/

walter-lippmann-political-analyst-dead-at-85-walter-lippmann.html.

Winfield, Betty H. 2008. "Introduction: Emerging Professionalism and Modernity." In *Journalism 1908: Birth of a Profession*, edited by Betty H. Winfield, 1–16. Columbia: University of Missouri Press.

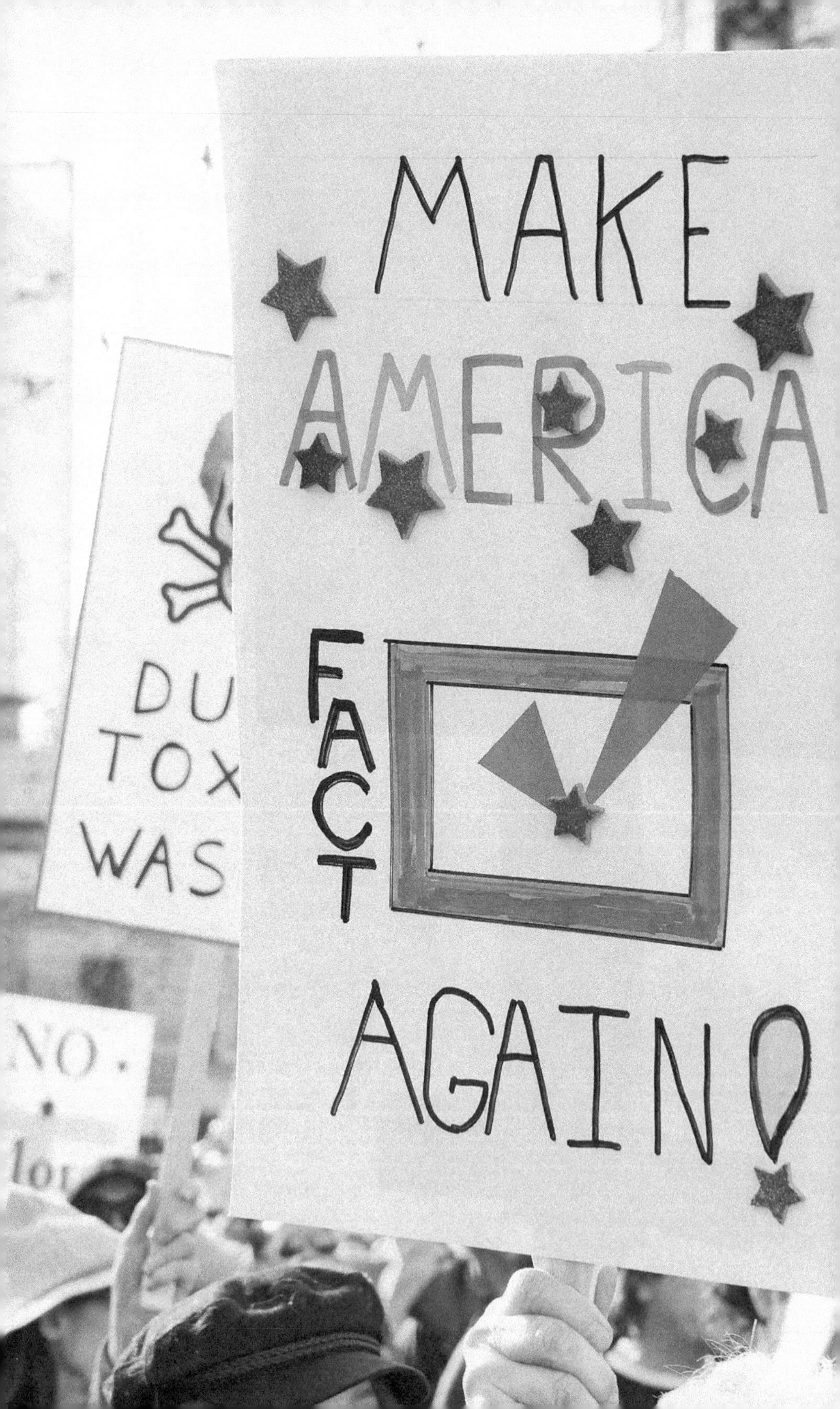
MAKE
AMERICA
FACT
AGAIN!

Introduction

This chapter explores some of the dominant problems and concerns present in the contemporary news and information landscape. The chapter is organized into five main sections. The first section, Economic Challenges in the News Industry, overviews aspects of the shifting news industry landscape. The second section, News and Audiences, overviews what current research reveals about trust in the news media and how this may be connected to partisanship, perceptions of media bias, and newsroom diversity. The next section, Challenges to Reliable Information: A Contemporary Exploration of Terms, defines and discusses categories of information—from so-called fake news to "fabricated content" to "conspiracy theories"—that have populated recent discussions of news media. The fourth section, Digital Technologies and News and Information, summarizes how algorithms, social bots, and deep fake videos contribute to the information ecosystem. Finally, the last section, Solutions, reviews what initiatives are being implemented and what ideas are being discussed to address some of the challenges in the complex news and information landscape.

This sign at the 2019 Women's March highlights a participant's concern about the spread of false information. (Sheila Fitzgerald/Dreamstime.com)

Economic Challenges in the News Industry

The News Business Model

As noted in Chapter 1, a dominant issue that all news organizations continue to grapple with is finding a business model that will generate enough revenue to support quality reporting at a time when technology continues to drive the way news organizations operate in digital spaces. Many news organizations have adapted to, and taken advantage of, digital technology in ways that for now have made them financially viable. The *New York Times*, for example, has ultimately settled on promoting a reader subscription model that has resulted in revenue from more than four million subscribers, about three-quarters of them digital-only subscribers (Peiser 2018). Local television news, a main source of information for Americans, has the financial stability to adapt to new forms of digital storytelling and social media reporting that younger demographics expect (Knight Foundation 2018b). Many digital-only news organizations have thrived in the online environment. However, other legacy news organizations and digital-only news organizations have not been as successful and continue to face challenges. In January 2016, Cayleigh Parrish of *Fast Company* summarized what about a dozen news industry professionals and experts believed would be the biggest challenges of the year. Several highlighted such technological initiatives as improving mobile and other platform experiences and continuing to develop virtual reality journalism. Others spoke to the need to improve the public's trust in news by encouraging journalists to be more accountable, transparent, and more willing to engage in community-oriented reporting that was inclusive of new audiences. Many spoke about developing new revenue streams that would allow news organizations to be less reliant on advertising dollars.

Although television news remains popular among Americans, it too faces declining audiences as a result of the internet. Network news at the beginning of the twenty-first century had already "endured a very painful, decade-long process of retrenchment," whereby news bureaus had been closed and spending on news reporting had been cut (Ponce de Leon 2015, 241). For example, in 2001, ABC News had seven overseas news bureaus to assist in reporting following the September 11, 2001, terrorist attacks; in 1989, the organization had seventeen (Ponce de Leon 2015). Cable news, a network television news disrupter, has also cut overseas news operations. In addition, the television audience is aging, and younger generations are less likely to get their news from television. As a result, legacy television news providers are developing news-oriented initiatives using online video and online streaming but face competition from other streaming services (Nielsen and Sambrook 2016). While television news broadcasters address the differences between producing news for television and mobile devices, digital news organizations are already producing mobile video, and Facebook Live and Twitter's Periscope already livestream events (Nielsen and Sambrook 2016).

A recent *Nieman Reports* article summarizes that the local television news market is also dealing with changing demographic preferences; people watch less television, and younger people, in particular, do not watch much local television news (Morrison and Carlson 2018). Local news stations are being encouraged to innovate in ways beyond simply having a social media presence to attract younger audiences. Several grants and projects, supported by organizations and universities, are funding initiatives that sustain local news, advance innovative news reporting, and report on stories "using non-traditional methods—perhaps adding animation or data visualizations" (18). The report suggests, however, that while some stations have been successful in implementing new approaches, progress is slow. Additionally, given a recent Federal Communications Commission (FCC) rule change that eliminates some media ownership caps, it is unclear how further potential media consolidation will impact local television stations.

Despite the new emphasis on digital news reporting, elements of its future are also a little unclear. In 2017, Talking Points

Memo's Josh Marshall predicted a soon-to-be "digital media crash" because he believed that the current system is unsustainable. Marshall argued that digital publishing had arrived at a moment where there were too many news outlets to be economically supported by advertisers. He pointed out that because venture capitalists were not seeing returns on their investments in digital news, they were not investing at the same rate, and that "platform monopolies" such as Google and Facebook have "gobbled up almost all of the growth in advertising revenue." The *Journalism, Media and Technology Trends and Predictions* report elaborates on this fact: "Although online advertising is still growing very fast, very little of that finds its way to publishers because giant tech platforms like Google and Facebook can target audiences more efficiently and with greater scale and have the volume to offer lower rates" (Newman 2019, 21–22). This economic instability has led to more industry-wide layoffs where declines in newsroom staff have become common. Numbers of newsroom employees have decreased every year from 2006 through 2016 (Farhi 2018). A Pew Research report shows that layoffs occurred at 36 percent of the largest newspapers in the United States and at 23 percent of high-traffic digital news outlets between January 2017 and April 2018 (Grieco, Sumida, and Fedeli 2018). News staff layoffs seem to be continuing. In the first months of 2019, numerous layoffs and restructuring that took place in a number of news organizations underscored the economic struggles facing the industry. In total, newspaper publishers like GateHouse Media, the Gannett Company, and the McClatchy Newspaper Company laid off over one thousand journalists and other staff (Goggin 2019). Vice Media, the Huffington Post, BuzzFeed, magazine publisher Conde Nast, and the *Dallas Morning News* also dealt with staff reductions (Goggin 2019). BuzzFeed News, a division of BuzzFeed that has established itself in the political reporting landscape, began laying off 15 percent of their staff and eliminated news teams focused on national security, national news features, and health (Jackson 2019).

News Deserts

The sector particularly hurt by these economic challenges and layoffs continues to be the newspaper business. One of the outcomes of the shift to the production and consumption of online news was the increasing merging and closing of local newspapers, resulting in news deserts popping up throughout the country. According to Penelope Muse Abernathy, a news desert is "a community, either rural or urban, with limited access to the sort of credible and comprehensive news and information that feeds democracy at the grassroots level." Abernathy is the author of several important reports produced at the Center for Innovation and Sustainability in Local Media at the University of North Carolina at Chapel Hill that examine in detail the changing landscape of newspapers, their readers, and their owners in the first part of the twenty-first century. In *The Rise of the New Media Baron and the Emerging Threat of News Deserts*, Abernathy (2016) documents how new newspaper owners and their approaches to business management result in decreasing the ability for local and regional papers to provide comprehensive news coverage of their area and, in some cases, remain operational. Abernathy documents the rise of "the new media baron"—newspaper owners that consist of "private equity funds, hedge funds and other newly formed investment partnerships" whose decision makers do not have journalism experience and "prioritize short term earnings" (7). These newspaper owners prioritize cost-cutting measures that result in staff layoffs and decreased reporting capabilities, which, as Abernathy points out, may have assisted in some newspapers surviving but did not result in any profits being reinvested in their journalism. Investment groups acquire newspapers as investments; "they are constantly buying, trading, and selling newspapers in their portfolio," closing papers that underperform, and "leaving communities without a newspaper or any other reliable source of local news or information" (8).

A *Washington Post* story provides an example of what this looks like in practice. Reporter Paul Farhi (2018) explains that the hedge fund Alden Global Capital controls Digital First Media, a company of one hundred daily and weekly papers, including the *San Jose Mercury News*, the *Denver Post*, the *St. Paul Pioneer Press*, and multiple papers in California. To generate profits, Digital First has been laying off large numbers of newspaper staff, selling newspaper assets, and reducing overhead, but the profits have not been reinvested in the papers. While newspaper reporters are trying to raise awareness of this practice, community and regional news coverage is suffering. Meanwhile, attempts by these companies to acquire more newspapers continue. In January 2019, Digital First expressed an interest in buying the Gannett Company, an offer that worried journalists working for such Gannett papers as *USA Today*, but the offer was unanimously rejected in February (Patterson 2019).

In the most recent report, *The Expanding News Desert*, Abernathy (2018) details what the local newspaper landscape currently looks like as more and more news deserts emerge in an era of increasing newspaper consolidation. Abernathy points out that in 2004, newspaper staffs and advertising revenue looked similar to figures in 1990, but since 2004, almost eighteen hundred local newspapers have stopped operating. Collected data indicate that 1,449 counties out of the 3,143 counties in the country only have one newspaper, and many of these newspapers are weekly publications. More than 2,000 counties in the country do not have a daily paper at all, and 200 counties in the country do not have a newspaper at all. Although local and regional newspapers provide news coverage of community issues relevant to residents, many are struggling financially. The reader and advertiser shift to digital news has shown that the previous newspaper business model that relied on advertising and subscription revenue for operations is no longer sustainable.

Abernathy (2018) points out that the "consolidation of the newspaper industry, which places the ownership of many media properties into the hands of a few large corporations, shifts editorial and business decisions to people without a strong stake in the local communities where their papers are located" (30). The largest twenty-five newspaper chains, which include New Media/Gatehouse, Gannett, Digital First Media, and Adams Publishing Group, own almost one-third of the 7,100 newspapers in the United States, showing a 20 percent increase in their holdings since 2004. The largest ten newspaper companies own "1,500 papers, including almost half—572—of the country's 1,283 dailies" (31). Many of the newspapers in operation, Abernathy suggests, are "ghosts" of their former selves as their failing business models and owners' profit-oriented strategies have prompted them to scale back on their coverage of communities they used to serve.

The lack of local news is problematic for several reasons. Without reliable local news, voter turnout and other political participation decrease, and there are less reporters in place to report on and hold local government officials accountable for their actions (Bergstein 2019). Often the "primary source of journalism," others suggest, are print journalists and their investigations; deep reporting and beat coverage inform much of television, radio, and internet news, particularly sites that aggregate news or offer analysis by bloggers (McChesney and Nichols 2010, 15). Abernathy (2018) also points out that "the people with the least access to local news are often the most vulnerable—the poorest, the least educated and most isolated" (8). Finally, if a printed newspaper is unavailable in rural communities where there is no easy access to the internet, the online news substitute is not a viable option.

Media Consolidation

While newspapers are being consolidated, operate on small staffs, or go out of business, large media conglomerates that control a huge sector of the news and information industry are increasing their holdings. Media reform advocates continue to argue that media consolidation threatens the democratic exchange of ideas and suppresses minority voices. Recent debates about net neutrality, big media's influence over governmental media policy, and the increasing amount of corporate money that influences media messaging, politicians, and elections raise concerns about decreasing citizen agency (Corcoran 2016; Nichols and McChesney 2013). Critics are alarmed that over twenty years after the Telecommunications Act of 1996 eased ownership rules, the media industry is controlled by a handful of corporations that have the resources to donate to and lobby politicians who enact policies that are in their favor (Corcoran 2016). Additionally, as noted in Chapter 1, big media may not sufficiently report on aspects of the media culture that threaten their business model, even when the majority of the public has voiced their concerns about consolidated media ownership (McChesney and Nichols 2010). Further, the increasing power of technology companies and their influence over news has added a new dimension to this discussion. A few main players dominate the technology industry (e.g., Facebook, Google, Apple, and Microsoft), the internet service provider industry (e.g., Comcast, Verizon, and AT&T), and the media industry (e.g., Comcast, Disney, and 21st Century Fox). The lines are blurring between the services technology companies, content distributors, and content providers offer, potentially leading to further consolidation and horizontal integration (Molla and Kafka 2018). Critics warn that growing internet monopolies do not serve the public as providers charge high fees and oppose net neutrality rules that ensure all websites are treated the same way by internet providers (Nichols and McChesney 2013).

Given that such companies as Facebook and Google (who owns YouTube) are so ubiquitous as sources for information, David Chavern (2018), president and CEO of the News Media Alliance, argues that the technology companies primarily control the distribution of online news by deciding "what news is delivered and to whom" (15). Chavern points out that

Facebook and Google have "immense filtering and decision making power" and their choices can prevent the presentation of comprehensive journalistic coverage to their users (15). Additionally, because of the powerful, and often problematic, role some technology companies play in distributing content ranging from conspiracy theories to disinformation, representatives from Facebook, YouTube, and Twitter were called to testify at U.S. government judiciary hearings in 2018 to speak to the nature of their platforms and content-filtering policies.

Critics continue to be concerned about the easy and fast spread of false information, hateful content, and situations where violence is streamed live, as was the case on March 15, 2019, when the terrorist shootings at New Zealand mosques were distributed online before the companies had a chance to intervene. In this case, Facebook was criticized for not removing the video from its platform fast enough; the company admitted that its artificial intelligence monitoring systems did not "catch" the livestream (Gold 2019). However, technology companies' use of artificial intelligence to identify and stop problematic content can be effective and has improved over the past few years (Lapowski 2019). Content moderation is also complicated; *Wired*'s Issie Lapowski (2019) points out that although Facebook and YouTube's policies do not allow graphic and violent content, they do allow newsworthy content: "The same clip that aims to glorify the shooting on one YouTube account, in other words, might also appear in a news report by a local affiliate."

Media consolidation can raise concerns within particular news industries such as the previously explained newspaper industry and the local television news market where single companies own large numbers of local television stations. In December 2018, it was announced that Nextar, who owns 174 local television stations in the country, planned to purchase Tribune Media, which would give Nextar another 42 television stations, and the most in the country, if the FCC approves the deal (Snider 2018). Proponents of easing the media ownership rules, recently implemented by the FCC, argue that in a competitive digital world where technology companies, streaming services, and paid television services can serve unlimited customers, limits on traditional broadcast station ownership don't make sense (Hoffman 2018).

However, consolidated television ownership can raise questions about local news station operations and independence. In April 2018, reports surfaced that Sinclair Broadcast Group, owner of over 190 television stations, required local television anchors to read previously written copy about fake news, expressing sentiments that mirrored President Donald Trump's characterizations of news unfavorable to his presidency as "fake" (Burke 2018; Fortin and Bromwich 2018). Sinclair has a history of requiring its television broadcasts to include conservative viewpoints and what some call "right-wing propaganda" (Burke 2018). Additionally, Sinclair routinely requires stations to air previously produced video segments, referred to as "must runs," raising concerns among employees and others that Sinclair is using its television stations to advance a conservative political agenda (Cohen, S. 2018). While journalists at these stations did not believe that their local news coverage was being influenced by Sinclair, and Sinclair argues that their previously produced commentary is always labeled as such, others criticize the use of a television broadcast to deliver systematic, conservative messaging (Cohen, S. 2018; Fortin and Bromwich 2018).

News and Audiences

News Polarization, Partisanship, and Trust

In 2014, the Pew Research Center's national survey of over ten thousand adults found that Republicans and Democrats were more ideologically split than they have been in twenty years. The research indicated that "ideological overlap between the two parties had diminished," resulting in the expressed opinions by the two groups of party members falling along ideological lines. Additionally, the research identified that more than two times as many people in each party think unfavorably—going so far to view the opposing party as "a threat to the nation's well-being"—of the opposing party as was noted in 1994. These findings were most salient among study participants who were most politically active; the *majority* of Americans "do not have uniformly conservative or liberal views," do not "see either party as a threat to the nation," and do "believe their representatives in government should meet halfway to resolve contentious disputes." However, Pew notes that despite this majority, those who are the most partisan are the ones whose voices are heard through "greater participation in every stage of the political process." In 2019, Pew found that ever-widening partisan divisions among political parties remain and that 71 percent of those surveyed believe that their representatives in government will not effectively work together in the coming year.

The divide between partisan citizens may carry over into what news media they consume. When it comes to news commentary, those on the political right tune into Fox News programming, political talk radio, or, increasingly, conservative YouTube commentators, referred to as the "YouTube Right" (Herrman 2017). Political comedy programming and programming on MSNBC tend to attract those on the political left. A Pew Research study (2014) that examined media habits and political polarization noted key differences between "consistent conservative" and "consistent liberal" citizens. Forty-seven percent of citizens who consistently express conservative views and 31 percent of citizens who mostly express conservative views say they are more likely to get their news from Fox News. In comparison, consistent and mostly consistent liberals identified a range of news sources they get information from, not relying collectively on one source. The sources they consult include CNN, NPR, the *New York Times*, MSNBC, and local television. Those who have mixed political views note CNN and local television as their top news sources (Mitchell et al. 2014).

News polarization occurs when people choose news sources based on their self-interests and ideology, which, in turn, creates audience groups where collectives of people share similar perspectives (Tewksbury and Riles 2015). MSNBC and Fox News, for example, produce prime-time programming that "have consistently given an entirely different view of America and its top stories each night," given the channels' choices around what stories to cover and how to discuss them (Ball 2017, 96). Some suggest that this segmentation of the audience is present in the online environment where content that resonates with similarly minded individuals may contribute to citizens finding themselves in information spaces referred to as "echo chambers" and "filter bubbles." An echo chamber emerges when users make content choices that result in exposure to similar sets of opinions; for example, a user may read a blog that links to other blogs that express similar views (Sumpter 2018). Eli Pariser (2011) coined the term "filter bubble" while critiquing how information from internet search queries was personalized for users by Facebook and Google. Pariser expresses concern that because search results are informed by previous online activity, including looking at news stories suggested by friends who may share similar ideas, users will find themselves in a filter bubble of information that is reflective of their own political and cultural views, thus potentially contributing to online news polarization. Whereas echo chambers result from individual choices about what content to look at, one's chosen online activity informs an algorithm that dictates filtered search results, or as David Sumpter (2018) puts it, "the difference between 'filtered' and 'echoed' cavities lies in whether they are created by algorithms or by people" (137).

An *MIT Technology Review* report that looked at how online accounts link to, follow, and cite sources indicates that online activity takes place on the political left and political right more so than in the political center or across partisan lines (Kelly and Francois 2018). Because diverse quality information is needed for citizens to understand and engage with current issues and the

political process, news polarization is a problem. David Tewksbury and Julius M. Riles (2015) point out that "when people
consume an imperfect diet from news sources, the quality of
their political knowledge can be threatened. Indeed, political
perceptions and behaviors can become skewed when people
rely on information and opinion that represent only once slice
of political reality" (382). Others point out that because of the
strength of confirmation bias, where people tend to believe
information that supports their perspectives even when faced
with facts that challenge an aspect of it, it may be difficult for
some to acknowledge their information is incorrect or inaccurate (Singer and Brooking 2018).

Although concerns about news polarization are well documented, other research suggests that adults' engagement with
online news sources across the political spectrum is happening.
For example, one research study found that the demographic
groups least likely to use the internet were ones that displayed
increased levels of political polarization (Boxell, Gentzkow,
and Shapiro 2017). In their discussion and examination of
adults' online news behavior, Jacob L. Nelson and James G.
Webster (2017) point to several studies that suggest people
are not engaging with only partisan media that reflects their
own views. Nelson and Webster's own investigation found that
popular political news sites were visited by "ideological diverse
audiences." They write, "A few brand-name news sites attract
a majority of the political news audience, while the remaining
news sites attract negligible amounts of audience visits. Ideologically mixed audiences are not only visiting the same political news sites but also are spending considerable amounts of
time on them. This is a world not of echo chambers and filter
bubbles but of political news consumption that looks surprisingly similar regardless of visitors' political preferences" (10).
Nelson and Webster do not dispute the presence of political polarization. They call for further research that examines
ways audiences engage with political news rather than relying
on research that only looks at how often users visit particular

sites. Additionally, in his discussion of what is known about online algorithms, Sumpter (2018) points out that research suggests that filter bubbles generated on Facebook may not be as impactful as supposed, noting that users were exposed to fewer opposing views because of individual preferences, but the difference between the filtered view and a view supplied by random Facebook news posts was "negligible" (147).

Another concept that informs discussions of news polarization has to do with thoughts about the news media's role as a watchdog on elected government officials. Research has shown that over the past thirty years, the public consistently believed that the news media's watchdog role has kept those in power from engaging in things they should not be doing (Pew Research Center 2013). However, in 2017 and 2018, Republicans and Democrats were divided more than they ever had been before in their support of the watchdog role of the news media, with many more Democrats than Republicans supporting this particular press function (Gottfried, Stocking, and Grieco 2018). These findings emerge in a partisan climate where the relationship between the news media and President Trump is fraught. Though there is a long history of tension between American presidents and the press, Trump has been overt in his disdain of media coverage he does not perceive as favorable and clear in his praise of Fox News programming, perhaps indicating to his supporters that only Fox can be trusted. Trump has called the press "the enemy of the American people" and uses the words "fake" and "phony" to refer to verifiable news content, prompting many to voice concern that his rhetoric can be interpreted as anti-free press, anti-democratic, and dangerous to both journalists and democracy (Grynbaum 2017; Keith 2018; Landler 2018). Trump's attacks on the media have prompted some in his base of supporters to act aggressively toward the news media Trump does not like (Grynbaum 2017).

News polarization discussions can also be informed by what is known about citizens' trust of the news media. The changes in the journalism industry, the addition of online sources of news, the partisan polarization of active members of the electorate, and the presence of misinformation and disinformation in news content may all contribute to citizens' trust in, and engagement with, certain news media. A Pew Research report has shown that trust in news media sources, however, often falls along partisan lines. Politically left-leaning citizens trust far more news sources than politically right-leaning citizens, with those on the left indicating "more trust than distrust" of mainstream news sources such as NPR, BBC, every broadcast television news network but Fox, CNN, the *New York Times*, the *Washington Post*, Google News, and the *Wall Street Journal* (Mitchell et al. 2014). Right-leaning citizens indicated they "trusted more than distrusted" far fewer sources—primarily Fox News and the *Wall Street Journal* (Mitchell et al. 2014).

How citizens make sense of news media content may also be a factor in understanding this environment. Opinions about the news populate the information landscape. Numerous television programs feature political pundits discussing current news along partisan lines. Political talk radio, podcast hosts and their guests, opinion writers, and columnists all discuss current events and news developments from ideological standpoints. Research not only suggests that consumers are more engaged in political talk show discussions when talk show hosts' positions are similar to their own but also shows that consumers believe discussions of positions they don't agree with should be present for the program to be credible (Bode et al. 2018). Journalism experts point out that there are different ways opinions can be expressed. Some commentators fall into the category of "opinion journalists," those who offer their points of view within a journalistic tradition where facts presented in a fair context are used to support their point of view (Kovach and Rosenstiel 2010, 141). On the other hand, there are others, often hosts of political talk shows, who offer their opinions outside of this framework, relying on little evidence and taking on the role of a passionate "culture warrior" to express their views (Kovach and Rosenstiel 2010, 142–143).

Informed citizens need to be able to identify the nature of the opinions being expressed, and they need to be able to distinguish facts from perspectives. However, a Pew Research study that looked at whether adults can determine the difference between factual and opinion statements revealed that this was a difficult task for many of the over five thousand who participated (Mitchell, Gottfried, Barthel, and Sumida 2018). Results indicated that just 26 percent of participants could identify all five factual statements presented to them in the study, and just 35 percent could identify all five opinion statements. Results also determined that "overall, Republicans and Democrats are more likely to see factual and opinion news statements as factual when they favor their side" (Mitchell et al. 2018). Additionally, research completed by the Media Insight Project (2018) reveals that both journalists and the public want the same things—"verified facts, supplemented by some background and analysis"—but that 42 percent of the surveyed public believes news is populated with too much opinion and commentary. This research also found that some basic news concepts are not understood by the public; for example, 50 percent of the public indicate that they don't completely understand what an op-ed is (opinions written by guest writers or columnists, usually "opposite" or alongside the editorial content in a newspaper), 43 percent state that they don't know what attribution means in news reporting (how journalists attribute or source their material to people, organizations, or other research), and 57 percent are unable to define what native advertising is (paid content that may look like reporting but is marketing oriented).

According to the national polling agency Gallup, the percentage of Americans who indicated that they had trust in the news media fell from 54 percent in 2003 to 32 percent in 2016, and in 2017, Gallup reported an increase in trust to 41 percent (The Knight Foundation 2018a). As a follow-up to these findings, the Knight Foundation (2018a) worked with Gallup to examine the indicators of news media trust. The research suggested that the top reasons why people indicated distrust in news organizations had to do with the inaccuracy (inaccurate reporting, misleading reporting, fake news, etc.) and bias (slanted or unfair reporting) they viewed news organizations perpetuating. Respondents also expressed frustration with sensational news, negative reporting, and a lack of serious news. The research indicated that Republicans and Democrats were less likely to trust news sources that had a partisan reputation opposite their own but that people trusted some news organizations that they perceived reported in fair, nonpartisan, and balanced ways. On perhaps a positive note, 69 percent of adults who have lost trust in the media say it can be restored. Other research has suggested that trust in the news media will increase if journalists explain their use of sources more clearly, are more transparent about their reporting, and are mindful of the ways they are interpreting and giving context to the facts (Media Insight Project 2018).

Other Media Insight Project findings indicate that the public thinks the accuracy of media reporting on race, ethnicity, religion, people who earn low incomes, and people who live in rural areas could be improved. The Media Insight Project also noted that Republicans, in particular, express concerns about media coverage. Fifty-one percent of Republicans believe that the press does not accurately report on Republicans, and 53 percent of Republicans believe that the press does not accurately report on conservatives. Additionally, Republicans believe Democrats are not accurately portrayed by the news media. A recent Pew Research study further highlights differences in republican and democrat perceptions of the news media. While the majority (58 percent) of those surveyed claim the "media do not understand people like them," 73 percent of Republicans believe that news organizations don't understand them as opposed to 40 percent of Democrats who express the same sentiment (Gottfried and Grieco 2019).

Research by the Knight Foundation (2018c) and Gallup provides some additional insight into the complicated relationship between citizens' trust and news organizations. An experimental study looked at whether trust in specific news articles is influenced by participants' knowledge of the news organization that advances the article. Researchers found that the news articles that earned the highest trust ratings were from the Associated Press and the *New York Times* as sources for the news, whether or not these news sources were identified. Additionally, articles from Breitbart News, Media Matters, and 100 Percent Fed Up earned the lowest trust ratings regardless of whether the article was attributed to one of these sources. The study noted, however, that trustworthy ratings of articles from Vox, Fox News, and Breitbart News dropped when these organizations were revealed as the source. The study authors suggest that overall the partisan leaning of a news organization is influential in inspiring trust in the reported story. Democrats, for example, alter their trust assessment of news content the most when the source is revealed to be Fox News or Breitbart, suggesting that these findings might point to the idea that "the 'brand' reputation" of some news sources "affects perceived trustworthiness of the content more than the information presented" (8).

News Customization

On any given day, there are infinite numbers of possible news stories that could be reported on. News organizations have to make choices about what stories to cover, how much time to spend on a story, and how prominently featured a story should be. Because news organizations cannot report on everything, what they do cover, particularly the stories they give the most attention to, set the news agenda. Called agenda setting, these choices determine what citizens might think about, and be informed on, when they consume news. The agenda-setting function of the news media is a product of choices having to be made by news organizations; however, these choices can be criticized. Sometimes "more useful information" is set aside in news reporting in favor of sensational stories that may attract more audience members in a fragmented market (Bennett 2016, 28). Other times, news organizations may not report on stories that threaten other interests. The organization Project Censored founded by Carl Jensen in 1976, for example, publishes a list of stories each year that were either not reported or underreported, often arguing that corporate media bias informs the news agenda.

The online news environment is identified as a place where individual interests could challenge mass media decisions around what is news. To an extent, people's ability to personalize their news has challenged the agenda-setting function of traditional media (Russell 2011). Famously referred to as "the Daily Me" by MIT's Nicholas Negroponte, digital technologies allow for consumers to choose what news interests them and create their own, personalized or customized, delivery of news they find relevant; this practice emerged alongside news producers' competition for audiences' attention in an increasingly fragmented news environment (Jones and Salter 2012). However, news customization raises other questions. Some wonder how much mainstream news agendas are truly disrupted in customized environments. Adrienne Russell (2011), a professor of digital media studies, suggests that "people were encouraged mostly to customize mainstream content, which of course is material spun from the taste-making, agenda-setting hierarchies of media industry executives" (73). Others point out that news customization "made it possible for readers to limit their exposure to ideas, stories and contrasting world views that weren't of their own choosing," which, in turn, leads to the creation of news consumed in personalized echo chambers (Jones and Salter 2012, 100).

Digital journalism experts Janet Jones and Lee Salter (2012) explain that news customization also resulted in news organizations monitoring what stories were popular by keeping track of which stories were clicked on the most. Called "click through" monitoring, news organizations began to use data about what stories were popular to revise their home pages. While this may result in the advancement of "important but under reported" stories, the public's voice in directing news agendas is complicated for news organizations that have to "navigate the tricky terrain between being popular and being credible" (110). Popular news stories, for example, are often celebrity oriented and may not be the ones serious news organizations want to prioritize in their reporting. Additionally, as Jones and Salter (2012) argue, social media sites "have been implicated in blurring the boundaries between news and non-news spaces allowing serious content to morph into entertainment and lifestyle. The concern is that, unchecked, news customization will narrow people's fields of interest in such a spectacular way that it will undermine the very function of news within a democratic public sphere" (113).

News Bias

When news stories are reported, they are framed, or told, in particular ways. Scholar Claes de Vreese (2005) explains that "a frame is an emphasis in salience of different aspects of the topic. While agenda setting theory deals with the salience of issues, framing deals with the presentation of issues" (53). News framing analysis examines how stories are reported by identifying what elements of the story are relied on to convey information. In any news story, certain elements may be focused on to suggest an interpretation; for example, one story on climate change may emphasize how the earth is changing, while another may detail ways environmental regulation might impact businesses (Bennett 2016, 33). News stories have to be framed in order for the content to be presented to the audience in an understandable structure or narrative. However, because news frames "may effect learning, interpretation and evaluation of issues and events," it is important to consider how framing choices may impact understanding and influence public opinion related to the topic at hand (de Vreese 2005, 52). Often when news coverage of a story is analyzed, elements of how the story is framed—what the central idea of the story is, what language is used, what images are used, and so forth—are discussed.

Political news bias occurs when a particular political position, interest, or perspective is framed more favorably than other perspectives in news reporting. Distinctions might be made between news organizations that produce content to appeal to a similarly politically minded audience and news organizations that strive for providing balanced reporting where stories are vetted by editors who have an interest in maintaining their news organizations' reputation for fairness (Bennett 2016). However, as noted earlier, one of the reasons citizens claim a mistrust of news is because they believe some news organizations are politically biased, and this is not a new assertion. Many, many article and book authors over the years have explored the topic of political media bias from both scholarly and professional vantage points, with both scholars and practitioners providing perspectives and evidence that inform how news content or coverage may align more with conservative or liberal perspectives. Additionally, even when news coverage is not particularly tilted one way or the other, audiences may perceive it as such. Scholars have identified a phenomenon called the hostile media effect, where audience members who are actively politically partisan view news media coverage of controversial topics as biased against their perspectives (Feldman 2018). Scholars consider this effect to be both "robust," meaning that it has been a present finding in many diverse research studies, and problematic for democracy. Lauren Feldman (2018) notes, "Although the hostile biases that partisans project on media coverage are, in many cases, not objectively real, these perceptions—justified or not—have been found to influence how people perceive the public opinion climate, the way they consume news, and their participation in political life."

Citizens are interested in discussing news media bias in the current partisan climate. In 2016, Vanessa Otero, an attorney, created a Media Bias Chart and has updated it a few times since its first release and viral dissemination. Seen at Media-BiasChart.com (2019), the chart plots news organizations on a continuum of liberal to conservative and by descriptions of quality, that is, factual reporting, analysis, fair persuasion, unfair persuasion, propaganda, and inaccurate/fabricated information. The chart also attempts to determine whether news organizations are likely to report news, fairly interpret news, unfairly interpret news, or advance "nonsense damaging to public discourse." Otero argues that fact-based news stories were once dominant, but now "many sources people consider to be 'news sources' are actually dominated by analysis and opinion pieces" (Langlois 2018).

Other organizations also try to address or call out political bias in news reporting. For example, AllSides.com is a website whose goal is to show users multiple perspectives on the same news story in an attempt to highlight how different sources, aligned with left-, center-, or right-leaning political positions, discuss the same issue. The site encourages consideration of different points of view to combat polarization and decrease the proliferation of filter bubbles. On the political right, Accuracy in Media (AIM) is a news media watchdog group that highlights news coverage they see as biased. On the political left, Fairness and Accuracy in Reporting (FAIR) does the same. These organizations provide news consumers with examples of how claims of media bias are articulated.

Others take a broader view of bias in news reporting. Bennett (2016) argues that the main motivator for news story selection and framing is profit, not partisanship. While intentionally partisan news organizations such as Fox and MSNBC produce content to appeal to their audience, nonpartisan news organizations focus more on "attention grabbing stories" that will attract large audiences (31). In pointing out that the current news environment is one where organizations need to maximize their profits, Bennett describes four "information biases" that populate news reporting. The first is *personalization*, where the human aspect of a story dominates reporting at the expense of exploring the complex social, economic, and political context the story takes place in. The second is *dramatization*, where the dramatized reporting of stories can be engaging but does not always "enlighten and explain"; rather it is used to "excite, anger and further personalize events" (38). *Fragmentation* refers to how stories can be isolated "from each other and their larger contexts," making it difficult for citizens to understand the "big picture" of what is going on (38). Finally, *politics as a game* is an information bias that prioritizes reporting on politics more often as a contest rather than reporting on policy issues in depth or on what politicians are saying.

Journalist Brooke Gladstone (2011) also argues that discussions of news bias should not be focused on political bias but instead should consider other aspects of journalistic news coverage. *Commercial bias*, she argues, results in prioritizing news with "conflict and momentum" over follow-up reporting that might broaden an understanding of a current story. Because people "are wired to care about anything that even remotely threatens us," *bad news bias* emerges when reporting on aspects of crime and danger is dominant. Gladstone argues that because of *status quo bias*, the media ignores any position that advocates radical change, pointing out that especially when it comes to the political system, the current structure is rarely critiqued. *Access bias* refers to the relationship journalists must maintain with those in power in order to get information from them; sources may not provide information if they are upset with the journalists' coverage. Reporters often socialize with administration officials, raising concerns that coverage of these officials is tempered by these relationships. Because images and stories often engage the public, *visual bias* (where visuals may result in a story being noticed more than other stories) and *narrative bias* (when reporting takes place in a narrative format of beginning, middle and end, even if the story doesn't really have an ending or if the story elements change) may work together in ways that contribute to misleading reporting.

Finally, Gladstone says that *fairness bias* (sometimes referred to as false equivalency) occurs when journalists try to assure their audience that they are not biased by offering multiple viewpoints the same amount of time, even when another side's position is false or inaccurate (62–69).

Being able to describe the type of news content one is engaged with may also contribute to an understanding of media bias. Journalism experts Bill Kovach and Tom Rosenstiel (2010) point out that consumers "may find competing models of news delivery, with different implicit values, even on the same news channel, on the same website, and even within a single TV program," so it is important to consider each piece of news content separately (34). When news content is verified, they write, it includes multiple sources, evidence of research, the assembly of facts in a context, and the presence of "healthy skepticism" (34–35). Other news content might fall into different categories that do not prioritize verifiable information. For example, live television may provide largely unchallenged spaces for politicians and other leaders to share talking points, leading to animated exchanges of partisan ideas that are broadly articulated, sometimes inaccurate, and more opinion driven than fact driven (Kovach and Rosenstiel 2010).

Kovach and Rosenstiel also point out that other news content is "neo-partisan," where "the practitioners of this work—whether on the air, online or in print—are strongly ideological, often demagogic" (45). This opinion-driven content is often present as other news stories are reported. Additionally, interest groups, political organizations, and think tanks also report on topics connected to their own agendas. Their reports might be picked up by the general news media whose reporters may or may not examine or identify the biased perspective that informs the information. Finally, Kovach and Rosenstiel emphasize that news aggregation, bloggers, and social media content have subjective components that consumers should look for when considering content that is shared by them.

Newsroom Diversity

Connected to discussions of what news stories are covered and how they are told is the issue of newsroom diversity. Over the course of history, as the news media industries developed, their white owners' and staffs' perspectives dominated the mainstream news, often playing "a pivotal role in spreading racist views among the American people," a theme that scholars Juan Gonzalez and Joseph Torres (2011) argue persists today (185). Gonzalez and Torres note that, for the most part, nonwhite journalists were not part of mainstream news production, resulting in news coverage of nonwhite communities being crafted from white journalists' vantage points. At times, this has led to problems of representation. Over the decades, scholars have examined how news media have represented particular demographic groups, pointing out that stereotypical, or otherwise problematic, representations can inform consumers' perceptions of these groups (Larson 2006). For example, research has examined news stereotypes and their potential impact on consumer attitudes and has documented that some demographic groups, such as black Americans, are disproportionally represented as criminals in local news reports (Arendt and Northup 2015; Dixon and Linz 2000).

In today's media climate, the internet has provided more space for journalists of color to do their work; however, media consolidation has resulted in a lack of minority media ownership of traditional media outlets. Gonzalez and Torres (2011) highlight this as problematic, arguing "given that people of color are expected to make up a majority of the population by 2050, a media system where a white minority controls virtually all the principal news production and dissemination would be inherently democratic" (188).

From media ownership to diverse reporting staffs, diversity in the news media is a current issue the industry is grappling with (Newman 2019). Lasharah Bunting (2018) of the Knight Foundation points out that "a deep relationship with readers leads to improved trust, stronger journalism and sustainable business" but "that authentic connection can be difficult to establish when newsroom leaders and staff don't reflect the communities they serve." A recent report by the Women's Media Center (WMC) (2018) compiles available data from several industry organizations to demonstrate that women, and particularly women of color, are in the minority across all levels of the news industry. The WMC reports that among almost 40 percent of newsrooms that responded to the most recent American Society of News Editors' annual survey, about 52 percent of all newsroom staff are white men and about 31 percent are white women. Among newsroom leaders, those who make choices about who covers what news, about 54 percent are white men and 33 percent are white women. These numbers highlight the gender disparity and also point to the finding that about 83 percent of all newsroom staff, and 86 percent of all newsroom leaders, are white. According to the Radio Television Digital News Association's (RTDNA) data reviewed in this report, local television news (the organization does not collect data from national or cable news organizations) is comprised of about 44 percent white men, 31 percent white women, 12 percent nonwhite men, and 13 percent nonwhite women. RTDNA's random survey of almost four thousand radio stations found that about 58 percent of radio staff were white men, 30 percent white women, 6 percent women of color, and 5.5 percent men of color. Given that many media professionals begin their careers in local media, these numbers may be predictive of what the future demographic picture may look like on a national level.

The WMC argues, through its exploration of the collected data and interviews with diverse female journalists, that the news media cannot report on what is happening in the country in an accurate and fair way without a diverse newsroom staff who have knowledge about certain aspects of stories and life experiences that white journalists do not have. News teams comprised of white journalists miss major stories and potential audiences for their work. Several journalists interviewed for the report provide additional points. For example, Rummana Hussain from the *Chicago Sun-Times* noted that individual biases may shape the nature of choices made about news coverage of minority groups. Joy-Ann Reid, a political analyst and columnist, argues that media coverage of the 2016 election resulted in attention paid to only some parts of the country, while other members of the electorate were ignored. Similarly, CNN Digital vice president Mitra Kalita states, "We are now in a moment of presenting the American people as so polarized, as the coastal elites versus people in fly over country. These terms are mostly wrong and have an element of insult to them" (35).

At a time when journalism jobs are disappearing, it may be difficult to diversify newsrooms; however, a diverse slate of reporters are needed to properly address the complexities of all news stories by using their various experiences and understandings of historical contexts (Bunting 2018). There are challenges that impede this goal. Journalists Ann Curry and Dorothy Tucker suggest that the structure of newsroom succession is one where men mentor other men to rise up (WMC 2018). Other research has examined news leaders' existing potential biases and perceptions of diverse journalists that may contribute to the challenges in transforming newsrooms to places where diverse journalists are covering full ranges of stories, not just stories connected to their particular demographic community (Somani and Hopkinson 2018).

News organizations are aware of the need to diversify not only their staff but also their content. Some newsrooms are using automated tools to determine how gender and ethnically diverse their content is, and some predict that journalists will pay special attention to their sources in the future to ensure that a diverse slate of voices contribute to any particular news story (Newman 2019). News organizations might also establish relationships with niche reporters and the ethnic press in order to appropriately understand and cover relevant issues. The American Press Institute advocates for collaborations with ethnic media outlets to generate reporting that is "for communities" rather than just being "about communities" (Gerson and Rodriguez 2018).

Challenges to Reliable Information: A Contemporary Exploration of Terms

The Need for Reliable Information

Access to reliable, verifiable information is necessary for citizens to make informed decisions about many aspects of their life, including their votes, their support of causes, their civic engagement, and their personal life choices. It is important to acknowledge that even the most credible information is not always perfect; within a human system of factual reporting, interpretation of facts, and analysis, mistakes can be made and the understanding of information can shift. Reporting can also achieve different levels of quality. However, good faith efforts to produce trustworthy information may share similar characteristics. In his article "Here's What Non-fake News Looks Like," journalism expert Michael Schudson (2017) suggests that reliable news "puts reality first" and is not influenced by partisans, business owners, or audience members. He notes that reliable news sources will comply with the ethical standards of the profession and have the "willingness to retract, correct, and implicitly or explicitly apologize for misstatements in a timely manner." Schudson also stipulates that journalists should be "calm and declarative," "present multiple positions or viewpoints" that are reasonable, "disclose sources when possible," "use commonly accepted data and databases," and "pursue evidence and leads" that may challenge their own belief systems.

In 2016, *Oxford Dictionary* identified "post-truth" as its international word of the year, defining the term as "relating to or denoting circumstances in which objective facts are less influential in shaping public opinion than appeals to emotion and personal belief." The choice of this word reflects what some describe as a time period, or era, in the culture where lies are used effectively to assert "ideological supremacy," where evidence or fact-checked information does not have the same power as it once did, and the distribution of untruthful material is widely spread on social media (Kingsbury 2018). In an interview about *Post-Truth*, a book that traces the history and application of the concept, author Lee McIntyre points out "that if the truth doesn't serve your agenda, you can challenge it, and you can create an environment in which, through disinformation and manufacturing doubt, you can get people to believe what you want them to believe" (Kingsbury 2018). Although the post-truth moniker may be commonly used when discussing politics, it also refers to a historical moment where citizens are particularly challenged to properly assess and evaluate information.

While currently a popular topic in the public discourse, challenges to assessing and evaluating information are not new. Lies, misleading information, propaganda, sensational reporting, poor journalism, falsified content, and promotional material have always been part of the information sphere. Entertainment and infotainment media—from television talk shows to documentaries to filmic portrayals of "real events" to some medical and health claims advanced by celebrity figures—have historically been criticized for advancing information that is "true" when it is less than accurate. However, the presence of unreliable content is amplified in a participatory culture where it is easy, and often profitable, for problematic information to be created and widely distributed, resulting in new discussions of accuracy that are largely situated in the digital sphere. Understanding commonly discussed phrases and concepts used to describe challenges to reliable information in the digital age will help citizens identify whether the information they come across is credible.

"Fake News"

Fake news, false reporting, made-up news stories—essentially the publication of information designed to look like "real" news—are not new phenomena. The first false news stories have been traced back to the fifteenth century after the invention of the printing press allowed for greater dissemination of printed information (Soll 2016). When newspapers were developed, captivating made-up stories were included to increase the sales of papers (Soll 2016). Sometimes these falsified reports, like the 1874 story in the *New York Herald* that reported animals had escaped from the Central Park Zoo and had killed many people, prompted action among readers, even if, as it was in this case, the story was marked as untrue at the bottom of the article (Uberti 2016). Much has been written about the period of yellow journalism where exaggeration and fabrication in sensational reporting dominated factual accounts of events, prompting the establishment of the objective journalism movement in the late 1800s (Soll 2016). More recently, the term has been used to refer to satirical news products, such as *The Onion* or *The Daily Show*.

Today, in our converged digital media environment, incorrect and misleading information is part of the landscape. Digital technology has contributed to the ubiquitous presence of information overload—there is more information, in the form of websites, social media content, videos, articles, books, blogs, and so forth than people are able to consider, process, and evaluate. Current technology makes it easy for anyone to fabricate a "news story" and share it in ways that prompt others to perpetuate the falsehood. Additionally, algorithmic computer programs called bots can automatically generate information, misleading some users to believe that these messages are coming from a person (Barclay 2018). Since the integration of the internet into American culture, there have been numerous examples of false reporting, internet hoaxes, and the perpetuation of lies that have been shared in digital spaces.

A recent application of the term "fake news" emerged during the 2016 American presidential campaign when made-up political-oriented stories were being widely read and shared via social media. "Fake news" refers to information that is false or inaccurate. Quotes are often used around these two words to convey that "fake news" is a broad, complicated term that can mean different things to different people. Brooke Borel (2017) of FiveThirtyEight notes, "Depending on who you talk to 'fake news' may refer to satirical news, hoaxes, news that's clumsily framed or outright wrong, propaganda, lies destined for viral clicks and advertising dollars, politically motivated half-truths and more." A study that examined how audiences understand fake news revealed that "fake news is only in part about fabricated news reports narrowly defined, and much more about a wider disconnect with the information landscape—including news media and politicians as well as platform companies" (Nielsen and Graves 2017, 1). In an article for *Columbia Journalism Review*, David Uberti (2016) argues, "Let's retire the dreaded moniker in favor of more precise choices: misinformation, deception, lies. Just as the media has employed 'fake news' to discredit competitors for public attention, political celebrities and partisan publications have used it to discredit the press wholesale."

The use of this term by politicians is often one that applies the moniker to "news organizations whose coverage they find disagreeable, and in this way, has become a mechanism by which the powerful clamp down upon, restrict, undermine and circumvent the free press" (Wardle and Derakhshan 2017). President Trump often appropriates the term "fake news" to refer to reporting he disagrees with or dislikes, whether said reporting is fact based or not, often spreading misinformation and disinformation himself (Ross and Rivers 2018). In their dismissal of the term "fake news," Claire Wardle and Hossein Derakhshan (2017) substitute a framework of "information disorder" that encompasses "three types of information using dimensions of harm and falseness: mis-information is when false information is shared but no harm is meant, disinformation is when false information is knowingly shared to cause harm, mal-information is when genuine information is shared to cause harm, often by moving private information into the public sphere."

While the mainstream use of the term "fake news" may not be going away anytime soon, an overview of the different types of information that this term might broadly refer to can assist in one's understanding of the complexities of information in the current digital media environment. It is important to be able to identify the type of content that is being created and shared, what motivations might prompt the creation of this content, and how the content is being distributed in order to best understand the "information ecosystem" that supports problematic material (Wardle and Derakhshan 2017).

Misinformation and Disinformation

In 2018, Dictionary.com dubbed "misinformation," which it defines as "false information that is spread, regardless of whether there is intent to mislead," as the word of the year. The site clearly notes that "misinformation" differs from "disinformation," defined as "deliberately misleading or biased information; manipulated narrative or facts; propaganda," because disinformation's definition requires there to be intent. In explaining their choice, the organization noted the problem of misinformation and disinformation being spread across social media sites through posts and memes, even as some companies tried to squash it. Dictionary.com also states that because people don't fact-check information on social media, they may play a role in the spread of misinformation that is actually disinformation, stating "if a politician strategically spreads information that they know to be false in the form of articles, photos, memes, etc., that's disinformation. When an individual sees this disinformation, believes it, and then shares it, that's misinformation." A UNESCO report that addresses this issue adopts a similar definition, noting "misinformation is information that is false, but the person who is disseminating it believes that it is true. Disinformation is information that is false, and the person who is disseminating it knows it is false" (Wardle and Derakhshan 2018).

Social media has provided people and organizations with an easy method of spreading misinformation and disinformation. Given the low cost of creating and distributing false content, the practice is financially lucrative if the content is sensational or engaging enough to attract viewers who will in turn share the story with others. For example, many made-up stories about Donald Trump and Hillary Clinton during the 2016 election season were traced to a small town in Macedonia where teenage authors of false websites and fake news stories made money from web advertising companies each time their made-up content was clicked on by millions of viewers (Subramanian 2017). Other fake sites try to manipulate users into spending money. BuzzFeed News' Craig Silverman (2016a) reported on a series of fake Native American Facebook pages operated by non-Native Americans in Vietnam and Kosovo. These contrived, but popular, Facebook pages capitalized on the protests at Standing Rock against the pipeline construction to sell fraudulent Native American merchandise, often using designs Natives claim were stolen from them.

Writer and journalist James Ball (2017) suggests that if money is not a motivation, purveyors of false information fall into two broad categories: "one group is made up of hoaxers and pranksters, making fake news for the thrill, for the attention, or to enjoy the 'stupidity' of groups they dislike. The other type is a partisan who invents news which they think will help the cause or the candidate they've decided to champion" (134). After the Boston Marathon bombing in 2013, many false stories about victims, potential subsequent attacks, and conspiracy theories spread via Twitter, providing a contrasting use of the platform that was also effectively and appropriately used by officials to communicate information (Gross 2013). So-called anti-vaxers, a vocal group of people who argue against childhood vaccinations despite widespread scientific evidence that demonstrates their safety and contributions to eliminating diseases, harnessed Twitter to advance their cause, imply that large numbers of people agreed with their point of view, and craft tweets "designed to erode confidence in vaccination" (Diresta and Lotan 2015). Scholars continue to examine the presence of "fake news" stories and websites during the 2016 presidential election. One recent study suggests that information from fake news domains was rarely shared among Facebook friends during the election from April to November 2016, but when it was, it was most likely shared by conservatives and Americans over the age of sixty-five (Guess, Nagler, and Tucker 2019). However, a BuzzFeed analysis shows that "fake news" generated more shares, reactions, and comments on Facebook than "real news" during the past three months of the election campaign, a pattern that was not seen prior to that point (Silverman 2016b).

Social media scholar danah boyd (2017) points out that some sophisticated computer users want to "attack the emergent attention economy" in order to "manipulate the media narrative, just to show that they could." "Hacker-minded folks," as boyd refers to them, discovered ways to manipulate or take advantage of social media algorithms and otherwise coordinate online actions in ways that achieve their goal—to "shape information within a networked ecosystem." While sometimes the information that the hackers aim to call attention to is innocuous, other times it is not. Wardle (2018) of First Draft News explains that the trajectory of spreading disruptive, and potentially dangerous, information can be visualized in what she calls the "trumpet of amplification." Here, "disinformation often starts on the anonymous web (platforms like 4chan and Discord), moves into closed or semi-closed groups (Twitter DM groups, Facebook or WhatsApp groups), onto conspiracy communities on Reddit Forums or YouTube channels, and then onto open social networks like Twitter, Facebook and Instagram." Wardle points out that if professional media picks up the information at this point—either to debunk it or use it irresponsibly in a story—"the agents of disinformation have won. Amplification, in any form, was their goal in the first place."

Misinformation, disinformation, and especially systematically organized disinformation campaigns threaten the democratic process, and despite more widespread acknowledgment of the presence of false news both by consumers and technology companies that have implemented measures to prevent the spread of misinformation and disinformation, the problem persists. In the time period leading up to the 2018 midterm elections in the United States, social media companies disclosed the presence of inaccurate posts, some of which were false and others were "hyperpartisan and sensationalized that may not be entirely accurate but still contain some kernel of truth" (Breland 2018). Though it did not seem to be a coordinated effort led by a particular group, users who seemed to share similar ideologies spread these misinformed posts, eventually resulting in the content being shared with larger and larger pools of people (Breland 2018).

Finally, as the country prepares to consider candidates for the next presidential primaries and eventual election, it is expected that misinformation and disinformation will continue to persist and remain potentially influential. Authors of this content include political operatives. A recent *New York Times* article highlighted how a political campaign staffer has anonymously put together webpages designed to look like candidates' campaign websites (Rosenberg 2019). The most "successful" of these mock campaign sites is the one for former Vice President Joseph Biden, as some users believe it to be an authentic campaign site (Rosenberg 2019). Reporter Matthew Rosenberg (2019) points out that not only is the website fake but it "offers a preview of what election experts and national security officials say Americans can expect to be bombarded with for the next year and a half: anonymous and hard-to-trace digital messaging spread by sophisticated political operatives whose aim is to sow political discord through deceit." Rosenberg reports that these tactics are expected to be employed by both democrat and republican operatives in the upcoming election season.

Propaganda

"Propaganda" is a term that refers to the distribution of information that is designed to influence, or shift, people's opinions, points of view, and/or actions. Propaganda is often associated with advancing a political point of view, but it can be associated with any organization's goals. It is not a new practice, nor is it a concept that is inherently negative. Critic and professor Mark Crispin Miller (2004) suggests that while propaganda may have a negative connotation and is associated with lying or manipulation, propaganda can also serve a "worthy" cause provided it is absent lies or mistruths (Frontline 2004). He notes, "Any systematic attempt to move large numbers of people to some action is propaganda. Trying to get people to quit smoking, propaganda; to wear their seat belts, same thing" (Frontline 2004). During World War II, the Allied forces used propaganda to generate support for their objectives just as the Nazi regime did. Propaganda techniques are commonly used by public relations professionals, politicians, advertisers, and organizations.

Propagandists often use emotional appeals in their messaging, and "most propaganda mixes a small amount of fact with a large dose of fiction" (Barclay 2018, 34). According to Aaron Delwiche (2018), several basic propaganda techniques are used to advance the goals of the propagandist, including using fear, misusing logic, using euphemisms, generating positive or negative emotional responses to ideas, relying on notable people's testimonials, and linking culturally celebrated value systems with the ideas about the issue at hand. In the digital age, the use and reach of propaganda have expanded. Delwiche explains that problematic persuasive messaging is sometimes hard to detect: "Propagandists use computer controlled accounts called bots to control the flow of information in online forums, and they amplify the reach of these bots with the help of fake user profiles called *sockpuppets*. As if this were not enough, hidden persuaders are also able to use data about a user's online behavior to figure out which messages are most likely to influence that person."

The influential nature of propaganda has been recently discussed as part of the investigation into the Russian government's interference in the 2016 presidential election. The U. S. Office of Special Counsel has identified the propaganda tools used by Russian state actors to influence the election, tools that promoted content favorable to the Trump campaign. The Special Counsel's 2018 indictment against Russian organizations and related individuals details ways political messaging was created and disseminated on social media platforms, noting "defendants and their co-conspirators, through fraud and deceit, created hundreds of social media accounts and used them to develop certain fictitious U.S. personas into 'leader[s] of public opinion' in the United States" (14). Social media accounts addressed topics such as immigration, race relations, religion, and distaste for Hillary Clinton. Additionally, the indictment discusses how these foreign actors used social media to organize political rallies and describes how online political ads were purchased that declared support for Trump or advanced discourse against Hillary Clinton. While the concrete influence of this campaign is difficult to prove, these materials were viewed by thousands of people.

Promotional Information

Promotional content takes several forms in the information landscape. Authors, actors, and celebrities are often interviewed as part of publicity tours that promote their upcoming books, films, television shows, or other projects. Advertisements that exist online, in print publications, and on the radio and television are usually distinguishable forms of messaging that recognizably are in place to sell or promote a product or service. Public relations materials and efforts, in comparison, are designed to be invisible.

Wendall Potter (2010), a former high-level public relations professional, explains that "PR subtly convinces you to change the way you think" and notes that the best "PR usually gets free media space because it is presented as unbiased information"

(58). Public relations professionals might write news releases about what happened at an event before it takes place, train executives on how to interview with the media, and employ lobbyists and work closely with reporters to benefit the organization (Potter 2010). Public relations efforts can contribute to the democratic process by offering an exchange of ideas, highlighting worthy causes, promoting points of view, and selling products in a free marketplace (Stauber and Rampton 1995). However, some argue that many large industries have unfairly utilized public relations for their own interests and profits, what one industry critic describes as "the undemocratic power of the multi-billion dollar PR industry to manipulate and propagandize on behalf of wealthy special interests, dominating debate, discussion and decision making" (Stauber and Rampton 1995, 205). Some detailed and critical analysis of certain public relations efforts, including PR "spin," reveal campaigns that engage in unethical practices that mislead the public on such issues as health care, environmental issues, food safety, and economics (Potter 2010; Rampton and Stauber 2001; Stauber and Rampton 1995). As news organizations face economic challenges, incorporating free promotional content into their papers and broadcasts becomes a viable option, and it can be difficult to distinguish the difference between promotional content provided by a public relations firm and editorial content that is created by a news organization (Farsetta and Price 2006; Potter 2010).

Other promotional content that provides information is aligned more with the advertising, rather than public relations, tradition. In an attempt to continually target fragmented markets of consumers, advertising companies have developed new promotional techniques that seamlessly integrate promotional material into information providers' platforms and track and target customers in digital spaces. As a component of many news and information organizations' business models to secure financing, native advertising and/or sponsored content posts often appear alongside editorial reporting. According to Valerie Turgeon (2017) of the content marketing agency Brandpoint, native ads look similar to the type of content they appear next to in the digital space but are labeled as advertising, while sponsored content is "brand journalism," an article or video that details the positives of a brand or product. Native advertising might take the form of an advertorial that explains and/or promotes a product and might further prompt users to explore branded articles by using attention-grabbing headlines or images that appear in a section of the digital space called "suggested content" (Keller 2019).

Some publishers "erect a strict wall between their marketing and editorial departments," but others hire people from editorial to create customized, branded, promotional content, like social media posts, videos, and articles, so it matches the form and aesthetic of the space it appears in (Levy 2019). Because the ad and the journalistic content look similar, users may not always distinguish between the sponsored content and the editorial content, content that is independently produced by an organization's reporters and writers, on a particular website. Another promotional practice is called "influencer marketing." Usually taking place on social media, online influencers promote brands, products, or services to their numerous followers, not always disclosing their commercial objectives. While some influencers are notable people or celebrities, others, referred to as micro influencers or nano influencers, have fewer followers and work in niche markets (Bloom 2019).

Scholars have expressed concerns that native advertising–oriented techniques trick readers into thinking what they are seeing is editorial rather than promotional content, blurring the lines between what is news and what is not (Carlson 2015; Glasser, Varma, and Zou 2019). Trust in the media may erode when consumers are not initially aware of the promotional tactics being used to persuade them. Some scholars have also explored the ethics of the deceptive tactics used in native advertising, suggesting that consumers are more likely to react negatively to advertising when promotional intentions are not disclosed (Han, Drumwright, and Goo 2018). Currently, a

Federal Trade Commission policy that addresses native advertising asks that advertisers appropriately label their promotional content, subscribing to the "view that promotional messages not readily identifiable as advertising can deceive consumers, who are likely to view such material as unbiased and independent" (Mudge and Shaheen 2017, 10).

Finally, at a time when large amounts of information, called "big data," can be easily collected from individuals, companies have the ability to analyze these data to create psychographic profiles of people who they may then organize in similarly minded groups (Burleigh 2017). These groups can then be micro-targeted, where messages that are expected to provoke, persuade, and resonate with them are shared, with the hopes of prompting a desired reaction. Persuasive micro-targeting techniques have been used by presidential campaigns to analyze, group, and market to pockets of citizens (Burleigh 2017). The collection and use of people's private information for commercial and persuasive purposes have resulted in anger among some users; Facebook, in particular, has been criticized for its use and selling of private information without users' knowledge or consent.

Content Fabricated by Journalists

Journalism is supposed to rely on "facts, reality and trust" (Borel 2017), and sometimes journalists themselves break this credo, producing fraudulent work that is initially thought to be credible given their roles as professional journalists. For example, Pulitzer Prize winners Louis Seibold (in 1921) and Janet Cooke (in 1981) fabricated the stories that "earned" their honors. Seibold worked with President Woodrow Wilson's wife and chief of staff to fake an interview feature story with the president who was recovering from a stroke at the time, and Cooke wrote about an eight-year-old heroin addict who didn't exist (Robillard 2012). Writer Stephen Glass made up stories, sources, and quotes supported by faked notes from imagined events and interviews to construct articles for the *New Republic* as well as for publications such as *Harper* and *Rolling Stone* (Bissinger 2007). The *New York Times* reporter Jayson Blair "committed frequent acts of journalistic fraud" during his four years at the *New York Times*, making up quotes, fabricating article material, and lying to editors about where he reported from (Barry et al. 2003). Other journalists and columnists over the years have been found committing similar transgressions—making up sources or information or plagiarizing others—to support their story (Silverman 2012). In 2018, internationally recognized writer Claas Relotius of Germany's highly regarded newsmagazine *Der Spiegel* was found to have "fabricated facts and sources in more than a dozen articles over a seven-year period" (Pham 2018). While these fraudulent actions are discouraging and problematic, reputable news organizations typically disclose and investigate such revelations, knowing that actions of individual reporters reflect on the organization's credibility.

Conspiracy Theories

As with other forms of problematic information, conspiracy theories, which are unsubstantiated beliefs in covert organizations and their activities, are not new, but the spread of them has increased in the digital age due to the ease of sharing and the powerful outcomes of the algorithms used by social media companies that result in suggesting provocative material. A popular conspiracy theorist is Alex Jones, who hosts a radio show and runs a website called InfoWars. Though Jones has been advancing his conspiracy theories for over twenty years, which include the assertions that the government staged terrorist attacks and, more recently, that the school shooting at the Sandy Hook Elementary School in Newtown, Connecticut, was a hoax, he gained more mainstream attention when Donald Trump appeared on his program in 2015 and thanked and complemented him. Jones has also argued that the government controls the weather, Microsoft's Bill Gates is a eugenicist, and millions of undocumented people were voting in elections (Killelea 2017). In 2018, Apple, the music platform Spotify,

Facebook, and YouTube largely banned Jones's content from their platforms in an attempt to combat the spread of his misinformation, conspiracy theories, and lies (Nicas 2018). While this move resulted in less views of Jones's inflammatory material, it also raised questions about issues of free speech and the powerful reach of today's technology companies in an era of media consolidation. As one technology reporter writes, "That Facebook and Google, which owns YouTube, muffled one of the internet's loudest voices so quickly illustrates the tremendous influence a few internet companies have over public discourse and the spread of information" (Nicas 2018).

Widely spread conspiracy theories run the risk of being socially irresponsible and can lead to trouble as it did during what is now called Pizzagate, the storming of a Washington, DC, pizza place in 2016 by a man with loaded weapons and a knife who falsely believed presidential candidate Hillary Clinton was operating a child sex ring at the restaurant. This falsehood appeared on Facebook, Twitter, Brietbart.com, and InfoWars.com and was shared by many—from ordinary people to bots to activists to Trump campaign associates to Russian operatives (Robb 2017). Conspiracy theories have also been created and/or spread by political pundits to advance their political agenda (Roose 2018a). For example, after explosive devices were sent to CNN and several prominent Democrats, commentators on the political right disseminated a narrative that the devices were planted by activists on the far left in an attempt to make the political right appear violent in advance of the 2018 midterm elections (Roose 2018a).

The video sharing site YouTube has been identified as a problematic host of highly viewed conspiracy theory–oriented content. YouTube has been criticized for suggesting conspiracy-oriented videos to viewers even when they have not previously viewed similar content (Wakabayashi 2019). Vox's Jane Coaston (2018) argues that, although there is nothing illegal about conspiracy theories and they are an element of free expression, YouTube's algorithms, like other social media algorithms, tend to recommend sensational and provocative videos, leading to the spread of information that is socially irresponsible. Examples of conspiracy theories that have thrived on YouTube include different narratives about the terrorist attacks on September 11, 2001, suggestions that the Sandy Hook school shooting tragedy did not happen, the idea that President Trump and investigator Robert Mueller are working together to uncover a pedophile ring, videos associated with Pizzagate, and something called Frazzledrip, which asserts that Hillary Clinton cut off a child's face and wore it as a mask (Coaston 2018). Recently, YouTube-hosted conspiracy videos have convinced an increasing number of viewers that the earth is flat (Sample 2019).

YouTube has also been criticized for allowing a video that asserted "crisis actors" were part of the February 14, 2018, Parkland, Florida, school shooting (it was eventually removed) and for not hiring enough staff to better monitor videos that advance conspiracy theories or other misinformation and dis-information (Graham 2019). Recently, the company has made further changes to try to combat conspiracy-oriented information. In January 2019, YouTube issued a statement that they would put measures in place to stop recommending conspiracy theory–oriented videos to users (Wakabayashi 2019).

Digital Technologies and News and Information

News Algorithms

The web allows consumers to easily access news and information from a diverse slate of sources. However, it is not possible for any one user to keep track of all the multiple news updates posted online. News aggregators were developed to create a feed of information that displays updates from a user-chosen group of websites. Such news aggregators as Inoreader, Feedly, and Flipboard are helpful to users because they collect and provide content in one place for easy viewing. Sophisticated algorithms, or formulaic computer programs, may also be used with aggregation to collect and present news-related content to users; this curated content may direct consumer traffic to particular websites. For example, the Google News algorithm prioritizes news organization websites that first break a story; these stories then appear at the top of Google News and get more attention (Ball 2017). News aggregators that curate content "spotlight stories and often package content based on algorithms and/or the work of editors" who make choices on how to contextualize the information (Skaggs 2012).

Because algorithms drive what content users are exposed to via their social media feeds, James Cohen (2018) argues that citizens need to be aware of how others write algorithms to create each person's individual stream of information. Cohen explains that "algorithms collect, convert, and organize user actions into data to create unique media environments through various methods of data collection and data tracking (occasionally referred to as 'dataveillance') of digital media activity on apps and browsers as well as tracking data in physical spaces" (141). Essentially, the algorithm collects and analyzes large amounts of personal data to determine what information would be most favorably received in a social media feed. Cohen points out that whereas traditional, or legacy, media presents fixed information, such as the stories on a radio news program or in a daily newspaper, "the algorithmic media environment is a custom, unique environment that changes as the user changes, but also with the culture surrounding the user" (145). Social media companies want to use algorithms that will increase users' time spent online.

The "custom" online environment that Cohen refers to may contribute to the creation of filter bubbles and echo chambers. As noted earlier, filter bubbles are problematic because they may limit people's exposure to content that challenges their perspectives and belief systems, possibly preventing the consideration of multiple, and valuable, ideas needed to understand the complexity of contemporary issues. In a recent interview with *Wired* magazine, Eli Pariser highlights the algorithmic power of the Facebook News Feed, noting that it "shapes what we get to know" and argues that "unintended biases in those algorithms can have enormous effects" (Hempel 2017). Experts P. W. Singer and Emerson Brooking (2018) point out that people are likely to share information they've seen on a friend's social media feed, which algorithmically results in similar content being suggested to that user, resulting in a feedback loop of additional similar content. When one sees a familiar claim, they write, "The less likely you are to assess it critically. And the longer you linger in a particular community, the more its claims will be repeated until they become truisms—even if they remain the opposite of the truth" (124). While this may be the case some of the time, users have been found to share information without reading more than the article headline. A recent study about Twitter use indicated that people were more likely to retweet information than read it; 59 percent of links shared were not read (Dewey 2016).

Technology companies' use of, and tweaking of, their algorithms to curate and suggest content may have powerful implications. For example, given the enormous reach of Facebook News Feed, much has been written about the algorithm that drives the content, including online news stories, that appears on it. Because web publisher advertising revenue is often correlated with website traffic, "a change to Facebook's algorithm can make or break publishers, as making posts or shares a little bit more or less vulnerable can mean thousands or millions more—or fewer—clicks" (Ball 2017, 146). Because Facebook is invested in keeping their users on their site for as long as they can in order to generate revenue from advertisers, the company will make changes to their algorithm to achieve this, sometimes to prioritize news and other times to prioritize entertainment or friend and family updates on the feed (Ball 2017).

The Facebook News Feed

The influential and pervasive presence of "fake news" on Facebook corresponds with the rapid growth of the popular social media company, a company whose initial mission was to "make the world more open and connected" (Bourg and Jacoby 2018). After the social media site became available outside of colleges and universities in 2006, the number of users increased dramatically. By 2008, Facebook claimed thirty-five million users, and these numbers increased each month, adding between five hundred thousand and eight hundred thousand users a day (Madrigal 2012). In 2015, the company claimed to have 1.59 billion active monthly users, and in 2016, this number increased to 1.86 billion (Fiegerman 2017). Despite numerous controversies ranging from the presence of "fake news" on the site to the company's use of private customer data, Facebook's popularity increased to two billion users a month by the fall of 2018 (Bourg and Jacoby 2018). A Pew Research study additionally found that in 2018, 68 percent of adults were on Facebook, with 43 percent of these users noting that they obtain news from the platform (Gramlich 2018).

A 2018 *Frontline* investigative report highlights how Facebook News Feed's algorithm contributes to the site's perpetuation of misinformation and disinformation. Introduced in 2009, the News Feed is a stream of information provided to each user that is customized based on the user's previous Facebook activity; the company's algorithms analyze people's activity on Facebook and preferred content to determine what information to prioritize in an individual feed that offers a personalized stream of information. Because users tend to click on provocative content, the algorithmic News Feed responds in kind, prioritizing sensational, often polarizing, and sometimes "fake" posts, which, in turn, inspire more clicks (Bourg and Jacoby 2018). Additionally, in 2014, Facebook debuted a feature called "Trending Topics" on users' Facebook pages. This compilation of suggested stories from around the web was initially selected by journalists and backfired when those running the feature were accused of limiting and blocking conservative-oriented topics (Ball 2017). The "Trending Topics" team was replaced with an algorithm, a decision that some also point to as informing the proliferation of "fake news" on the site (Ball

2017). Facebook discontinued "Trending Topics" in June 2018 and is experimenting with different ways to share legitimate news stories on its platform (Newcomb 2018).

Today there is an understanding that Facebook and other social media companies, such as Twitter, can be, and are being, used by others to promote disinformation and misinformation. These companies, along with the U.S. government, are trying to prevent the spread of disinformation and identify its perpetrators. After it became clear that misinformation and disinformation were pervasive on Facebook in the run-up to the 2016 presidential election, ABC News, the Associated Press, Snopes, and Politifact began working with Facebook to fact-check and highlight incorrect news that appeared in users' News Feeds (Ananny 2018). Facebook also implemented a news verification service and employed a security firm to help identify misinformation and fake sites on Facebook (Bourg and Jacoby 2018; Frier 2018b).

Despite these efforts, the presence of misinformation and disinformation on Facebook remains a problem. Even after it was determined that Russia employed a social media influence campaign to disrupt the 2016 presidential election, Russian intelligence pages remained on the site (Frier 2018b). Additionally, on October 11, 2018, Facebook announced in a company newsroom post that they were eliminating 559 pages and 251 accounts. The company explained:

Given the activity we've seen—and its timing ahead of the US midterm elections—we wanted to give some details about the types of behavior that led to this action. Many were using fake accounts or multiple accounts with the same names and posted massive amounts of content across a network of Groups and Pages to drive traffic to their websites. Many used the same techniques to make their content appear more popular on Facebook than it really was. Others were ad farms using Facebook to mislead people into thinking that they were forums for legitimate political debate. (Gleicher and Rodriguez 2018)

The company determined that creators of these accounts lived in the United States and constructed "click bait"–oriented political content that was false (Frier 2018a). Just a few months before, in August, the company stated that it removed 652 fake sites it traced to Iran and additionally removed an undisclosed number of Russian intelligence pages (Frier 2018b). Social media users need to be vigilant when considering information that crosses their screens as it likely will not be possible for all incorrect information to be eliminated. Additionally, as Wardle and Derakhshan (2017) of First Draft News point out, consumers need to be aware that misinformation and disinformation are often encountered in an "ecosystem" of other content, including reliable news, promotional material, personal updates, and partisan perspectives.

Social Media Bots

A social media bot is a computer program that is written to look as if a person is posting and interacting on social media sites. Social media bots can be useful tools—they can be programmed to collect information in a transparent way, widely disseminate beneficial information, make people laugh, and engage citizens (Wooley and Howard 2016). Bots—the term is derived from "robot"—range in their level of sophistication and purposes but, given their automation capabilities, can promote particular messages on social media sites at a rate far higher than humans (Singer and Brooking 2018). Bots can continually promote a particular hashtag on Twitter, for example, over and over to digitally "bury" an opposing view (Singer and Brooking 2018, 140). Given that it is estimated that the majority of web traffic is generated by computers, the pervasiveness of bots is something citizens should recognize as information sharers and generators (Reed 2018; Singer and Brooking 2018).

Bots have been used as political disruptors, sometimes launched by authoritarian governments to counter information

(Singer and Brooking 2018). Samuel Wooley of PoliticalBots. org and Professor Phil Howard (2016) argue that given the fact that bots and botnets (bots that are networked together) have been used during election campaigns, "automated campaign communications are a very real threat to our democracy." One of the first uses of a botnet in an American election was during the Massachusetts special election to fill a Senate seat vacated by Senator Ted Kennedy's passing; bots commissioned by conservatives in favor of candidate Scott Brown populated social media (Singer and Brooking 2018). The success of this strategy informed the use of botnets in subsequent elections. Other research shows "in past elections, politicians, government agencies, and advocacy groups have used bots to engage voters and spread messages. We've found bots disseminating lies, attacking people and poisoning conversations" (Wooley and Howard 2016).

Social media bots spread false information during the 2016 presidential campaign, where Twitter bots disproportionally spread information from sources with little credibility (Shao et al. 2018). Two-thirds of these bots were in favor of Trump, and "as Election Day approached, pro-Trump bots swelled in intensity and volume, overpowering pro-Clinton voices by a five-to-one ratio" (Singer and Brooking 2018, 143). Bots have also been used to share untrue or misleading information to generate unrest and amplify charged conversations, making it look like lots of people are engaged in a conversation when, in reality, the social media participation is bot driven (Recode 2018). Despite numerous initiatives to stifle problematic social bots, concerns remain over how bots are being used to spread false information. For example, bots advocating against vaccinations contribute to problematic misunderstandings of this disease-preventing measure (Wooley and Howard 2016). After the school shooting in Santa Fe, Texas, in May 2018, numerous bots were found advancing disinformation about the tragedy (Morris 2018). However, bots alone cannot be blamed for the spread of misinformation and disinformation. MIT Media Lab scholars

Soroush Vosoughi, Deb Roy, and Sinan Aral (2018) found, in their comprehensive analysis of what kinds of stories were spread on Twitter from 2006 to 2017, that bots tweeted false and true stories at relatively equal rates but that humans were more likely to tweet false stories. The authors suggest that perhaps the novelty of the false content or the emotional response to the content prompts people to pass false content along.

Public awareness of bots and botnets has increased. A 2018 Pew Research report found that two-thirds of Americans have heard of bots, and within this group, the majority believe bots are used "maliciously." The study further indicated that many do not feel confident in their ability to detect bots and share concerns that bots' spreading of information contributes to a misinformed citizenry. While people in the study acknowledge that some bot uses are acceptable, such as sharing emergency updates or for promotional purposes, researchers also found that the more people knew about bots, the less favorably they felt about them (Stocking and Sumida 2018).

Deepfake Videos

In April 2018, actor and film director Jordan Peele participated in creating a video of former president Barack Obama speaking to viewers in a seemingly official setting with the American flag in the background. The video itself, however, was a forgery where Obama appeared to be saying words actually spoken by Peele. Seen by millions, Peele produced this "deepfake" video to raise awareness of the dangers inherent in this emerging technology. Deepfake videos are fake videos that are created using sophisticated software programs. The computers use artificial intelligence to produce the videos. Security and legal experts Robert Chesney and Danielle Citron (2019) explain that "deep fakes are the product of recent advances in a form of artificial intelligence known as 'deep learning,' in which sets of algorithms called 'neural networks' learn to infer rules and replicate patterns by sifting through large data sets" (148). Deepfake programs, like the easy-to-obtain OpenFaceSwap, are able to replicate an individual's gestures, movements, and expressions while making adjustments to the video so that it appears authentic (Knight 2018). Face-swapping, where one face is used in place of another, and increasingly sophisticated audio technology have been used to depict politicians, actors, and others fictitiously (Chesney and Citron 2019; Knight 2018). Because there is so much audiovisual material available of high-profile people to draw from and alter to create these deepfakes, they are most at risk for being fraudulently portrayed in deepfakes, possibly serving the interests of an adversary (Howcraft 2018).

While acknowledging that technology has always assisted in deception, Chesney and Citron (2019) suggest that deepfakes are "unprecedented" because of "their combination of quality, applicability to persuasive formats such as audio and video, and resistance to detection" (150). The development of deepfake technology is aided by a "generative adversarial network," or GAN, which can be trained to produce "surprisingly realistic fake imagery" (Knight 2018, 40). As the technology is perfected, it may become harder for people to identify some of the minor glitches that currently raise a red flag that the video is not authentic. If people cannot determine the authenticity of a video that appears on social media, for example, disinformation campaigns that employ these tactics may threaten elections or provoke tensions among social groups (Chesney and Citron 2019).

Experts are working on developing ways to use artificial intelligence to detect deepfake videos and are brainstorming ways to authenticate content (Chesney and Citron 2019). Citizens can look carefully at videos to try to discern any visual inconsistencies or changes in pixilation (Knight 2018). Deepfakes are emerging at a time when digital spaces are already populated with misinformation and disinformation, and the public is already skeptical of sometimes even the most reliable information. As broader knowledge of the presence of deepfakes increases, some warn that this skepticism will be manipulated. *MIT Technology Review* senior editor Will Knight argues, "As the powerful become increasingly aware of AI fakery it will become easy to dismiss even clear-cut video evidence of wrongdoing as nothing more than GAN-made digital deception. The truth will still be out there. But will you know it when you see it?" (41).

Solutions

Organization Initiatives

In order for the public to trust information that crosses their screens, the reliability of that information needs to be confirmed. Such fact-checking organizations as Politifact, Snopes, and FactCheck.org are relied upon by citizens and journalists as helpful tools in understanding the veracity of information in its given context. Foundations and journalism organizations are addressing these issues with funded initiatives, research, and journalism trainings. Technology platforms are continuing to identify and shut down fake accounts, have partnered with fact-checkers, and have developed systems to promote reliable news, identify bots, and appropriately label content. Preliminary research suggests these tactics are working to decrease interaction with unreliable material (Newman 2019). The Digital News Project's *Journalism, Media and Technology Trends and Predictions* report suggests that news publisher credibility will eventually influence whether or not news is shared on social media or via search platforms or aggregators (Newman 2019). Aware of the percentages that indicate public distrust in the news media, some news organizations are publishing "trust indicators," explanations of their newsgathering policies and ethics, as a way of assuring citizens of their legitimacy. Additionally, such new initiatives as NewsGuard, a start-up that "aims to rate (as green or red) every significant site in the United States," may help consumers in identifying reputable news (Newman 2019, 16). Other novel news "trust" initiatives include Trusting News, The Trust Project, and The News Integrity Initiative (Schmidt 2018b).

In March 2018, Google announced the creation of the Google News Initiative, a multifaceted project that Google pledges will support journalism by helping news organizations. Perhaps implicitly acknowledging its part in sharing unreliable information and conspiracy theories in Google and YouTube search results, the company has pledged $300 million over three years to "support authoritative journalism" (Roose 2018b). The initiative builds on current Google programs that support newsroom grants, trainings and partnerships, and plans to implement new ideas designed to help news organizations obtain subscribers (Ingram 2018). The company also plans to start a Disinfo Lab with First Draft News that helps journalists monitor disinformation during elections and improve their search algorithms to prioritize stronger sources in search results (Ingram 2018).

Experts also point out that news organizations need to be transparent with the public about how they gather information, verify facts, and use sources. Transparency requires journalists to admit what they don't know and honestly share what they know and how they know it, embodying "the original meaning of what came to be called objectivity in news" (Kovach and Rosenstiel 2010, 185). Others point out that news organizations have to do a better job at identifying the quality news they produce and think about whether they should report on items that may catch people's attention but are of little substance. As Ball (2017) argues, "If newspapers don't differentiate the stories that they've put time and reporting resources into from those they run based on a single tweet, why should readers give any more credence to one than another?" (93). Similarly, Ethan Zuckerman (2018) from the Center for Civic Media points out that producing quality news is expensive, and it can be difficult for news organizations to encourage people to pay attention to it. Zuckerman writes, "One of the disturbing aspects of this situation is that democracy requires not only high quality journalism, but an audience of citizens to consume it. Our problem is not just paying for stories—it may include paying for these stories to reach the audiences who need them if journalism can't win the battle for attention in our discovery engines/attention markets." Zuckerman wonders if the technology, coupled with public funding, might be appropriated to direct news to populations of citizens by using social media in a new way.

Increasing News and Information Literacy

Even as news organizations work to gain more of the public trust and technology companies filter out information that is suspect, unreliable, or false, problematic information is likely to remain part of the news and information landscape. Though many would argue it is not a "solution" to the issues problematic information poses, media literacy initiatives aim to educate citizens to access, analyze, evaluate, and create media across all forms and platforms. The core questions of media literacy, phrased in slightly different ways by different media literacy organizations, invite media consumers to ask questions when evaluating media texts. The Media Education Lab at the University of Rhode Island lists them as "Who created the message and what is the purpose? What techniques are used to attract and hold attention? What lifestyles, values and points of view are depicted? How might different people interpret this message? What is omitted?" Asking these broad questions while thoughtfully and deliberately looking at and listening to such texts as videos, blogs, news reports, memes, and tweets may help consumers decide on the quality and nature of the information. Media literacy curricula focus on all media and approach the study of news and information as an element of the complex media landscape, drawing connections between news media and other media constructions (Jolly 2014).

News literacy programs focus specifically on evaluating news and information, empowering consumers to develop critical thinking skills in ways that help them determine what information is trustworthy. For example, the Center for News Literacy at Stony Brook University in New York, which began in 2005, is just one of the now many educational institutions and nonprofit organizations focusing on increasing news and information literacy skills (Jacobson 2017). As the *Columbia Journalism Review*'s Lindsay Beyerstein (2014) writes, "The need for news literacy has only grown. Where the movement once worried about blogs, left-right bias, and how to decode the front page of a newspaper, it now confronts a booming content-marketing business that is cranking out native advertising, all manner of 'sponsored content,' and glossy magazines and slick docu-ads produced by corporations that look and sound a lot like journalism."

Even though scholars debate over how to characterize the educational initiatives aiming to increase people's abilities to critically assess and evaluate information, they hope that increasing the public's literacy skills will result in more informed engagement with, and discernment of, media content (Jolly 2014). There is a demonstrated need for these initiatives. A recent Stanford History Education Group (SHEG) study assessed students' abilities to evaluate information. Researchers who analyzed 7,804 student responses to questions that asked them to evaluate information found that students across middle school, high school, and undergraduate levels are not proficient in the skills needed to critically consider and evaluate information they come across online (Wineburg et al. 2016).

There are growing lists of resources and curricula available for teachers, community leaders, journalists, and the public who address these topics. For example, a national nonprofit called the News Literacy Project contracts with a range of news organizations in the United States to provide educational programming. Poynter's MediaWise, a teen-oriented digital literacy project, is expected to debut a new media literacy curriculum in the fall of 2019. The American Press Institute provides free news literacy resources for students, teachers, and professionals.

Such national and regional media literacy organizations as the National Association for Media Education host conferences for teachers, academics, and interested citizens. On the international level, UNESCO's Global Alliance for Partnerships on Media and Information Literacy supports initiatives that promote media and information literacy (MIL) for all.

In addition, there are several steps that people can take to increase their ability to evaluate content and avoid being deceived by false information. In the contemporary landscape of print journalism, television and radio news, podcasts, talk shows, online news, mobile video, and social media, citizens are more active in selecting information from their own group of sources and need to be able to critically evaluate the content from these sources. Kovach and Rosenstiel (2010) list six questions citizens can ask about the information they encounter to assist in this process: "What kind of content am I encountering? Is the information complete; and if not, what is missing? Who or what are the sources, and why should I believe them? What evidence is presented, and how was it tested or vetted? What might be an alternative explanation or understanding? Am I learning what I need to?" (168). Ball (2017) suggests that citizens can also refrain from sharing information before they evaluate it and make choices that move themselves out of their personalized filter bubble of information that likely reinforces existing viewpoints. He also challenges consumers to learn basic statistics to be less fooled by numbers, treat all stories with skepticism, whether they align with a personal viewpoint or not, and resist subscribing to conspiracy theories, no matter how small.

Others offer more specific advice. Eugene Kiely and Lori Robertson (2016) of the Annenberg Public Policy Center's FactCheck.org describe ways consumers can detect "fake news." They ask people to look carefully at the source of information to determine whether it is an imposter, satiric, fictional, or made-up news site. They also advise consumers to "read beyond the headline and look at the author, sources, and satirical, suspicious or obviously disqualifying information that indicates the story is made up." The authors encourage people to be aware of their confirmation bias—the willingness to accept information that supports their own belief system and reject information that may not. First Draft News offers an hour-long, free online course on identifying misinformation called "Verification Training" to teach "the general public how to verify online media so they don't fall for hoaxes, rumors and misinformation" (Rinehart 2018).

Searching for New Models of News

One of the areas of the news landscape that has demonstrated growth and success is the nonprofit news sector. Founded in 2009 as a public interest–oriented investigative journalism effort, the Institute for Nonprofit News (INN) now claims a membership of 189 nonprofit news organizations that operate around the country; examples include Aspen Journalism, the Center for Investigative Reporting, Eye on Ohio, ProPublica, and the Seattle Globalist. In their 2018 survey of the state of nonprofit news, INN found that nonprofits are performing well, and although the sector relies heavily on donations, these news organizations are generating other forms of revenue. The report also highlights that much of nonprofit news organization reporting is not centered on breaking news but is instead focused on investigative journalism, often situated in the organization's region. Many of these nonprofit news organizations aim to fill the void in local reporting that is a by-product of the emergence of news deserts.

In emphasizing that reliable local news is crucial for a democracy, reporter Brian Bergstein (2019) suggests that even more attention needs to be paid to funding local investigative and other reporting. While nonprofits such as ProPublica cover various communities in depth, he argues that more support is needed. Bergstein wonders if more funding should be directed to PBS or if the private sector should be prompted to support more local news, incentivized by tax breaks. Essentially, Bergstein argues that a funding structure must be established in order to subsidize quality newsgathering and reporting. Zuckerman (2018) suggests that there are ways to finance quality news, but in order for them to work, a shift away from the current thinking about news as dependent on market forces needs to happen. Zuckerman states that "news may be too important to leave to the whims of the market" and proposes that public media financing, something he admits might be difficult to implement in the United States, might be what is needed to preserve the crucial service that quality news provides in a democracy.

Bergstein and Zuckerman are echoing similar calls for media reform advanced by Robert McChesney and John Nichols in several of their articles and books. Most notably, in *The Death and Life of American Journalism*, McChesney and Nichols (2010) argue for the establishment of a public news media system. News is a public good, they state, and journalism should hold people in power accountable, serve the information needs of all citizens, distinguish truth from lies, and "produce a wide range of opinions on the most important issues of our times" (163–164). To do this properly, journalism needs to operate free of corporations or government influence and be publicly funded. McChesney and Nichols detail ways public money could, and should, be used to pay for such a system, relying on numerous examples of precedent that show the government has historically acknowledged, supported, and subsidized the free press because its existence is central to a functioning democracy.

It is uncertain whether broad news media reform will take place. In the meantime, news organizations are trying to remain economically viable by looking at subscription models, bundling options for news subscribers that mimic the idea of Netflix, reader donation models, and philanthropic support (Newman 2019, 25). Foundations, in particular, have played a role in supporting newspapers, magazines, and public media over the past few years, but while some nonprofits like Pro-Publica and the Texas Tribune receive lots of philanthropic support, allocations to other news organizations are uneven (Schmidt 2018b). The aforementioned Google News Initiative may assist in funding newsroom innovations. Journalism programs, such as the Tow-Knight Center for Entrepreneurial Journalism at City University of New York's (CUNY) Graduate School of Journalism, have begun exploring and developing financially prosperous models of journalism that align with new media's modes of reporting (Claussen 2011).

There are some successes that may suggest future directions for the industry. The *Guardian*, a newspaper based in London that has an international reach, is finding success with its reader donation model; readers support the paper with monetary contributions in the amount they choose (Newman 2019). Newspapers such as the *Boston Globe* and the *Washington Post* are now owned by wealthy business owners, John Henry and Jeff Bezos, respectively, who have so far been successful in supporting their papers' journalistic goals while increasing their economic stability (Kennedy 2018). Relying on foundations, reader donations, and wealthy individuals to support news reporting, however, may not be realistic.

As the industry wrestles with these issues, new platforms for news reporting emerge. An initiative referred to as the "slow news movement" is being enacted by Tortoise Media, a news service in the UK that opened its membership in 2019 and features open news conferences and coverage of four to five stories each day (Newman 2019). Another anticipated news service is The Correspondent, an English language version of De Correspondent, an online journalism site in the Netherlands. De Correspondent began in 2013 after a record-breaking crowd-funding campaign and, according to its website, is currently is "one of the largest ad-free, member funded journalism platforms in Europe, currently supported by more than 60,000 paying members." When he asked citizens to fund The Correspondent on his blog and press tour, prominent journalism professor Jay Rosen (2018) emphasized why he thought this news platform was so valuable, suggesting that as a member-supported organization, The Correspondent would produce quality, in-depth journalism without advertising, corporate sponsorship, and tracking of customers' web use or "click bait". In January 2019, Rosen updated his blog to announce The Correspondent succeeded in raising $2.6 million and will formally launch later in the year.

Conclusion

The ways citizens access news and information will continue to change as technology evolves and new forms of reporting continue to evolve and emerge. Predictions for the future include the further development of social media "stories" (like the Instagram story) in reporting, the continual use of online video, and the increased use of Facebook Watch, the social media company's TV platform (Newman 2019). It is an open question whether some of the initiatives being implemented to address the pressing concerns about news and information in the United States will result in positive change. Consumers might reflect on how partisanship impacts their trust in news sources and adherence to news routines and consider how, or if, their online news media habits subject them to filter bubbles and echo chambers of similar ideas and perspectives. Continually developing an understanding of how different types of information, from reputable reporting to sensational headlines to disinformation, coexist in digital spaces might decrease one's chances of being taken in by problematic content. Developing media and news literacy skills empower citizens to be critical information consumers. As the news industry continues to try to build trust among consumers, develop sustainable business models, diversify newsrooms and reporting, and thwart disinformation campaigns, it is likely that new controversies and issues will arise that pose additional challenges to producing and accessing quality information.

Bibliography

Abernathy, Penelope M. 2016. *The Rise of the New Media Baron and the Emerging Threat of News Deserts.* The Center for Innovation and Sustainability in Local Media, School of Media and Journalism, University of North Carolina at Chapel Hill. Accessed March 1, 2019. https://www.usnewsdeserts.com/reports/rise-new-media-baron/executive-summary/.

Abernathy, Penelope M. 2018. "The Expanding News Desert." The Center for Innovation and Sustainability in Local Media, School of Media and Journalism, University of North Carolina at Chapel Hill. Accessed March 1, 2019. https://www.usnewsdeserts.com/.

Ananny, Mike. 2018. "Checking In with the Facebook Fact Checking Partnership." *Columbia Journalism Review,* April 4. https://www.cjr.org/tow_center/facebook-fact-checking-partnerships.php.

Arendt, Florian, and Temple Northup. 2015. "Effects of Long-Term Exposure to News Stereotypes on Implicit and Explicit Attitudes." *International Journal of Communication* 9: 2370–2390.

Ball, James. 2017. *Post-Truth: How Bullshit Conquered the World.* London: Biteback Publishing Ltd.

Barclay, Donald. 2018. *Fake News, Propaganda, and Plain Old Lies: How to Find Trustworthy Information in the Digital Age.* Lanham, MD: Rowman & Littlefield.

Barry, Dan, David Barstow, Jonathan Glater, Adam Liptak, and Jacques Steinberg. 2003. "Correcting the Record: Times Reporter Who Resigned Leaves a Long Trail of Deception." *New York Times,* May 11. https://www.nytimes.com/2003/05/11/us/correcting-the-record-times-reporter-who-resigned-leaves-long-trail-of-deception.html.

Bennett, W. Lance. 2016. *News: The Politics of Illusion, 10th ed.* Chicago, IL: University of Chicago Press.

Bergstein, Brian. 2019. "An Old Way to Fix New Media." *Boston Globe*, March 3. Kindle Edition.

Beyerstein, Lindsay. 2014. "Can News Literacy Grow Up?" *Columbia Journalism Review*, September/October. https:// archives.cjr.org/feature/can_news_literacy_grow_up.php.

Bissinger, Buzz. 2007. "Shattered Glass." *Vanity Fair*, September 5. https://www.vanityfair.com/magazine/ 1998/09/bissinger199809.

Bloom, David. 2019. "Five Key Trends Shaping Influencer Marketing in 2019." *Forbes*, January 1. https://www.forbes.com/sites/dbloom/2019/01/01/ influencer-marketing-top-trends-2019/#34fd51506b25.

Bode, Letica, Emily Vraga, German Alvarez, Courtney Johnson, Magda Konieczna, and Michael Mirer. 2018. "What Viewers Want: Assessing the Impact of Host Bias on Viewer Engagement with Political Talk Shows." *Journal of Broadcasting & Electronic Media* 62, no. 4: 597–613. doi:https://doi.org/10.1080/08838151.2018.1519567.

Borel, Brooke. 2017. "Fact Checking Won't Save Us from Fake News." FiveThirtyEight.com, January 4. https://five thirtyeight.com/features/fact-checking-wont-save-us-from-fake-news/.

Bourg, Anya, and James Jacoby. 2018. "The Facebook Dilemma, Parts One and Two." *Frontline*. PBS. Boston: WGBH, October 29; October 30. https://www.pbs.org/ wgbh/frontline/film/facebook-dilemma/.

Boxell, Levi, Matthew Gentzkow, and Jesse Shapiro. 2017. "Is the Internet Causing Political Polarization? Evidence from Demographics." Working Paper No. 23258, National Bureau of Economic Research, March. https://www.nber .org/papers/w23258.pdf.

boyd, danah. 2017. "Hacking the Attention Economy." Medium, January 5. https://points.datasociety.net/hacking-the-attention-economy-9fa1daca7a37.

Breland, Ali. 2018. "Social Media Companies Grapple with New Forms of Political Misinformation." *The Hill,* November 11, 2018. https://thehill.com/policy/technology/416062-social-media-companies-grapple-with-new-forms-of-political-misinformation

Bunting, Lasharah. 2018. "What We Need to Know to Improve Diversity in Newsrooms." Knight Foundation, September 26. https://knightfoundation.org/articles/what-we-need-to-know-to-improve-diversity-in-newsrooms.

Burke, Timothy. 2018. "How America's Largest Local TV Owner Turned Its News Anchors into Soldiers in Trump's War on the Media. Deadspin, March 31. https://theconcourse.deadspin.com/how-americas-largest-local-tv-owner-turned-its-news-anc-1824233490.

Burleigh, Nina. 2017. "How Big Data Mines Personal Info to Craft Fake News and Manipulate Voters." *Newsweek,* June 16. Accessed via ProQuest.

Carlson, Matt. 2015. "When News Sites Go Native: Redefining the Advertising–Editorial Divide in Response to Native Advertising." *Journalism* 16, no. 7: 849–865.

Chavern, David. 2018. "Statement of David Chavern." Serial No. 115–156. "Filtering Practices of Social Media Platforms." Hearing before the Committee on the Judiciary House of Representatives. April 26. https://www.govinfo.gov/app/details/CHRG-115hhrg32930/CHRG-115hhrg32930.

Chesney, Robert, and Danielle Citron. 2019. "Deepfakes and the New Disinformation War." *Foreign Affairs* 98, no. 1: 147–155.

Claussen, Dane S. 2011. "Editor's Note: CUNY's Entrepreneurial Journalism: Partially Old Wine in a New Bottle, and Not Quite Thirst-Quenching, But Still a Good Drink." *Journalism & Mass Communication Educator* 66, no. 1: 3–6.

Coaston, Jane. 2018. "YouTube's Conspiracy Crisis, Explained." Vox, December 14. https://www.vox.com/ technology/2018/12/12/18136132/ google-youtube-congress-conspiracy-theories.

Cohen, James. 2018. "Exploring Echo-Systems: How Algorithms Shape Immersive Media Environments." *Journal of Media Literacy Education* 10, no. 2: 139–151.

Cohen, Stephen. 2018. "KOMO Attacks 'Biased and False News' in Sinclair Written Promos." SeattlePI.com, April 3. https://www.seattlepi.com/seattlenews/article/KOMO-fake-news-Sinclair-promos-12792032.php.

Corcoran, Michael. 2016. "Twenty Years of Media Consolidation Has Not Been Good for Our Democracy." Bill Moyers.com, March 30. https://billmoyers.com/story/ twenty-years-of-media-consolidation-has-not-been-good-for-our-democracy/.

Delwiche, Aaron. 2018. "What Is Propaganda Analysis?" Propaganda Critic. Last modified August 8, 2018. Accessed January 22, 2019. https://propagandacritic.com/index.php/ how-to-decode-propaganda/what-is-propaganda-analysis/.

de Vreese, Claes. 2005. "News Framing: Theory and Typology." *Information Design Journal* 13, no. 1: 51–61. doi:10.1075/idjdd.13.1.06vre.

Dewey, Caitlin. 2016. "6 in 10 of You Will Share This Link without Reading It According to a New and Depressing Study." *Washington Post*, June 16. https://www.washington post.com/news/the-intersect/wp/2016/06/16/six-in-10-of-you-will-share-this-link-without-reading-it-according-to-a-new-and-depressing-study/?noredirect=on&utm_term= .dad4cfbd06b9.

Dictionary.com. 2018. "Our Word of the Year Is . . . Misinformation." Accessed January 7, 2019. https://www .dictionary.com/e/word-of-the-year/.

Diresta, Renee, and Gilad Lotan. 2015. "Anti-Vaxxers Are Using Twitter to Manipulate a Vaccine Bill."

Wired, June 8. https://www.wired.com/2015/06/ antivaxxers-influencing-legislation/.

Dixon, Travis, and Daniel Linz. 2000. "Overrepresentation and Underrepresentation of African Americans and Latinos as Lawbreakers on Television News." *Journal of Communication* 50: 131–154.

Farhi, Paul. 2018. "As a Secretive Hedge Fund Guts Its Newspapers, Journalists Are Fighting Back." *Washington Post*, April 12. https://www.washingtonpost.com/lifestyle/ style/as-a-secretive-hedge-fund-guts-its-newspapers- journalists-are-fighting-back/2018/04/12/8926a45c-3c10- 11e8-974f-aacd97698cef_story.htmlFarsetta, Diane, and Daniel Price. 2006. "Fake TV News: Widespread and Undisclosed." Center for Media and Democracy, April 6. Accessed January 25, 2019. https://www.prwatch.org/ fakenews/execsummary.

Feldman, Lauren. 2018. "The Hostile Media Effect." In *The Oxford Handbook of Political Communication*, edited by Kate Kenski and Kathleen H. Jamieson. Oxford Handbooks Online. http://www.oxfordhandbooks.com/ view/10.1093/oxfordhb/9780199793471.001.0001/ oxfordhb-9780199793471-e-011. doi:10.1093/ oxfordhb/9780199793471.013.011_update_001.

Fiegerman, Seth. 2017. "Facebook Is Closing In on 2 Billion Users." CNN.com, February 1. https://money.cnn.com/ 2017/02/01/technology/facebook-earnings/index.html.

Fortin, Jacey, and Jonah E. Bromwich. 2018. "Sinclair Made Dozens of Local News Anchors Recite the Same Script." *New York Times*, April 2. https://www.nytimes.com/2018/04/02/ business/media/sinclair-news-anchors-script.html.

Frier, Sarah. 2018a. "Facebook Removes 559 Pages, 251 Accounts Spreading U.S. Misinformation." Bloomberg, October 11. https://www.bloomberg.com/news/articles/ 2018-10-11/facebook-removes-over-800-accounts- spreading-u-s-misinformation.

Frier, Sarah. 2018b. "Facebook Says It Removed Influence Campaigns from Iran, Russia." Bloomberg, August 21. https://www.bloomberg.com/news/articles/2018-08-21/facebook-says-it-removed-influence-campaigns-from-iran-russia.

Frontline. 2004. "Interview with Mark Crispin Miller." PBS.org. Posted November 9. Accessed January 7, 2019. https://www.pbs.org/wgbh/pages/frontline/shows/persuaders/interviews/miller.html.

Gerson, Daniela, and Carlos Rodriguez. 2018. Going Forward: How Ethnic and Mainstream Media Can Collaborate in Changing Communities. The American Press Institute, July 19. https://www.americanpressinstitute.org/publications/reports/strategy-studies/ethnic-and-mainstream-media-collaborations-in-changing-communities/.

Gladstone, Brooke. 2011. The Influencing Machine. New York: W.W. Norton & Company.

Glasser, Theodore, Anita Varma, and Sheng Zou. 2019. "Native Advertising and the Cultivation of Counterfeit News." Journalism 20, no. 1: 150–153.

Gleicher, Nathaniel, and Oscar Rodriguez. 2018. "Removing Additional Inauthentic Activity from Facebook." Facebook Newsroom, October 11. https://newsroom.fb.com/news/2018/10/removing-inauthentic-activity/.

Goggin, Benjamin. 2019. "More Than 2,200 People Lost Their Jobs in a Media Landslide So Far This Year." Business Insider, February 10. https://www.businessinsider.com/2019-media-layoffs-job-cuts-at-buzzfeed-huffpost-vice-details-2019-2.

Gold, Hadas. 2019. "Facebook: Our AI Failed to Catch the New Zealand Shooter Video." CNN.com, March 21. https://www.cnn.com/2019/03/21/tech/facebok-new-zealand-artificial-intelligence/index.html.

Gonzalez, Juan, and Joseph Torres. 2011. "News for All: The Epic Story of Race and the American Media." In Will The Last Reporter Please Turn Out the Lights, edited by Robert

McChesney and Victor Pikard, 185–193. New York: The New Press.

Gottfried, Jeffrey, and Elizabeth Grieco. 2019. "Nearly Three-Quarters of Republicans Say the News Media Don't Understand People Like Them." Pew Research Center, January 18. https://www.pewresearch.org/fact-tank/2019/01/18/nearly-three-quarters-of-republicans-say-the-news-media-dont-understand-people-like-them/.

Gottfried, Jeffrey, Galen Stocking, and Elizabeth Grieco. 2018. "Partisans Remain Sharply Divided in Their Attitudes about the News Media." Pew Research Center, September 25. Accessed February 12, 2019. http://www.journalism.org/2018/09/25/partisans-remain-sharply-divided-in-their-attitudes-about-the-news-media/.

Graham, Jefferson. 2019. "YouTube to Curb Recommending Conspiracy Videos." *USA Today*, January 25. https://www.usatoday.com/story/tech/talkingtech/2019/01/25/youtube-stop-recommending-conspiracy-videos-misinform-users/2677506002/.

Gramlich, John. 2018. "10 Facts about Americans and Facebook." Pew Research Center, October 24. http://www.pewresearch.org/fact-tank/2018/10/24/facts-about-americans-and-facebook/.

Grieco, Elizabeth, Nami Sumida, and Sophia Fedeli. 2018. "About a Third of Large U.S. Newspapers Have Suffered Layoffs since 2017." Pew Research Center, July 23. http://www.pewresearch.org/fact-tank/2018/07/23/about-a-third-of-large-u-s-newspapers-have-suffered-layoffs-since-2017/.

Gross, Doug. 2013. "5 Viral Stories about Boston Attacks That Aren't True." CNN.com, April 17. https://www.cnn.com/2013/04/16/tech/social-media/social-media-boston-fakes/index.html.

Grynbaum, Michael. 2017. "Trump Calls the News Media 'The Enemy of the American People.'" *New York Times*, February 2. https://www.nytimes.com/2017/02/17/

business/trump-calls-the-news-media-the-enemy-of-the-people.html?module=inline.

Guess, Andrew, Jonathan Nagler, and Joshua Tucker. 2019. "Less Than You Think: Prevalence and Predictors of Fake News Dissemination on Facebook." *Science Advances* 5, no. 1: 1–8. http://advances.sciencemag.org/. doi:10.1126/sciadv.aau4586.

Han, Jiyoon, Minette Drumwright, and Wongun Goo. 2018. "Native Advertising: Is Deception an Asset or a Liability?" *Journal of Media Ethics* 33, no. 3: 102–119.

Hempel, Jessi. 2017. "Eli Pariser Predicted the Future. Now He Can't Escape It." *Wired*, May 24. https://www.wired.com/2017/05/eli-pariser-predicted-the-future-now-he-cant-escape-it/.

Herrman, John. 2017. "For the New Far Right, YouTube Has Become the New Talk Radio." *New York Times Magazine*, August 3. https://www.nytimes.com/2017/08/03/magazine/for-the-new-far-right-youtube-has-become-the-new-talk-radio.html.

Hoffman, Adonis. 2018. "TV Owners Need New Rules to Keep Pace." *Hill*, September 4. https://thehill.com/opinion/technology/404861-tv-owners-need-new-rules-to-keep-pace.

Howcraft, Elizabeth. 2018. "How Faking Videos Became Easy and Why That's So Scary." Bloomberg, September 10. https://www.bloomberg.com/news/articles/2018-09-10/how-faking-videos-became-easy-and-why-that-s-so-scary-quicktake.

Ingram, Matthew. 2018. "The Media Today: Google Offers News Business as $300 Million Olive Branch." *Columbia Journalism Review*, March 21. https://www.cjr.org/the_media_today/google-news-initiative.php.

Institute for Nonprofit News. 2018. *INN Index: The State of Nonprofit News*. Accessed March 31, 2019. https://inn.org/

wp-content/uploads/2018/10/INN.Index2018FinalFull
Report.pdf.

Jackson, Abby. 2019. "BuzzFeed News Has Eliminated
Its Health, National, and National-Security Desks as It
Lays Off 15% of the Entire Company." Business Insider,
January 25. https://www.businessinsider.in/BuzzFeed-
News-has-eliminated-its-health-national-and-national-
security-desks-as-it-lays-off-15-of-the-entire-company/
articleshow/67696040.cms.

Jacobson, Linda. 2017. "Schools Fight Spread of Fake
News through News Literacy Lessons." Education Dive,
October 24. https://www.educationdive.com/news/
schools-fight-spread-of-fake-news-through-news-literacy-
lessons/507057/.

Jolly, Jihii. 2014. "News Literacy vs. Media Literacy."
Columbia Journalism Review, September 4. https://archives
.cjr.org/news_literacy/news_literacy_vs_media_literac.php.

Jones, Janet, and Lee Salter. 2012. *Digital Journalism*. Los
Angeles, CA: Sage.

Keith, Tamara. 2018. "President Trump's Description
of What's 'Fake' Is Expanding." National Public Radio,
September 2. https://www.npr.org/2018/09/02/64376
1979/president-trumps-description-of-whats-fake-is-
expanding.

Keller, Joshua. 2019. "Native Advertising: The New Pillar of
Digital." *Forbes*, January 24. https://www.forbes.com/sites/
forbesagencycouncil/2019/01/24/native-advertising-the-
new-pillar-of-digital/#241880e85e0e.

Kelly, John, and Camille Francois. 2018. "This Is What Filter
Bubbles Actually Look Like." *MIT Technology Review*,
August 22. https://www.technologyreview.com/s/611807/
this-is-what-filter-bubbles-actually-look-like/.

Kennedy, Dan. 2018. *The Return of the Moguls*. Lebanon,
NH: ForeEdge.

Kiely, Eugene, and Lori Robertson. 2016. "How to Spot Fake News." Factcheck.org, November 18. https://www.factcheck.org/2016/11/how-to-spot-fake-news/.

Killelea, Eric. 2017. "Alex Jones' Mis-Info Wars: 7 Bat-sh** Conspiracy Theories." *Rolling Stone*, February 21. https://www.rollingstone.com/culture/culture-lists/alex-jones-mis-infowars-7-bat-sht-conspiracy-theories-195468/satanists-are-taking-over-america-116484/.

Kingsbury, Alex. 2018. " 'Post-truth,' the Ultimate Form of Cynicism." *Boston Globe*, May 18. https://www.bostonglobe.com/ideas/2018/05/18/post-truth-ultimate-form-cynicism/jHR0TbsLmksAlwTKcYHU2L/story.html.

Knight, Will. 2018. "Fake America Great Again." *MIT Technology Review*, August 17. https://www.technologyreview.com/s/611810/fake-america-great-again/.

Knight Foundation. 2018a. *Indicators of News Media Trust. A Gallup/Knight Foundation Survey*. September 11. Accessed February 15, 2019. https://knightfoundation.org/reports/indicators-of-news-media-trust.

Knight Foundation. 2018b. *Local TV News and the New Media Landscape*. April 5. Accessed January 11, 2019. https://kf-site-production.s3.amazonaws.com/publications/pdfs/000/000/251/original/TVNews_bundle-v5.pdf.

Knight Foundation. 2018c. *An Online Experimental Platform to Assess Trust in Media. A Gallup/Knight Foundation Survey*. July 18. https://knightfoundation.org/reports/an-online-experimental-platform-to-assess-trust-in-the-media.

Kovach, Bill, and Tom Rosenstiel. 2010. *Blur: How to Know What's True in the Age of Information Overload*. New York, NY: Bloomsbury.

Landler, Mark. 2018. "New York Times Publisher and Trump Clash over President's Threats against Journalism." *New York Times*, July 7. https://www.nytimes.com/2018/07/29/us/politics/trump-new-york-times-sulzberger.html.

Langlois, Shawn. 2018. "How Biased Is Your News Source? You Probably Won't Agree with This Chart." Marketwatch.com, April 21. https://www.marketwatch.com/story/how-biased-is-your-news-source-you-probably-wont-agree-with-this-chart-2018–02–28.

Lapowski, Issie. 2019. "Why Tech Didn't Stop the New Zealand Attack from Going Viral." *Wired*, March 15. https://www.wired.com/story/new-zealand-shooting-video-social-media/.

Larson, Stephanie G. 2006. *Media & Minorities: The Politics of Race in News and Entertainment*. Lanham, MD: Rowman & Littlefield.

Levy, Nicole. 2019. "The New Native Advertising Narrative." *Folio*, January 23. https://www.foliomag.com/the-new-native-advertising-narrative/.

Madrigal, Alexis. 2012. "The Surprising Trajectory of Facebook's Growth to a Billion Users in 1 Chart." *Atlantic*, October 4. https://www.theatlantic.com/technology/archive/2012/10/the-surprising-trajectory-of-facebooks-growth-to-a-billion-users-in-1-chart/263259/.

Marshall, Josh. 2017. "There's a Digital Media Crash. But No One Will Say It." Talking Points Memo, November 17. https://talkingpointsmemo.com/edblog/theres-a-digital-media-crash-but-no-one-will-say-it.

McChesney, Robert, and John Nichols. 2010. *The Death and Life of American Journalism*. Philadelphia, PA: Nation Books.

McDonald, Natalie H. 2019. "Popping the Filter Bubble: How Newspapers Are Navigating through Social Media Bots, Trolls and Misinformation to Bring Readers the Truth." *Editor & Publisher* 152, no. 2: 46–50.

Media Insight Project. 2018. *Americans and the News Media: What They Do—and Don't—Understand about Each Other*. The American Press Institute and the

Associated Press-NORC Center for Public Affairs Research, June 11. Accessed March 1, 2019. https://www.americanpressinstitute.org/publications/reports/survey-research/americans-and-the-news-media/.

Mitchell, Amy, Jeffrey Gottfried, Michael Barthel, and Nami Sumida. 2018. "Distinguishing between Factual and Opinion Statements in the News." Pew Research Center, June 18. http://www.journalism.org/2018/06/18/distinguishing-between-factual-and-opinion-statements-in-the-news/.

Mitchell, Amy, Katerina E. Matsa, Jeffrey Gottfried, and Jocelyn Kiley. 2014. "Political Polarization and Media Habits." Pew Research Center, October 21. Accessed February 28, 2019. http://www.journalism.org/2014/10/21/political-polarization-media-habits/.

Molla, Rani, and Peter Kafka. 2018. "Here's Who Owns Everything in Big Media Today." Recode, June 18. https://www.recode.net/2018/1/23/16905844/media-landscape-verizon-amazon-comcast-disney-fox-relationships-chart.

Morris, David Z. 2018. "Trolls and Bots Moved Fast to Politicize Texas School Shooting on Social Media." *Fortune*, May 19. http://fortune.com/2018/05/19/santa-fe-shooting-trolls-bots-conspiracy-theory/.

Morrison, Sara, and Eryn Carlson. 2018. "Reinventing Local News." *Nieman Reports*, April 18. https://niemanreports.org/articles/reinventing-local-tv-news/.

Mudge, Amy R., and Randal Shaheen. 2017. "Native Advertising, Influencers and Endorsements: Where Is the Line between Integrated Content and Deceptively Formatted Advertising?" *Journal of Internet Law* 21, no. 5: 1–16.

Nelson, Jacob L., and James G. Webster. 2017. "The Myth of Partisan Selective Exposure: A Portrait of the Online Political News Audience." *Social Media + Society* 3, no. 3. doi:10.1177/2056305117729314. Accessed at https://journals.sagepub.com/doi/10.1177/2056305117729314.

Newcomb, Alyssa. 2018. "Facebook Trending Section Is Dead as Company Offers New Approach to Breaking News." NBC.com, June 1. https://www.nbcnews.com/tech/social-media/facebook-trending-section-dead-company-offers-new-approach-breaking-news-n879226.

Newman, Nic. 2019. "Journalism, Media and Technology Trends and Predictions 2019." Reuters Institute for the Study of Journalism, January. Accessed March 3, 2019. https://reutersinstitute.politics.ox.ac.uk/our-research/journalism-media-and-technology-trends-and-predictions-2019.

Nicas, Jack. 2018. "Alex Jones Said Bans Would Strengthen Him. He Was Wrong." *New York Times*, September 4. https://www.nytimes.com/2018/09/04/technology/alex-jones-infowars-bans-traffic.html.

Nichols, John, and Robert McChesney. 2013. "Free the Media!" *Nation*, November 6. https://www.thenation.com/article/free-media/.

Nielsen, Rasmus K., and Lucas Graves. 2017. " 'News You Don't Believe': Audience Perspectives on Fake News." Reuters Institute for the Study of Journalism. Accessed January 11, 2019. https://reutersinstitute.politics.ox.ac.uk/our-research/news-you-dont-believe-audience-perspectives-fake-news.

Nielsen, Rasmus K., and Richard Sambrook. 2016. "What Is Happening to Television News?" Reuters Institute for the Study of Journalism. Accessed January 11, 2019. https://reutersinstitute.politics.ox.ac.uk/our-research/what-happening-television-news.

Pariser, Eli. 2011. *The Filter Bubble: What the Internet Is Hiding from You*. London: Penguin Press.

Parrish, Cayleigh. 2016. "The Biggest Challenges Facing the News Industry in 2016." *Fast Company*, January 4. https://www.fastcompany.com/3054408/the-biggest-challenges-facing-the-news-industry-in-2016.

Patterson, Philana. 2019. "Gannett Rejects Takeover Offer from MNG/Digital First Media." *USA Today*, February 4. https://www.usatoday.com/story/money/business/2019/02/04/gannett-rejects-mng-enterprises-digital-first-media-proposal/2765975002/.

Peiser, Jaclyn. 2018. "New York Times Tops 4 Million Mark in Total Subscribers." *New York Times*, November 1. https://www.nytimes.com/2018/11/01/business/media/new-york-times-earnings-subscribers.html.

Pew Research Center. 2013. "Amid Criticism, Support for Media's 'Watchdog' Role Stands Out." Pew Research Center, August 8. http://www.people-press.org/2013/08/08/amid-criticism-support-for-medias-watchdog-role-stands-out/.

Pew Research Center. 2014. "Political Polarization in the American Public." Pew Research Center, U.S. Politics & Policy, June 12. http://www.people-press.org/2014/06/12/political-polarization-in-the-american-public/.

Pew Research Center. 2019. "Public's 2019 Priorities: Economy, Health Care, Education, and Security All near Top of List." Pew Research Center, U.S. Politics & Policy, January 24. http://www.people-press.org/2019/01/24/publics-2019-priorities-economy-health-care-education-and-security-all-near-top-of-list/.

Pham, Sherisse. 2018. "Germany's Der Spiegel Says Star Reporter Claas Relotius Wrote Fake Stories 'on a Grand Scale.'" CNN.com, December 20. https://www.cnn.com/2018/12/20/media/claas-relotius-spiegel/index.html.

Ponce de Leon, Charles. 2015. *That's the Way It Is: A History of Television News in America*. Chicago: University of Chicago Press.

Potter, Wendall. 2010. *Deadly Spin*. New York: Bloomsbury Press.

Rampton, Sheldon, and John Stauber. 2001. *Trust Us, We're Experts*. New York: Jeremy P. Tarcher/Putnam.

Read, Max. 2018. "How Much of the Internet Is Fake? Turns Out, a Lot of It, Actually." *New York Magazine*, December 26. http://nymag.com/intelligencer/2018/12/how-much-of-the-internet-is-fake.html.

"Read the Special Counsel's Indictment Against the Internet Research Agency and Others." 2018. *The New York Times*, February 16. https://www.nytimes.com/interactive/2018/02/16/us/politics/document-The-Special-Counsel-s-Indictment-of-the-Internet.html.

Recode. 2018. "How Bots Amplify Hoaxes and Propaganda on Social Media." Recode, August 2. https://www.recode.net/2018/8/2/17636264/josh-ginsberg-zignal-bot-recode-decode.

Rinehart, Aimee. 2018. "Free Online Course on Identifying Misinformation." First Draft News, March 19. https://firstdraftnews.org/free-online-course-on-identifying-misinformation/.

Robb, Amanda. 2017. "Anatomy of a Fake News Scandal." *Rolling Stone*, November 16. https://www.rollingstone.com/politics/politics-news/anatomy-of-a-fake-news-scandal-125877/.

Robillard, Kevin. 2012. "10 Journos Caught Fabricating." *Politico*, July 31. https://www.politico.com/story/2012/07/10-journos-caught-fabricating-079221.

Roose, Kevin. 2018a. " 'False Flag' Theory on Pipe Bombs Zooms from Right-Wing Fringe to Mainstream." *New York Times*, October 25. https://www.nytimes.com/2018/10/25/business/false-flag-theory-bombs-conservative-media.html.

Roose, Kevin. 2018b. "Google Pledges 300 Million to Clean Up False News." *New York Times*, March 20. https://www.nytimes.com/2018/03/20/business/media/google-false-news.html.

Rosen, Jay. 2018. "Letter to My Network: Join The Correspondent." PressThink [blog], November 17, 2018. http://pressthink.org/2018/11/letter-to-my-network-join-the-correspondent/

Rosenberg, Howard, and Charles Feldman. 2008. *No Time to Think: The Menace of Media Speed and the 24-Hour News Cycle*. New York: Continuum International Publishing Group.

Rosenberg, Matthew. 2019. "Trump Consultant is Trolling Democrats with Biden Site That Isn't Biden's." *New York Times*, June 29, 2019. https://www.nytimes.com/2019/06/29/us/politics/fake-joe-biden-website.html

Ross, Andrew S., and Damian J. Rivers. 2018. "Discursive Deflection: Accusation of 'Fake News' and the Spread of Mis- and Disinformation in the Tweets of President Trump." *Social Media + Society* 4, no. 2. doi:10.1177/2056305118776010. Accessed at https://journals.sagepub.com/doi/full/10.1177/2056305118776010.

Russell, Adrienne. 2011. *Networked: A Contemporary History of News in Transition*. Malden, MA: Polity Press.

Sample, Ian. 2019. "Study Blames YouTube for Rise in Number of Flat Earthers." *Guardian*, February 17. https://www.theguardian.com/science/2019/feb/17/study-blames-youtube-for-rise-in-number-of-flat-earthers.

Schmidt, Christine. 2018a. "A Look at How Foundations Are Helping the Journalism Industry Stand Up Straight." Nieman Lab, June 18. http://www.niemanlab.org/2018/06/a-look-at-how-foundations-are-helping-the-journalism-industry-stand-up-straight/.

Schmidt, Christine. 2018b. "So What Is That, er, Trusted News Integrity Trust Project All About? A Guide to the Many (similarly named) New Efforts Fighting for Journalism." Nieman Lab, April 5. http://www.niemanlab.org/2018/04/so-what-is-that-er-trusted-news-integrity-trust-project-all-about-a-guide-to-the-many-similarly-named-new-efforts-fighting-for-journalism/.

Schudson, Michael. 2017. "Here's What Non-Fake News Looks Like." *Columbia Journalism Review*, February 23. https://www.cjr.org/analysis/fake-news-real-news-list.php.

Shao, Chengcheng, Giovanni Luca Ciampaglia, Onur Varol, Kai-Cheng Yang, Alessandro Flammini, and Filippo Menczer. 2018. "The Spread of Low-Credibility Content by Social Bots." *Nature Communications* 9, no. 1: 4787. doi:10.1038/s41467-018-06930-7.

Silverman, Craig. 2012. "There Were 31 Incidents of Plagiarism/Fabrication in 2012." Poynter, December 21. https://www.poynter.org/reporting-editing/2012/there-were-31-incidents-of-plagiarismfabrication-in-2012/.

Silverman, Craig. 2016a. "These Big Native American Facebook Pages Are Actually Being Run by People in Kosovo and Vietnam." BuzzFeed News, December 12. https://www.buzzfeednews.com/article/craigsilverman/facebook-scammers-profiting-from-standing-rock.

Silverman, Craig. 2016b. "This Analysis Shows How Viral Fake News Election News Outperformed Real News on Facebook." BuzzFeed News, November 16. https://www.buzzfeednews.com/article/craigsilverman/viral-fake-election-news-outperformed-real-news-on-facebook#.emA15rzd0.

Singer, P. W., and Emerson Brooking. 2018. *LikeWar: The Weaponization of Social Media*. New York: Houghton Mifflin.

Skaggs, Kevin. 2012. "What's New in News Aggregation?" *Guardian*, July 17. https://www.theguardian.com/media-network/media-network-blog/2012/jul/17/what-is-new-news-aggregation.

Snider, Mike. 2018. "Nextar to Buy Tribune Media for 4.1 Billion, Become Largest Local TV Group in U.S." *USA Today*, December 3. https://www.usatoday.com/story/money/media/2018/12/03/nexstar-tribune-media-largest-tv-group/2189402002/.

Soll, Jacob. 2016. "The Long and Brutal History of Fake News." *Politico*, December 18. Accessed June 7, 2018. https://www.politico.com/magazine/story/2016/12/fake-news-history-long-violent-214535.

Somani, Indira, and Natalie Hopkinson. 2018. "Color, Caste and the Public Sphere." *Journalism Practice.* https://www .tandfonline.com/doi/full/10.1080/17512786.2018 .1426999. Accessed March 2, 2019.

Stauber, John, and Sheldon Rampton. 1995. *Toxic Sludge Is Good for You: Lies, Damn Lies and the Public Relations Industry.* Monroe, ME: Common Courage Press.

Stocking, Galen, and Nami Sumida. 2018. "Social Media Bots Draw Public's Attention and Concern." Pew Research Center, October 15. http://www.journalism.org/2018/10/ 15/social-media-bots-draw-publics-attention-and-concern/.

Subramanian, Samantha. 2017. "Inside the Macedonian Fake News Complex." *Wired,* February 15. https://www.wired .com/2017/02/veles-macedonia-fake-news/.

Sumpter, David. 2018. *Outnumbered: From Facebook and Google to Fake News and Filter Bubbles—The Algorithms That Control Our Lives.* London: Bloomsbury Sigma.

Tewksbury, David, and Julius M. Riles. 2015. "Polarization as a Function of Citizen Dispositions and Exposure to News on the Internet." *Journal of Broadcasting & Electronic Media* 59, no. 3: 381–398. doi:10.1080/08838151.2015.1054996.

Turgeon, Valerie. 2017. "Native Advertising vs. Sponsored Content: What's the Difference?" Brandpoint.com, November 15. Accessed January 23, 2019. https://www .brandpoint.com/blog/native-advertising-vs-sponsored-content-whats-the-difference/.

Uberti, David. 2016. *The Real History of Fake News. Columbia Journalism Review,* December 15. https://www.cjr.org/ special_report/fake_news_history.php.

Vosoughi, Soroush, Deb Roy, and Sinan Aral. 2018. "The Spread of True and False News Online." *Science* 359, no. 6380: 1146–1151. doi:10.1126/science.aap9559.

Wakabayashi, Daisuke. 2019. "YouTube to Stop Directing Users to Conspiracy Videos." *Boston Globe,* January 26. Kindle Edition.

Wardle, Claire. 2018. "Five Lessons for Reporting in an Age of Disinformation." First Draft News, December 27. https://firstdraftnews.org/5-lessons-for-reporting-in-an-age-of-disinformation/.

Wardle, Claire, and Hossein Derakhshan. 2017. "One Year On, We're Still Not Recognizing the Complexity of Information Disorder Online." First Draft News, October 31. https://firstdraftnews.org/coe_infodisorder/.

Wardle, Claire, and Hossein Derakhshan. 2018. "Thinking about 'Information Disorder': Formats of Misinformation, Disinformation and Mal-information." In *Journalism, "Fake News," & Disinformation: A Handbook for Journalism Education and Training*. UNESCO. https://en.unesco.org/fightfakenews.

Wineburg, Sam, Sarah McGrew, Joel Breakstone, and Teresa Ortega. 2016. "Evaluating Information: The Cornerstone of Civic Online Reasoning." Stanford Digital Repository. Accessed January 11, 2019. https://purl.stanford.edu/fv751yt5934.

Women's Media Center. 2018. *The Status of Women of Color in the U.S. Media 2018*. Accessed January 11, 2019. http://www.womensmediacenter.com/assets/site/reports/the-status-of-women-of-color-in-the-u-s-media-2018-full-report/Women-of-Color-Report-FINAL-WEB.pdf.

Wooley, Samuel, and Phil Howard. 2016. "Bots Unite to Automate the Presidential Election." *Wired*, May 15. https://www.wired.com/2016/05/twitterbots-2/.

Zuckerman, Ethan. 2018. "Four Problems for News and Democracy." Medium, April 1. https://medium.com/trust-media-and-democracy/we-know-the-news-is-in-crisis-5d1c4fbf7691.

Introduction

This chapter is comprised of a series of essays authored by professionals and scholars who offer different perspectives on aspects of journalism, media, and "fake news" in the United States. To begin, Dennis Lein shares what newsrooms used to be like and details how they've changed from his perspective as a reporter. Sean R. Sadri discusses the types of sourcing used in modern journalism, pointing out source strategies that have remained consistent and others that have emerged in the digital age. Julie Frechette argues why, especially given current events, it is crucial for consumers to increase their news literacy skills. Determining the nature of informational content is important, and in her essay, Lori Bindig Yousman describes the blurred lines between journalism and public relations. Considering that news media representations may influence consumer perceptions of different demographic groups, Nahed Eltantawy offers her thoughts on news media coverage of Muslims. Randall Livingstone shares his understanding of social media bots and offers advice for those hoping to become more aware of these computer programs. Implicitly referencing journalism's beginning, Erica Drzewiecki defends the value of the local printed newspaper in the digital age. News satire is a popular form of entertainment

Members of the news media await a press conference in New York City on May 19, 2017. (Erin Alexis Randolph/Dreamstime.com)

and, for some, a news source; Bill Yousman's essay critically considers this genre. Finally, Kate Felsen conveys the human component of journalistic work in her reflections on experiencing and covering traumatic events when she was a foreign news editor at ABC News.

The 1970s Newsrooms Balanced Past and Future
Dennis Lein

Walk into any newsroom in the early to mid-1970s, and here is what you heard and saw: the clickety-clack of typewriters, cigarette smoke, someone yelling to someone else because that was the only way to make yourself heard over all the other background chatter, the typewriter noise, and some other guy yelling. There seemed almost always to be another guy yelling.

Paper was everywhere, stacked or strewn about on tops of desks in old government reports or in sheets glued end to end and impaled by reporters on long metal spikes or placed in wire baskets for editors to examine and polish.

Those last days of the precomputerized newsrooms are barely recognizable now. When computers were installed, change came quickly. Newsroom systems upgraded technology constantly. Every year brought advances. Ways to communicate kept getting faster and quieter. The pace of change itself quickened.

Looking back, that stretch in the 1970s was clearly transitional. Newsrooms had one foot in the past and one in the future, but they operated more like those of ten, twenty, thirty, even forty years earlier, a romanticized era that evoked images of the play and movie *The Front Page*.

It was a crazy, colorful place filled with odd personalities, people who got into the business, not always because they graduated from journalism schools but because they knew someone or they were news junkies willing to work the long, odd hours for little pay. Most were white men.

There was a coziness between reporters and columnists and the people they wrote about that doesn't exist as much now.

Journalists then had easier access to locker rooms, fires, and crime scenes and to coaches, players, and public officials who weren't yet coached by public relations types. There was an immediacy to what was written because there were fewer filters. But there was a trade-off: personal stuff that might be considered news now sometimes wasn't then.

The telephones, old-time rotary types, were always ringing, and they rang loudly. Reporters taking notes cradled handsets in the crooks of their necks while punching away on typewriter keys, many using just their index fingers, or scribbling in notebooks.

Stories were written on paper, glued together, cluttered with editing marks, and then sent off to a series of editors, who marked them up more, and slapped on headlines before they were typeset and stuck onto paste-up pages by hand in a composing room. As for color photos, they were still a rarity. Almost all news photos were in black and white and remained that way until the 1980s.

There were no cell phones, no internet, no emails, and no text messages; as a result, there were fewer ways to communicate. Reporters leaving telephone messages with sources often had to wait long periods for return calls.

It was more cumbersome and labor-intensive. Reporters out of the office on assignment had to borrow someone else's phone or plug coins into a pay phone to call the office with breaking news. Without a way to write and transmit from afar, they had to know how to craft a story on the cuff and dictate to a newsroom colleague. Otherwise, they had to wait until they returned to write their stories.

With no internet, basic background information wasn't readily available. Newsrooms had clip libraries, where all earlier stories had been cut out of the paper, folded and cross-indexed by names and subjects. Reporters had to spend more time working sources, poring over public records in public buildings, or viewing microfilm in libraries.

There were morning and afternoon newspapers, and there were strict deadlines to hit because everyone, from the pasteup folks to the printers, counted on them. You wrote one story—not a tweet, a blog item and then something online, before the main piece. You got one chance, and you couldn't make changes as easily as now. Once you turned in your story, you had to wait for the paper to be printed to see it for the first time.

Waiting was often nerve wracking. With no instant online publication of facts and tidbits, reporters guarded their scoops jealously. Once their stories were published, the competition had to wait until the next news cycle to catch up.

By the mid- to late 1970s, the first video display terminals were finding their way into most newsrooms. They weren't always reliable, and it wasn't unusual to lose entire stories when they crashed.

When change came, it came quickly.

Within a decade, the typewriters were gone, replaced by personal computers that didn't make as much noise. Over time, instead of yelling across the room to a colleague, you could send a text or an email. Smoking was banned. Reporters accustomed to a constant drone of noise became comfortable with silence. More and more women and minorities got jobs. Laptops and cell phones became the thing.

The way journalism was done didn't change much. It was still about playing a watchdog role, and it was still about gathering information, verifying facts, and writing and then presenting those findings fairly and cleanly to the public.

But the platform changed dramatically.

By the early twenty-first century, the pace had quickened even more. News was tweeted, blogs were written, and online stories were posted. Stories were even being written differently. Instead of traditional, time-tested approaches, more stories were put together to read better on a short form on a phone, or some type of multimedia presentation was being done.

Since then, the news business has continued to evolve, getting more sophisticated, more efficient, and more professional. But much of the color and the types of characters who made those bygone days so distinctive have been largely lost along the way.

Dennis Lien was a reporter and editor for thirty-seven years, thirty-four of them at the St. Paul Pioneer Press. His first story was written on a typewriter; one of his last on a smartphone.

From Anonymous Sources to Analytics and Embedded Tweets: The Evolution of News Sourcing in Modern Journalism
Sean R. Sadri

Every successful journalist needs an interesting story to tell. These stories are told through investigation, eyewitness reporting, interviews, Freedom of Information Act (FOIA) requests, and a bevy of other avenues from which a journalist can uncover the facts. At the heart of every news story are reputable sources that can articulate details or corroborate information. Before the internet became the primary avenue for news and knowledge, there was a straightforward process for disseminating information through traditional media (i.e., print, television, and radio). Journalists would interview sources that they deemed credible, and they would rearrange and package that information into a coherent story that the audience would see. The online ecosystem has changed the newsgathering process for reporters. Finding credible sources and conducting interviews are still a necessary part of the process, but journalists now have many other factors to consider.

Editors are also putting more pressure on journalists to land a story first. Reporters with the scoop on a story receive added exposure, and competing news outlets acknowledge their news organization as the source of the story. Thus, anonymous sources are becoming more common as a way to break a story immediately without the backlash that source might face publicly (Farhi 2013). When anonymous sources feel the need to share insider information on their company, political party, sports team, and so forth with a reporter, they want the information exposed to the public. However, potential repercussions from their organization forbid their name from being attached to the comments, so their names are omitted and replaced with a phrase like "a person with knowledge of the situation" or "a person close to the matter."

This type of sourcing has become ubiquitous throughout modern journalism, and audiences have become more accepting of confidential sources in news stories. Conversely, journalists using unnamed sources open themselves up to criticism from readers who argue that these stories limit journalistic accountability (Bacon 2017). However, many investigative stories (particularly those in Washington, DC) are often impossible to write without the use of anonymous sources. Journalists can combat claims of inaccurate reporting by providing as many details about the source being quoted without providing names. Essentially, audiences will find "officials within the Department of Homeland Security" as a more reliable source than "administration officials."

Prior to the digital age, journalists uncovered primary sources for their stories through eyewitness accounts, interviews, public speeches, legal documents, as well as audio and video recordings. These sources would make up the crux of their news stories, and audiences were only exposed to the quotes and sound bites that the journalist deemed essential to the story. However, new media has altered the news landscape and streamlined the sourcing process, eliminating several steps. For example, verified social media accounts (particularly those on Twitter and Instagram) have become primary news sources. Politicians, political commentators, celebrities, professional athletes, and so forth can speak directly to the public at any time or place from their mobile phones. Tweets can be embedded in an online article, and any number of journalists can have a half dozen quotes from Twitter for their articles without conducting a single interview. However, ethical journalists still have a duty to put all the tweets in a larger context. Readers and viewers should have a proper understanding of a tweet's intended meaning, but a reporter's need to conduct a formal interview has diminished.

A contemporary reporter must also have a skill set that transcends text, audio, and video. Primary sources for an article can simply be data points that paint a larger picture of the story. Using advanced analytics, journalists can use data to discover consistencies and uncover anomalies in the raw numbers. The onus, then, lies on the reporter to describe the findings and use data visualization for these sources to reach their full potential. For example, the website FiveThirtyEight.com publishes dozens of articles a month that use analytics to provide readers a better understanding of politics, sports, science, economics, and culture. Data scientists at FiveThirtyEight develop algorithms to predict an outcome, and data journalists articulate (through text and visuals) the possible outcomes to readers.

Using a sports example, every soccer match of the 2018 FIFA World Cup was simulated twenty thousand times, and the percentage of each possible outcome was provided in real time (Boice and Dottle 2018). Before each match, teams were given a Soccer Power Index (SPI) rating, which is a combination of a team's recent match results and the overall strength of their World Cup roster. The statistical models predict the winner before the match begins but adjust predictions as the game progresses. If a team scores a goal, the percentages of a win, loss, or draw are recalculated. Simulations like this are applicable to virtually any discipline or topic. Using national polling data, the site routinely publishes articles about the likely outcomes of national and state elections (Bacon and Mehta 2018). Traditional news organizations, such as the *New York Times* and *Washington Post*, have adapted this storytelling model and are using data journalism and graphic design throughout their online platform. The *New York Times*, for example, published a three-part feature story on climate change in the Antarctic using scientific data and simulations to predict the potential impact of global warming on coastal cities (Gillis 2017). As readers scroll down each article, they are shown interactive maps that simulate the movement of glaciers, areas on the continent vulnerable to ocean heat, as well as visual representations of areas that have lost or gained significant amounts of ice.

While these newer forms of sourcing are growing in popularity among journalists, audiences are still coming to terms with the changes. Journalists need to maintain best ethical practices (including fact-checking information and finding corroborating sources) to avoid a story being labeled "fake news."

Bibliography

Bacon, Perry, Jr. 2017. "When to Trust a Story That Uses Unnamed Sources." FiveThirtyEight. Last modified July 18, 2017. https://fivethirtyeight.com/features/when-to-trust-a-story-that-uses-unnamed-sources/.

Bacon, Perry, Jr., and Dhrumil Mehta. 2018. "An Updated Look at the Race for the Senate." FiveThirtyEight. Accessed June 22, 2018. https://fivethirtyeight.com/features/why-republicans-may-have-a-narrow-senate-advantage/.

Boice, Jay, and Rachael Dottle. 2018. "2018 World Cup Predictions." FiveThirtyEight. Accessed June 22, 2018. https://projects.fivethirtyeight.com/2018-world-cup-predictions/.

Farhi, Paul. 2013. "Anonymous Sources Are Increasing in News Stories, Along with Rather Curious Explanations." *Washington Post*, December 15. https://www.washington post.com/lifestyle/style/anonymous-sources-are-increasing-in-news-stories-along-with-rather-curious-explanations/2013/12/15/5049a11e-61ec-11e3-94ad-004fefa61ee6_story.html?utm_term=.ed67cc592a62.

Gillis, Justin. 2017. "Looming Floods, Threatened Cities." *New York Times*, May 17. https://www.nytimes.com/interactive/2017/05/18/climate/antarctica-ice-melt-climate-change-flood.html.

Dr. Sean R. Sadri is an assistant professor in the Department of Journalism and Creative Media at the University of Alabama, teaching sports media and journalism courses. His research is focused primarily on online sports and news credibility as well as the information-seeking behavior of modern sports media consumers.

Unlocking the Keys to the Brave "News" World: News Literacy as the World's Most Important Resource
Julie Frechette

Watch any dystopian science fiction film today, and you'll uncover signs of the changing landscape of U.S. news and information. In Netflix's sci-fi anthology series *Black Mirror*, audience ratings, social media "clout" scores, and trashy entertainment enslave the human spirit. The *Hunger Games* series depicts a new world order in which life and death are exploited by a mega-entertainment industry that controls news and information through censorship, spin, and Orwellian tactics. In Steven Spielberg's film adaptation of *Ready Player One*, news and information are obscured by virtual reality, avatars, and mass-mediated entertainment. Today, as top leaders bypass establishment news through tweets and dismiss facts and headlines that don't suit them as "fake news," the temptation may be to believe that the search for any credible information is futile—that trustworthy and reliable news have been corrupted by bias, propaganda, sensationalism, profit-driven ratings, corporate interests, and trending stories. So why bother becoming informed?

Here is the thing—being informed means staying attuned to how news and information *have* changed and are profoundly altering our world. In the digital age, information finds *us* through news feeds, sending us trending headlines and updates on our cell phones and digital devices. Companies like Google, Comcast, and Facebook use surveillance software, apps, and data mining to track us as we use cell phones, websites, and social media. Ever taken a free personality test online offered by your favorite social media site? Market researchers use the information provided by such "quizzes" to create psychographics that classify us according to our personality, opinions, values, attitudes, and lifestyles. The results are sold to information brokers who use big data—analytics, algorithms, and trends—to combine all the bits of data collected about us to sell to companies that are interested in our profiles.

In today's news economy, the flow of information is altered by surveillance, data mining, hate speech, hacking, trolling, click-bait, and even "likes." Rollbacks by the Federal Communications Commission (FCC) over net neutrality rules governing the internet mean that big cable companies like Comcast, Time Warner, AT&T, and Verizon can favor their own content over competitors, and internet service providers can block, throttle, or paywall content, thereby compromising a free and open internet. As for social media, we've only just begun to unravel how powerful information brokers and data mining shape public opinion and even affect the outcome of political elections.

In the 2016 presidential election, corporate news industries treated Americans as customers rather than as citizens by offering spectacle over reliable facts and solid political reporting. As Donald Trump launched his presidential campaign and emerged onto network news, ratings spiked by roughly 40 percent over the previous year on Fox News; CNN overcame near twenty-year rating lows with a 170 percent increase in prime time that year; and on March 8, 2016, Trump's primary night news was shown in full across cable news networks, while Hillary Clinton's victory speech went uncovered. Just a few months into the campaign cycle, "Trump had received nearly $1.9 billion worth of news coverage; his next closest Republican competitor, Ted Cruz, received a little more than $300 million," and Hillary Clinton "received less than $750 million" (Rutenberg 2016). While the news industry made millions, the public was cheated out of substantive political news, fact-checking, and analysis.

Just as former president Obama's campaign understood how to effectively tap into crowdsourced support and digital fundraising from mobile devices in the 2008 and 2012 national elections, Trump's campaign advisors leveraged data mining and social media in a revolutionary bid to sway voters in 2016. In addition to using sophisticated state-by-state analytics acquired from the Republican National Committee's data hub, Trump's team hired the British public relations firm Cambridge Analytica for over $5.9 million (Price 2018). The firm combined data mining with analytics to produce social media marketing favoring Trump while infusing doubt about Clinton's credibility and trustworthiness.

So how do we avoid cynicism and nihilism in this Brave "News" World?

Information wars have always been part of how media moguls and their monopolies have retained power, profit, and ratings. Yet today's changing media environment requires us to understand the importance of finding reliable and verifiable information within the digital architecture that controls today's attention economy. In addition to cross-checking facts and information from multiple news sources, channels, and platforms, government regulation is needed to keep our media open, diverse, and aligned with the public interest.

The upside to having networked information in the digital age is that there are plenty of alternatives to those provided by corporations. However, the responsibility remains on us to become wise about where our information is coming from and how to find trustworthy independent news sources in a post–net neutrality world. Instead of only accessing news from private sources, or letting them find us, we must seek out publicly funded and alternative news. This includes independent news sources, foreign news, sites that report on censorship, independent reporters and whistle-blowers, and news from organizations dedicated to improving media.

As news continues to grow and flow through profitable digital companies, we need to carefully analyze and judge the credibility and intent of a whole host of digital news and social media providers. Professional and amateur journalists are indistinguishable from bloggers, trolls, and hackers. Moreover, social media companies can't keep up with the pace and scope of malicious efforts to abuse their platforms. In March 2018, Facebook was under fire after the data mining company Cambridge Analytica sold information from fifty million Facebook users to the Trump campaign, leading to the #DeleteFacebook movement.

While some Americans are just starting to understand how the 2016 presidential election was shaped by social media infiltration, Facebook has uncovered another set of coordinated disinformation campaigns on their site meant to disrupt the 2018 midterm election. Such findings call for a thorough examination of the credentials and practices of news sources by FCC regulators, information providers, and the public at large. In addition to public interest regulation, it is now the responsibility of today's online users to detect inaccuracies, slander, libel, and propaganda. Guidance can be found from watchdog groups such as Fairness and Accuracy in Reporting (FAIR), Truthout, Free Press, *Columbia Journalism Review*, Project Censored, the Action Coalition for Media Education, and other reputable organizations.

Just as dystopian film protagonists find themselves fighting to defend the democratic values of a free press and open society, we need to develop media literacy tactics, tools, and strategies for the digital age. As digital outlets pursue a broader national audience and localized news becomes scarce, we also need to take an active role in finding, funding, and producing quality community news that includes diverse social media distribution and participation. Lessons can be learned from the Free Press Action Fund, which persuaded New Jersey's legislation to create a nonprofit group to fund local public news reporting projects by setting aside "$5 million from the sale of old public television licenses" (Rojas 2018).

Finally, fostering a better understanding of the world requires us to scan a wide variety of sources from global contexts. By incorporating an inclusive approach through these key frameworks for news literacy, we can create a media reform movement for digital citizenship that thrives off an informed citizenry, civic engagement, and social justice as the cornerstones of society.

Bibliography

Price, Greg. 2018. "How Cambridge Analytica Helped Trump: Explaining Firm's Role in President's Campaign." *Newsweek*, March 20. https://www.newsweek.com/trump-cambridge-analytica-explain-852903

Rojas, Rick. 2018 "News from Your Neighborhood, Brought to You by the State of New Jersey." *New York Times*, July 30. https://www.nytimes.com/2018/07/30/nyregion/nj-legislature-community-journalism.html.

Rutenberg, Jim. 2016. "The Mutual Dependence of Donald Trump and the News Media." *New York Times*, March 21. https://www.nytimes.com/2016/03/21/business/media/the-mutual-dependence-of-trump-and-the-news-media.html.

Julie Frechette, PhD, is professor and chair of the Department of Communication at Worcester State University. She is the author of the book Media Education for a Digital Generation *and serves as copresident of the Action Coalition for Media Education.*

Fake News Is Old News: The Blurry Boundaries between Journalism and Public Relations
Lori Bindig Yousman

While many associate the rise of "fake news" with the 2016 presidential election, the practice originated over a century ago with the development of the public relations industry. Public relations, or PR, is the practice of strategically building and maintaining relationships to advance a specific agenda. Though commonly employed by corporations, nonprofits, activist and community groups, government agencies, public officials, and celebrities also utilize PR. Although the inherent bias of PR conflicts with the notion of objective journalism, the boundaries between PR and news have long been blurred.

Despite the changes in PR over the years, the news media has consistently played a key role in its attempt to shape public opinion. PR practitioners work tirelessly to influence journalistic gatekeepers in hopes of obtaining positive news coverage for their client. The news is an ideal vehicle for the dissemination of PR because of its agenda-setting function and its free, large audience. Journalism's association with unbiased truth also lends credibility to PR messages. Thus, since the early twentieth century, PR practitioners have considered themselves "news engineers" who were responsible for creating and supplying the news (Ewen 1996).

As news engineers, early PR practitioners employed a range of techniques that blurred the boundaries between PR and journalism that are still used today. For instance, press releases mimic the look and style of newspaper articles but are written entirely by PR practitioners. Likewise, video news releases provide newsrooms with fully packaged stories—complete with video footage, expert sound bites, and PR professionals acting as correspondents—ready to be inserted into broadcasts. However, when these materials are used by journalists, the PR origins of the stories are not disclosed to their audience.

PR practitioners also bombard journalists with pitches for "soft news" stories that present their clients favorably. They have been known to stage events to draw attention from the press such as the 1929 "Torches of Freedom" march, the 2003 "Mission Accomplished" photo op, and Toyota's 2016 "Wall Climb" stunt. While these PR tactics are not innately unethical, over the years unscrupulous practitioners have fabricated news, deceiving journalists and the American public. Some of these stories have been inconsequential like P. T. Barnum's false proclamations about his sideshow attractions, while others like PR firm Hill & Knowlton's false testimony of babies being ripped from incubators resulted in U.S. support for the Gulf War (Grunig 1993).

Even when journalists ignore traditional PR efforts, PR can still influence the news. For instance, journalists often use information gleaned from organizational websites and social media as the background for their stories. While these platforms allow journalists to avoid direct contact with PR professionals, they are still engaging with carefully constructed PR messages that present the organization in the best possible light. Through faux third-party organizations with innocuous names that mask the identity of PR firms and their clients, journalists may encounter covert PR propaganda as was recently the case with the sugar and corn syrup industry front groups, the Center for Consumer Freedom and Citizens for Health (Hamburger 2014).

Other times, journalists have no choice than to reach out to PR practitioners in order to obtain access to spokespeople, experts, and industry information that is crucial to their stories. In these situations, PR professionals often present themselves as invaluable resources rather than client advocates. Complicating matters further is that a number of practitioners begin their careers in journalism and are still viewed as colleagues by reporters despite having transitioned to PR. Through these relationships, journalists become acculturated to PR and are more likely to consider PR practitioners as trustworthy sources and good contacts for their stories (Macnamara 2016; Obermaier, Koch, and Reismeyer 2015).

The changing media landscape also blurs the boundary between journalism and PR. The advent of cable and internet news outlets heralded the 24-hour news cycle, requiring journalists to continuously produce more content. Shrinking newsrooms have also compounded journalists' reliance on PR, as there are a fewer reporters and editors writing original stories and vetting PR materials. Increasingly, digital platforms feature "sponsored content" that looks like and appears beside traditional content but only exists because of a financial agreement. In these partnerships, which include the *New York Times* and Samsung, *Forbes* and FedEx, and the *Huffington Post* and Johnson & Johnson, sponsored content may be written entirely by the corporate partner, in conjunction with the sponsoring organization, or by staff reporters assigned to cover the paid stories (Sirrah 2017; Vega 2013).

While there is never a guarantee that PR strategies will result in news coverage, scholars estimate that over the past one hundred years, "50% to 75% of mass media content is provided or significantly influenced by PR" (Macnamara 2016, 118). Despite the efforts of PR to shape the news, research suggests that the public is generally unaware of its influence and assumes that news originates with editors and reporters (Follis 2013). Even among journalists, there is a tendency to under-report their reliance on PR (Macnamara 2016). Although these blurry boundaries are nothing new, the inability to distinguish PR from journalism has profound impact on society. Widespread critical media literacy is needed for a truly informed citizenry that is able to differentiate between legitimate journalism, "fake news," and corporate interests in order to have a functioning democracy.

Bibliography

Ewen, Stuart. 1996. *PR! A Social History of Spin*. New York: Basic Books.

Follis, Laura. 2013. "The Impact of Public Relations on News." Thesis, California Polytechnic State University. https://digitalcommons.calpoly.edu/joursp/55/.

Grunig, James E. 1993. "Public Relations and International Affairs: Effects, Ethics and Responsibility." *Journal of International Affairs* 47, no. 1: 137–162.

Hamburger, Tom. 2014. " 'Soft Lobbying' War between Sugar, Corn Syrup Shows New Tactics in Washington Influence." *Washington Post*, February 12.

Macnamara, James. 2016. "The Continuing Convergence of Journalism and PR: New Insights for Ethical Practice from a Three-Country Study of Senior Practitioners." *Journalism & Mass Communication Quarterly* 93, no. 1: 118–141.

Obermaier, Magdalena, Thomas Koch, and Claudia Reismeyer. 2015. "Deep Impact? How Journalists Perceive the Influence of Public Relations on Their

News Coverage and Which Variables Determine This Impact." *Communication Research*: 1–23. https://doi.org/ 10.1177/0093650215617505.

Sirrah, Ava. 2017. "The Blurring Line between Editorial and Native Ads at the New York Times." MediaShift, October 3. http://mediashift.org/2017/10/ advertisers-underwrite-new-york-times-content/.

Vega, Tanzina. 2013. "Sponsors Now Pay for Online Articles, Not Just Ads." *New York Times*, April 7. https://www .nytimes.com/2013/04/08/business/media/sponsors-now-pay-for-online-articles-not-just-ads.html.

Lori Bindig Yousman, PhD, is an associate professor in the School of Communication, Media, and the Arts at Sacred Heart University. Her research is grounded in media literacy and popular culture. Most recently, she coedited Gender, Race, and Class in Media, *5th edition, published by Sage.*

Western News Media Coverage of Muslims and Arabs: From 9/11 to the Trump Era
Nahed Eltantawy

Historically, Western media has often been criticized for their Islamophobic and orientalist coverage of Muslims (Bravo López 2011; Modood 1991; Said 1979). Researchers attribute stereotyping of Muslim and Arab Americans to Hollywood's long history of depicting Arabs and Muslims as barbaric villains, rich oil sheikhs, and terrorists (Nacos and Torres-Reyna 2004; Shaheen 2003). News media coverage of Muslims is no different. For years, news coverage of Muslims depicted men as barbaric, dominating, and violent, whereas women were viewed as one monolithic group of veiled, oppressed, and voiceless victims in need of saving (Eltantawy 2013; Said 1979). The September 11 terrorist attacks yielded more media attention toward Arabs and Muslims. Some of that coverage generated positive portrayals, including articles that gave voice to Muslim men and women who explained Islamic practices to Western audiences (Nacos and Torres-Reyna 2004). Yet, much of the news media coverage remained negative, focusing on Muslims as violent terrorists, thus creating public distrust and fear of Muslims, who were viewed as the dangerous Other (Awan 2017).

In fact, when it comes to terrorism, news media coverage of Muslims has remained fairly consistent over the years. A recent University of Alabama study shows that terror attacks by Muslims receive about 357 percent more news coverage than attacks by non-Muslims (Kearns, Betus, and Lemieux 2018). Media bias in such coverage also extends to how reporters describe the perpetrators. When the perpetrator is Muslim, the reporters waste no time identifying him as a terrorist or jihadi, yet when the perpetrator is a white American, he is usually described as a lone wolf or disturbed (Lakshmanan 2017). Hence, the news media continues to associate Muslims with terrorism, even when there is little evidence to support this claim. A recent U.S. government report states that, since September 12, 2001, attacks by far right extremists totaled sixty-two, compared to twenty-three attacks committed by radical Islamists (Maurer 2017).

When it comes to Muslim women, for years, the news media paid too much attention to what Muslim women wore instead of what they did or thought (Fakhraie 2010). The veil received the bulk of attention and was usually associated with oppression (Macdonald 2006; Ruby 2006). Thus, the same news media that portrayed Muslim women as voiceless victims of the veil was in fact silencing these women by not allowing them to speak and, instead, speaking for them on the dangers of the veil (Eltantawy 2013; Macdonald 2006).

Such negative coverage impacts public opinion and plays a role in shaping policies that affect Muslims within and outside the United States (Terman 2017). In recent years, Muslims within the United States have experienced violent attacks, threats to Mosques, negative political statements by government officials and politicians, including President Trump, as well as anti-Muslim policies, including the Muslim travel ban

("Anti-Muslim Activities in the United States" 2018). Pew statistics show 75 percent of Muslim Americans are concerned about discrimination against Muslims, while 68 percent say they are worried under Trump ("US Muslims Concerned . . ." 2017).

Yet, despite these concerns, there is reason for optimism. The past two or so years have witnessed some improvement in the coverage of Muslims, with news outlets increasingly relying on Muslim voices in their reporting. Recent news stories on veiling, for example, are allowing audiences to change their perceptions of the veil, thanks to interviews with Muslim women, who voice their personal thoughts on veiling (Biagiotti 2016; Ingber 2015). Additionally, when President Trump introduced the Muslim travel ban, this triggered a wave of positive news media coverage, where the audience got to read and watch news about everyday Muslim American doctors, lawyers, and teachers instead of the usual focus on Muslim extremists (Eltantawy 2017). With statistics projecting that the number of Muslims in the United States is expected to jump from 3.45 million in 2017 to 8.1 million by 2050 (Mohamed 2018), there is reason to believe that the coverage will keep improving, as more Muslim voices participate in newsmaking as well as in other media productions.

Bibliography

"Anti-Muslim Activities in the United States." 2018. New America. Accessed January 1, 2019. https://www.new america.org/in-depth/anti-muslim-activity/.

Awan, Imran. 2017. "Opinion: 'The Muslims Are Coming!' Why Islamophobia Is So Dangerous." CNN.com, July 31. https://www.cnn.com/2014/12/03/opinion/islamophobia-opinion/index.html.

Biagiotti, Lisa. 2016. "Watch Muslim Women Explain What Their Hijab Means to Them." *Los Angeles Times*, May 5. http://www.latimes.com/visuals/video/la-me-american-women-in-hijabs-video-story.html.

Bravo López, Fernando. 2011. "Towards a Definition of Islamophobia: Approximations of the Early Twentieth Century." *Ethnic and Racial Studies* 34, no. 4: 556–573.

Eltantawy, Nahed. 2013. "Above the Fold and Beyond the Veil: Islamophobia in Western Media." *The Routledge Companion to Media & Gender*: 384–392.

Eltantawy, Nahed. 2017. "Travel Ban Unites Americans against Bigotry." Fair Observer, February 27. https://www.fairobserver.com/region/north_america/travel-muslim-ban-us-immigration-donald-trump-news-81221/.

Fakhraie, Fatemeh. 2010. "Opinion: The Media Is Obsessed with How Muslim Women Look." CNN.com, August 30. http://www.cnn.com/2010/OPINION/08/30/muslim.women.media/index.html.

Ingber, Hanna. 2015. "Muslim Women on the Veil." *New York Times*, May 27. https://www.nytimes.com/2015/05/28/world/muslim-women-on-the-veil.html.

Kearns, Erin, Allison Betus, and Anthony Lemieux. 2018. "Why Do Some Terrorist Attacks Receive More Media Attention Than Others?" *Justice Quarterly*, doi:10.1080/07418825.2018.1524507. https://papers.ssrn.com/sol3/papers.cfm?abstract_id=2928138.

Lakshmanan, Indira. 2017. "Lone Wolf or Terrorist? How Bias Can Shape News Coverage. *Poynter*, October 2. https://www.poynter.org/ethics-trust/2017/lone-wolf-or-terrorist-how-bias-can-shape-news-coverage/.

Macdonald, Myra. 2006. "Muslim Women and the Veil: Problems of Image and Voice in Media Representations." *Feminist Media Studies* 6, no. 1: 7–23.

Maurer, Diana. 2017. "Countering Violent Extremism: Actions Needed to Define Strategy and Assess Progress of Federal Efforts." U.S. Government Accountability Office. https://www.gao.gov/assets/690/683984.pdf.

Modood, Tariq. 1992. *Not Easy Being British: Color, Culture and Citizenship*. Stoke-on-Trent, England: Runnymede Trust and Trentham.

Mohamed, Basheer. 2018. "New Estimates Show U.S. Muslim Population Continues to Grow." Pew Research Center, January 3. http://www.pewresearch.org/fact-tank/2018/01/03/new-estimates-show-u-s-muslim-population-continues-to-grow/.

Nacos, Brigitte L., and Oscar Torres-Reyna. 2004. "Framing Muslim-Americans before and after 9/11." In *Framing Terrorism*, edited by Pippa Norris, Montague Kern, and Marion Just, 133–158. New York: Routledge.

Ruby, Tabassum F. 2006. "Listening to the Voices of Hijab." *Women's Studies International Forum* 29, no. 1: 54–66.

Said, Edward. 1979. *Orientalism*. New York: Vintage.

Shaheen, Jack G. 2003. "Reel Bad Arabs: How Hollywood Vilifies a People." *Annals of the American Academy of Political and Social Science* 588, no. 1: 171–193.

Terman, Rochelle. 2017. "Islamophobia and Media Portrayals of Muslim Women: A Computational Text Analysis of US News Coverage." *International Studies Quarterly* 61, no. 3: 489–502.

"U.S. Muslims Concerned about Their Place in Society, But Continue to Believe in the American Dream." 2017. Pew Research Center, July 26. http://www.pewforum .org/2017/07/26/findings-from-pew-research-centers-2017-survey-of-us-muslims/.

Nahed Eltantawy is Communication Department chair and associate professor at the Nido R. Qubein School of Communication at High Point University, North Carolina. Her research focuses on media representations, social media activism, and critical and cultural studies. Her work has been published in various books and peer-reviewed journals, including Feminist Media Studies *and the* International Journal of Communication. *You can follow Eltantawy on Twitter at @ntantawy or contact her at neltanta@ highpoint.edu.*

A Plea for Print
Erica Drzewiecki

As the last generation to grow up largely without personal cell phones and social media, mine has a peculiar place in this brave new world. Sandwiched between old and new schools of thought, we have faced the choice to eat, decline, or simply take a taste.

Facebook was really just being introduced in high schools during my senior year, and I had no interest. I went on to study communications with a concentration in contemporary journalism. I would come to learn that this focus did not mean newspapers, but podcasts, video, and harnessing the World Wide Web as a platform to share the news.

In the decade since, our society has become even more entrenched in digital journalism, as my professors predicted it would.

The profits for daily reporting are obvious and plentiful—breaking news is posted as soon as it is made and updated constantly thereafter. Readers provide instant feedback, calling for corrections or posing new questions to keep reporters on their feet. Page visits and shares are all on record. On the other hand, I dare say weekly and monthly publications still feel quite snug in the print medium.

As the point person for one weekly and one monthly paper, I have found that readers are picking these up more often than they are sharing them online. The latter isn't even available on the internet, and it is still one of the company's most popular products.

The weekly has a modest circulation in a medium-sized town. Still, stacks at the town's library, police station, town hall, and local stores disappear quickly. Many who don't subscribe seek it out in their community.

For those digital diehards who don't stoop to "outdated" news consumption, read on for a glimpse encounter inside a weekly paper.

The front page photo and headline put the top story of the past seven days front and center, no bones (or clicks) about it. Let's say it's an investigative piece on the school board's budget deliberations. The print exposé carries more weight than its online counterpart. Open to a spread of the last meeting on pages four and five, with deliberately placed photos capturing all the finger pointing and feuding faces. It's impossible to miss the superintendent's controversial blowup, pasted into a pullout quote box in the center. Of course, his words will still get skewed on social media and dissected six times over by the usual band of critics.

Turn to page two to find out your neighbor's daughter was arrested again. Also here, learn that the last name of the award-winning author featured on page seven last week was spelled incorrectly.

Receive an earful of the latest political rants in letters on pages six and seven, often rebuttals of the prior week's submissions.

Cut out coupons for a sixteen-dollar oil change on the outskirts of the town and happy hour specials at that new place in the west end.

Did you notice that Mrs. Dearborn sent in a photo of the garden club's latest project? Flip the page over for snapshots of the class of 1973s recent reunion.

Pages nine and ten might feature a spread of the oil spill's impact on the surrounding neighborhood, with opinions from residents highlighted in pullout boxes on the page borders.

Sports are often the most popular section, as coverage of the baseball team's spring sweep gets hung in the high school's main office and passed around the hallways. Discover your favorite band is performing next month in the event calendar, and learn the Lutheran church is selling its organ. Turn to the back page, and scan through the high school's last quarter honor roll.

How did the town fare through the week? Learn here in a succinct, tangible, sixteen-page package.

Advertising is virtually unlimited on a website, but paper poses a competition for local businesses and community groups, who pay for space on the front page or a prime spot in a special event section. The week before town elections, watch as story copy battles for space with letters and political committee ads. The heart of a community beats through these pages.

Call us "the local rag," and use us to shroud family keepsakes in the attic. When the kids move out in ten years, they'll blow the dust off that box and be flabbergasted to read the movie theatre on Second Street used to be a brothel.

"There was eight feet of snow in 1991? Where was I that winter?" They'll ask.

There is a grace to thoughts conveyed with the lick of an envelope and payment of postage, mailed as letters to the editor of the weekly newspaper. I would rather read these than follow every whim of a serial poster to social media, fingers spewing emotions like vomit at 2 a.m.

I would rather wait in anticipation for the monthly piece from my favorite columnist, knowing they had thirty days to craft it and another thirty before their next chance to share arrived.

How are newspapers dying when they are the only plain records of history, framed on restaurant walls and preserved by microfilm in library archives? Every mistake, misspelling, and mishap is accounted for, if not corrected—most certainly not deleted without a trace.

If monthly and weekly printing is the antithesis to breaking news, let it be known as bonding news: a list of the year's scholarship recipients, photographs from the Knights of Columbus fund-raiser, a feature on the farmer's market, and the identity of the woman in July's Mystery Photo from 1954.

The local world, in all its glory, no device required.

Perhaps these old-fashioned media can teach us newsmakers and readers patience, preparation, and presentation. For these are industry virtues that the newfangled, minute-to-minute journalism has yet to master.

Erica Drzewiecki is a senior writer at Central Connecticut Com-munications. She is the chief reporter for the Newington Town Crier, *a weekly paper covering town issues, events, and people, and* CT Prime Time, *a monthly magazine featuring happenings in the senior community across central Connecticut. She also provides event coverage on Sundays for two dailies, the* New Britain Herald *and the* Bristol Press.

Searching for the Source: Bots, Misinformation, and You
Randall Livingstone

Among the major controversies related to the 2016 U.S. presi-dential election is the use of propaganda and misinformation to influence public opinion and perhaps even voting behaviors. Much focus has been put on the efforts of Russian hackers to disrupt our electoral system and democratic faith, and with good reason; the U.S. intelligence community has repeatedly affirmed the existence of a Russian campaign to influence the 2016 election as well as future elections (Demirjian 2018). One prong of this campaign has been the use of social media bots, which are automated or semiautomated accounts posing as authentic human accounts. These bots are able to quickly and broadly amplify messaging by reposting, retweeting, friend-ing, following, or liking social media content, and the volume of their presence on Twitter, Facebook, Instagram, and other major social media has muddied much of the authentic com-munication on these platforms.

Not all bots are bad, however. There are many automated accounts on Twitter that are not meant to deceive or manipulate but rather to inform, experiment, or entertain. @congressedits tweets when someone from the U.S. Congress anonymously edits a Wikipedia article, and @earthquakeBot tweets when-ever a quake of 5.0 or higher occurs around the world. @Two-Headlines takes two recent news stories and stitches together a nonsequitur yet realistic sounding news headline, while

@Mazemerizing generates random colorful mazes every three hours. There are even bots that "BONG" hourly (@big_ben_clock) and scream "AAAAAAAHHHHHHHHH" every ten minutes (@infinite_scream). Indeed, programmers and artists have taken the open nature of Twitter's automation rules to create useful tools and inane oddities. On Facebook, a much more closed platform, legitimate bots have appeared in recent years as chatbots, providing interactivity and customer service for brands and organizations.

One lesson of the information/disinformation ecosystem around the 2016 election is something that harkens back to traditional media literacy: know the source of the content. Of course, this can be difficult on social media. In the past, the limited number of legacy media outlets would allow consumers to more narrowly focus their critical eye as well as to establish trust with particular sources of information. But in the social media era, when everyone can create and distribute information at low costs, the vetting of a source often requires more time and energy, as well as a willingness to chase that information down a rabbit hole. A memorable post about a social issue may not attribute its source, but that information or opinion may very well have originated somewhere else. It is this crisis of authenticity on social media that bots exploit. Malicious bot accounts often look like normal accounts, with profile images, selfies, bios, locations, and informal language. They count on looking just real enough to not elicit further scrutiny by other users, and they hope to get their content into the stream of a social media feed, where users are even less inclined to click through to their profile and check the source.

While government agencies investigate and take action against malicious bots and their creators, some notable non-profit and academic organizations are also researching the impact of bots on social media, often presenting results more quickly to the public. The Pew Research Center's Internet and Technology division has looked at link sharing by bots on Twitter, finding that 66 percent of all tweeted links to popular news and current events websites come from bots (Wojcik et al. 2018). The Computational Propaganda Project (2018) at the Oxford Internet Institute has found that "political actors have used bots to manipulate conversations, demobilize opposition, and generate false support on popular sites." Similarly, the Hamilton 68 project from the Alliance for Securing Democracy, which developed a real-time tool that monitors six hundred Twitter accounts linked to the Russian influence campaign, has shown these bots often amplify content attacking the United States and Europe and promote conspiracy theories, disinformation, extremism, and divisive politics (Alliance for Securing Democracy 2018).

So how can a social media user become more informed about bots? First, remember the nature of the medium: Facebook, Twitter, and other social media allow anyone to become a publisher. Think like a journalist; when you see information worth spreading, find corroborating sources. Second, become an investigator by scrutinizing account profiles for telltale signs of botness. Recently created accounts that have very little or quite a lot of content, accounts with odd usernames (random strings of letters and/or numbers), and accounts that post at odd hours or apparently never "sleep" all should raise your suspicions. Third, use online tools that can dig deeper into an account. Botometer, a free web tool developed by the Network Science Institute and Center for Complex Networks and Systems at Indiana University, offers statistics on any Twitter account's content, frequency, and network of connections, scoring how likely the account is a bot. This tool also allows users to scan their followers to identify possible bots.

The recent malevolent interference in the democratic process both in the United States and other nations has prompted major social media platforms like Twitter and Facebook to purge millions of suspicious accounts from their user bases, but these services acknowledge that the battle with bot is continuous (Confessore and Dance 2018; Wagner and Molla 2018). You, the user, need to be vigilant when interacting with information on social media, because whether that information came to you from a bot with bad intentions or a human with good intentions, you become part of the source when you post, tweet, or share.

Bibliography

Alliance for Securing Democracy. 2018. "How to Read This Dashboard." Hamilton 68. https://dashboard .securingdemocracy.org/.

Computational Propaganda Project. 2018. "Project Description." http://comprop.oii.ox.ac.uk/about-the-project/.

Confessore, Nicholas, and Gabriel Dance. 2018. "Battling Fake Accounts, Twitter to Slash Millions of Followers." *New York Times*, July 11 https://www.nytimes.com/ 2018/07/11/technology/twitter-fake-followers.html.

Demirjian, Karoun. 2018. "Senate Report Affirms Intelligence Community's Conclusion That Russia Favored Trump over Clinton." *Washington Post*, July 3 https://www .washingtonpost.com/powerpost/senate-report-affirms-intelligence-communitys-conclusion-that-russia-favored-trump-over-clinton/2018/07/03/4f0f03a2-7ef7-11e8-bb6b-c1cb691f1402_story.html.

Wagner, Kurt, and Rani Molla. 2018. "Facebook Has Disabled Almost 1.3 Billion Fake Accounts over the Past Six Months." Recode, May 15.

Wojcik, Stefan, Solomon Messing, Aaron Smith, Lee Rainie, and Paul Hitlin. 2018. "Bots in the Twittersphere." Pew Research Center, April 9. http://www.pewinternet.org/ 2018/04/09/bots-in-the-twittersphere/.

Randall Livingstone, PhD, is an associate professor in the School of Communication at Endicott College. His research focuses on automation and the internet from a social science perspective.

Is Television News Satire the Problem or the Solution?
Bill Yousman

When Jon Stewart took over *The Daily Show* in 1999, he transformed the program into a full-blown parody of broadcast journalism, opening his first episode with "news" about the Clinton impeachment proceedings.

Stewart quickly brought television news satire to the fore as a popular and influential subgenre of television comedy. Networks frequently try to duplicate successful formulas, and numerous news satire programs would soon emerge, including several featuring former *Daily Show* "correspondents" like Stephen Colbert's *The Colbert Report* and *Full Frontal* with Samantha Bee. Other programs like *Real Time with Bill Maher* and *Saturday Night Live* also carry on a long tradition of satire that takes on political issues while mocking media coverage of politics.

Some scholars celebrate the democratic potential of television news satire (Day 2011; Jones 2010; Warner 2007). Chuck Tryon (2016), for example, argues, "[F]ake news shows have played a vital role in equipping audiences to engage with the news in a more critical fashion" (17). Yet, in an era when the president treats rallies as stand-up comedy while dismissing critical coverage with the label "fake news," we should ask whether explicitly comedic fake news has contributed to a cynical perspective by framing everything as a joke and suggesting that no source can be trusted. Several researchers have indeed found a relationship between viewing satirical programs and holding cynical views on media and politics (Balmas 2014; Baumgartner and Morris 2006; Guggenheim, Kwak, and Campbell 2011).

Years ago, Jeffrey Jones (2010) approvingly wrote, "[S]hould citizens come to believe that news is inauthentic, untrue, or just another form of constructed spectacle . . . then they might yearn for other means of establishing truth and reality" (182). Jones was optimistic that the other sources that citizens would seek out would include programs like *The Daily Show* and *The*

Colbert Report, which, he contended, often provide more information and insight into politics than traditional news outlets.

However, Jones (2010) was writing before the emergence of platforms like Facebook and Twitter as purveyors of fabrications and outright lies. Candidate, and now president, Trump embraced Twitter as a means of circumventing journalists whom he labels "the enemy of the people." Jones was correct to point out that it is the shortcomings of traditional news that drive audiences to seek out other sources of information, but he and others did not anticipate that they would turn to unreliable social media posts and coordinated disinformation campaigns.

Thus, when Jones (2010) optimistically writes, "[T]he postmodern claim that the 'fake' is more real than the 'real' is perhaps not such an unsettling notion after all" (184), he does so without the context that subsequent years have provided, which leads to the crucial question of whether television news satire can still be considered a force for public enlightenment in the era of digital deception. After millions of social media users read that the pope endorsed Donald Trump, or that Hillary Clinton was running a child slavery operation from the basement of a pizzeria, can we still insist that the fake being more real than the real is *not* an unsettling proposition?

Thus, the key question is whether satiric news contributed to the cultivation of a cynical populace more receptive to embracing fake news and dismissive of the importance, or even possibility, of truth in media and politics.

Several observers have identified the blurring of politics and entertainment, and the embrace of irony, as contributing factors in the willingness of the public to adopt the cynical attitude that fake news is just as good as the real thing—because everything is just comedy anyway (Kakutani 2018). Stephen Marche (2017) argued, "Political satirists, and their audiences, have turned the news itself into a joke. . . . [T]hey have contributed to the post-factual state of American political discourse." Steve Almond (2012) questioned Stewart and Colbert's motivations, efficacy, and economic constraints: "[They] never . . . question the corrupt precepts of the status quo too vigorously. . . . The goal is to mollify people, not incite them. . . . After all, their shows air on Comedy Central, which is owned by Viacom, the fifth largest media conglomerate in the world."

The American public is indeed quite cynical about both media and politics (Barthel and Mitchell 2017; Doherty, Kiley, and Tyson 2015). But to place the blame for this on satiric news seems unfounded. Erosion of trust in media and politicians precedes the emergence of even cable television. Moreover, the case can be made that satire encourages healthy skepticism and critical thinking rather than bleak cynicism.

Dana Cloud (2018) offers a useful nuance to idealistic hopes when she points out that satire only works for people who get that the material is indeed meant ironically. Yet several studies (Fox, Koleon, and Sahin 2007; Kohut, Morin, and Keeter 2007; Young 2004) have suggested that news satire can be a useful source of both information and analysis. And there is a long history of satire exposing the deceptions of the powerful. Ultimately satire will not solve the problems of the post-truth society all by itself. But its potential to engage audiences while enlightening them about issues traditional news media neglect may just be part of the solution.

Bibliography

Almond, Steve. 2012. "The Joke's on You: Presenting. . . *The Daily Show* and *The Colbert Report*." *Baffler*, July. https://thebaffler.com/salvos/the-jokes-on-you.

Balmas, Meital. 2014. "When Fake News Becomes Real: Combined Exposure to Multiple News Sources and Political Attitudes of Inefficacy, Alienation, and Cynicism." *Communication Research* 41, no. 3: 430–454.

Barthel, Michael, and Amy Mitchell. 2017. "Americans' Attitudes about the News Media Deeply Divided along

Partisan Lines." Pew Research Center, May 10. http://
www.journalism.org/2017/05/10/americans-attitudes-
about-the-news-media-deeply-divided-along-partisan-lines/
pj_2017-05-10_media-attitudes_a-08/.

Baumgartner, Jody, and Jonathan Morris. 2006. "*The Daily
Show* Effect: Candidate Evaluations, Efficacy, and American
Youth." *American Politics Research* 34, no. 3: 341–367.

Cloud, Dana. 2018. *Reality Bites: Rhetoric and the Circulation
of Truth Claims in U.S. Political Culture*. Columbus: The
Ohio State University Press.

Day, Amber. 2011. *Satire and Dissent: Interventions in
Contemporary Political Debate*. Bloomington: Indiana
University Press.

Doherty, Carroll, Jocelyn Kiley, and Alec Tyson. 2015.
"Beyond Distrust: How Americans View Their
Government." Pew Research Center, November 23.
http://assets.pewresearch.org/wp-content/uploads/
sites/5/2015/11/11-23-2015-Governance-release.pdf.

Fox, Julia R., Glory Koloen, and Volkan Sahin. 2007. "No
Joke: A Comparison of Substance in *The Daily Show with
Jon Stewart* and Broadcast Network Television Coverage
of the 2004 Presidential Election Campaign." *Journal of
Broadcasting and Electronic Media* 51, no. 2: 213–227.

Guggenheim, Lauren, Nojin Kwak, and Scott W. Campbell.
2011. "Nontraditional News Negativity: The Relationship
of Entertaining Political News Use to Political Cynicism
and Mistrust." *International Journal of Public Opinion
Research* 23, no. 3: 287–314.

Jones, Jeffrey. 2010. *Entertaining Politics: Satiric Television and
Political Engagement*. Lanham, MD: Rowman & Littlefield
Publishers.

Kakutani, Michiko. 2018. *The Death of Truth*. New York:
Crown.

Kohut, Andrew, Richard Morin, and Scott Keeter. 2007.
"What Americans Know: 1989–2007." Pew Research

Center. http://assets.pewresearch.org/wp-content/uploads/sites/5/legacy-pdf/319.pdf.

Marche, Stephen. 2017. "The Left Has a Post-Truth Problem Too: It's Called Comedy." *Los Angeles Times*, January 6. http://www.latimes.com/opinion/op-ed/la-oe-marche-left-fake-news-problem-comedy-20170106-story.html.

Tryon, Chuck. 2016. *Political TV.* New York: Routledge.

Warner, Jamie. 2007. "Political Culture Jamming: The Dissident Humor of *The Daily Show with Jon Stewart.*" *Popular Communication* 51, no.1: 17–36.

Young, Dannagal G. 2004. "*Daily Show* Viewers Knowledgeable about Presidential Campaign." National Annenberg Election Survey. Accessed January 1, 2019. https://web.archive.org/web/20050308165738/http://www.annenbergpublicpolicycenter.org/naes/2004_03_late-night-knowledge-2_9-21_pr.pdf.

Bill Yousman, PhD, is an associate professor of media studies at Sacred Heart University. He is the author of Prime-Time Prisons *(2009) and* The Spike Lee Enigma *(2014) and a coeditor of* Gender, Race and Class in Media *(2018).*

Alive Day
Kate Felsen

The phone rang as we were walking past the ping-pong table on our way to lunch. "Yes," Clark answered, somewhat impatiently. He paused to listen and then exclaimed, "What?! Where? Where are they taking them?"

"What is it?" I asked. "What's wrong?"

"It's Vinnie," he said, cupping the receiver, blue eyes unblinking. "Bob and Doug were hit by an IED."

My mouth went dry. I pictured Bob two nights earlier, fastening a chin clasp while I held out another unfamiliar helmet for him to try for size. IED? They were supposed to be done shooting their piece by now. They were supposed to be back in the Green Zone in ninety minutes. We were supposed to anchor President Bush's State of the Union address from the street outside our Baghdad bureau two nights later.

Instinctively, I turned and ran, Clark at my heels, up the narrow stairwell into the converted Iraqi living room, now an ABC newsroom. "I'll call Slavin; you call Martha," Clark ordered. It was eight hours earlier in the States—4:30 a.m.

"Martha, it's Kate. Bob and Doug have been hurt. All I know is they were on patrol in Taji with the 4th ID and got hit by a roadside bomb. They're alive. They're being choppered to the Combat Support Hospital, Zone 1. Vinnie and Magnus are ok. Can you call General Casey?"

"I'm on it, Kate." That's all she said, "I'm on it." Thank God for Martha Raddatz.

We raced to the hospital in an armored car, urging our driver, Haider, to take the route with the fewest checkpoints. I clutched Clark—dependable, most competent Clark—as I repeated a desperate mantra, "Please, let them be alive, please. They've got to be ok. Please."

A perky major met us at the entrance—how did she manage to curl her hair that way over here? "They are being prepped for transport to Balad, for brain surgery," she told us, "they might have just left." I ran down the sterile hallway. An Iraqi soldier was rolled by on a gray gurney. He glanced up at me and dazed, and it took a moment before I noticed he was missing something, his left arm below the elbow. The tendons—were they tendons?—looked like linguine in a thick, dark, plum tomato sauce. If he looked like this, I wondered, what would Bob and Doug look like?

***

This is just one glimpse, one memory from my life as a journalist that I can never forget. It stands out, but it's not alone. I could have told you about the time I watched a college junior die after falling off a balcony in Cancun, or the time I asked a firefighter what it was like to lose his twin brother the day the

Twin Towers fell, or the time I stood beside the Sistine Chapel and watched gray smoke rising from the ancient chimney turn to white signaling the election of a new pope.

When I became a journalist, I wanted to be exposed to people, places, ideas, and events all over the world. I wanted to learn from my peers and from others. I wanted to get to the truth and share it. I wanted to help people make informed decisions about their lives, their communities, and their democracy. And in many ways, I got my wish. I rose through the ranks at ABC News to become the senior producer in charge of foreign news for *World News Tonight*, a position I held for eight years and five anchors, Peter Jennings, Bob Woodruff, Elizabeth Vargas, Charles Gibson, and Diane Sawyer.

I never took for granted the access granted to me when I dialed a stranger and explained that I was calling from ABC News or working with Peter Jennings. That association gave me entrée into factories, farms, operating rooms, palaces, dugouts, weddings, and funerals, with a correspondent and camera crew in tow. What a privilege! But it was also a lot to process.

Even now, as I search through my catalog of memories, the documentary library in my brain, and sort the images into words, I am aware that my most vivid recollections are also my most painful and traumatizing ones. I see Bob and Doug side by side in pre-op, their heads wrapped in gauze, tubes delivering fluids from their necks. I smell the antiseptic iodine swabbed over their shrapnel wounds, and the feelings of helplessness and fear return like a wave. I was responsible for these men, for their lives. "This is Bob Woodruff," I told the nurses as they lifted him gingerly into the medevac, "he has a wife and four children who love him. This is Doug Vogt. His wife, Vivianne, and three daughters need him."

Truthfully, I needed someone too. I needed the comfort, assurance, and shoulders of my colleagues who were part of my team on that horrible day and other horrible days, including September 11, including that day in Cancun when I called the U.S. consul to tell him that a college kid whose New Jersey driver's license I held in my hand had died, including the moment I learned Peter Jennings had lung cancer, and including that Memorial Day when my soundman, James Brolin, was killed by a remotely detonated car bomb. Television news is a team sport, which meant I was never alone in my grief and worry, and that is a salve.

Bob and Doug call January 29, the day they were grievously injured, the day U.S. military personnel saved their lives by providing superb care, Alive Day. Each year on January 29, I reach out to let Bob and Doug know how very grateful I am that they survived, and they reach back with deep gratitude and love.

Memory can be a strange thing. Reaching for my memory of January 29, 2006, triggers feelings I have spent a lot of energy cataloging away, feelings I both long for and fear. That's because being a journalist made me feel more alive than almost anything.

Kate Felsen leads the communications and marketing team at Turnaround for Children, an education nonprofit that translates emerging scientific research about how children learn into tools and strategies for schools. Kate joined Turnaround in 2012 after a distinguished career at ABC News. As foreign editor for the flagship evening news broadcast, she worked closely with Peter Jennings, Bob Woodruff, Charles Gibson, and Diane Sawyer, covering breaking and feature stories around the globe and garnering eleven Emmy, three DuPont, and two Peabody Awards along the way.

4 Profiles

Introduction

There are many, many credible sources for news and information in the United States. As the country's technology has developed from print to radio to television to the internet, new ways of creating and disseminating newsworthy content were established and evolved to keep pace with an ever-changing media culture. Additionally, as journalism as a profession grew, new forms of investigation, storytelling, and reporting became integrated into the culture. Different types of platforms from magazines to talk shows to public affairs programming to digital-only news sites are utilized by a range of people reporting on, discussing, and sharing information. Numerous journalists and bloggers, photographers and columnists, and teams of people who work at broadcast and cablecast stations, websites, and social media platforms consistently provide a wealth of information—from hard news to human interest—for the public to engage with and critically assess. This chapter profiles a short list of some of the many notable figures throughout history who pioneered, impacted, and currently contribute to the evolving news and information landscape in the United States. The chapter also provides some information on a few of the organizations that have impacted, and continue to impact, the ways news and information are produced and shared.

Many news organizations have developed news apps for mobile devices. (Sharaf Maksumov/Dreamstime.com)

People

Joseph Pulitzer (1847–1911)

An immigrant from Hungary, Joseph Pulitzer began his career as a journalist in Missouri. In 1883, he moved to New York and purchased a struggling newspaper called the *New York World*. Pulitzer envisioned the *New York World* as a paper that "will expose all fraud and sham; fight all public evils and abuses; that will serve and battle for the people with earnest sincerity" ("Joseph Pulitzer . . ." 1911). Over two years, his overhaul of the paper resulted in an increase in circulation from 15,770 to 153,213 copies, marking "the start of a revolution in journalism that eventually worked its influence upon every metropolitan and rural paper published in the United States" (Juergens 1966, 4, 50).

The successful techniques Pulitzer used to increase the circulation of the *New York World* included changing the appearance of the newspaper layout and including images as central to reporting (Juergens 1966). He championed aggressive interviewing by reporters to deliver a story and required that those being interviewed be described in detail, a technique that is used in many feature stories today (Juergens 1966). He transformed the editorial pages to give voice to democratic beliefs and challenge corruption ("Joseph Pulitzer . . ." 1911). Pulitzer is now credited for advocacy that led to the "passage of antitrust legislation and regulation of the insurance industry" (Topping 1999).

Pulitzer aimed for a high readership and, in turn, acknowledged that increasing circulation would result in more advertising revenue that would ensure the paper's independence (Juergens 1966). To appeal to a large number of readers, Pulitzer prioritized high-quality reporting written by journalists he paid well and extended news coverage to encompass politics, sports, and other aspects of society (Daly 2012). He also prioritized sensational, human interest–oriented stories "of timeless interest: sex, violence, crime, tragedy, farce" (Juergens 1966, 47). For the most part, Pulitzer did not apologize for the paper's provocative content; he viewed the reporting as reflective of what was happening in the world and believed in appealing to a mass audience, including immigrants whose English was limited but who could understand some of the paper's stories because of the use of less complex words and images (Juergens 1966). After ten years, the paper's circulation topped six hundred thousand, the largest circulating paper in the country (Topping 1999).

From 1896 to 1898, Pulitzer and *New York Morning Journal* publisher William Randolph Hearst engaged in a circulation war, each aiming to sell more newspapers than the other, using sensational, "yellow journalism" reporting tactics (Topping 1999). Yellow journalism, a name that emerged from a popular comic that ran in the papers at the time, was irresponsible, often factually incorrect reporting, practiced by those hoping to increase sales of newspapers. This type of sensationalism differed from the previous sensationalism seen in typical *New York World* reporting, and Pulitzer later regretted his decision to engage with it (Juergens 1966). Pulitzer is also remembered for his philanthropy. He donated money to educational scholarships and established an endowment to support a school of journalism at Columbia University ("Joseph Pulitzer . . ." 1911). The Pulitzer Prizes celebrate top-notch journalism and other art forms and are awarded annually in his honor.

Ida Tarbell (1857–1944)

Born in Pennsylvania, Ida Tarbell began her journalism career writing for the *Chautauqua Assembly Herald* newspaper and the *Chautauquan*, a magazine where she developed her writing, editing, and investigative reporting skills (Brady 1989). She later wrote a celebrated biography of Napoleon Bonaparte and a biographical series on Abraham Lincoln in *McClure's Magazine*—both highly read articles that contributed to the publication's success (Brady 1989).

Tarbell is perhaps best known for her work as a journalist during the muckraking era. It was during this time that she researched and reported on the Standard Oil Company, a business owned by John D. Rockefeller. Tarbell had a personal connection to the oil industry; she witnessed how independent oil companies like the one operated by her family were disadvantaged by Standard Oil's business practices (Brady 1989). Her investigation into the company, however, was meticulously researched and detailed. The result of her years of work included a review of official documents, interviews with employees, and a key interview with a Standard Oil executive. In nineteen investigative articles for *McClure's Magazine*, Tarbell revealed how Rockefeller built his oil company monopoly by engaging in shady business practices that made it difficult for others to compete (King 2012). The series was eventually published as a book, *The History of the Standard Oil Company*, a title that is ranked highly on lists of exceptional examples of twentieth-century journalism.

Eventually Tarbell left *McClure's* and collaborated with others to purchase and develop the *American Magazine*. Tarbell wrote two main series for the publication, one on working conditions and tariffs and one on American women, writing that revealed her to, somewhat ironically, hold conservative views of women and to be anti-suffragist (Brady 1989). She continued to write books and articles, including her own autobiography, for as long as she was able (Brady 1989).

Adolph Ochs (1858–1935)

An American newspaper publisher, Adolph Ochs began his newspaper career in Chattanooga, Tennessee, working for the *Chattanooga Dispatch* and later, at the age of twenty, purchasing and overhauling the struggling *Chattanooga Times* into a leading newspaper in the South (Ezzel 2017). This experience helped Ochs transform the *New York Times*, a paper facing financial difficulties when he purchased it in 1896. The *New York Times* was founded in 1851 and had developed a reputation as a newspaper with a straightforward reporting style. Its circulation was small compared with other papers at the time, and Ochs implemented practices that increased the paper's circulation and stature (Daly 2012). Ochs asked that subscribers be solicited by phone. He spent time branding the newspaper as "accurate," "decent," and "respectable," crafting the slogan "all the news that's fit to print," an approach that stood in contrast to the yellow journalism and more sensational and story-driven news that was prevalent at the time (Schudson 1978). Two years after Ochs took over the *Times*, he decreased the price from three cents to one cent to be in line with the penny papers' pricing. Over the course of a year, the circulation tripled and kept growing (Schudson 1978).

The *Times* emphasized financial news and presented a conservative viewpoint, earning the nickname "Business Bible" and, by 1913, was publishing an index of its content, something that assisted in the development of its reputation of the "paper of record" (Daly 2012; Schudson 1978). Ochs also reinstated the idea (originally expressed by Benjamin Franklin) that the newspaper should operate as a public forum where divergent ideas on issues could be discussed; this commitment led to the establishment of the op-ed page in the *Times* and many other papers (Daly 2012). Journalism expert Michael Schudson (1978) points out that the *Times* positioned itself as an elevated publication: "the Times attracted readers among the wealthy and among those aspiring to wealth and status, in part, because it was socially approved. It was itself a badge of respectability" (117). Ochs used the paper's profits to continually improve the publication, and although he was slow to approve the use of news photography and did not permit comic strips, two elements readers favored, the paper thrived. Over the years, the *Times* became a highly respected publication due to its breadth of coverage and the high standards editors and reporters had to adhere to (Daly 2012).

William Randolph Hearst (1863–1951)

William Randolph Hearst was a media mogul who built a large media empire that dominated the United States during the early decades of the twentieth century. The Hearst

Corporation, an organization that traces its origins to William Randolph Hearst, remains a key player in the contemporary media landscape, owning cable networks and television stations, newspapers, and magazines.

Hearst started working in the journalism business when he took over the *San Francisco Examiner* in 1887. He later moved to New York and took over the *New York Morning Journal*, entering into a "circulation war" with Joseph Pulitzer and his paper, the *New York World*, and engaging in the period's yellow journalism practices (Topping 1999). While Hearst is often credited with fabricating some news reporting to sell papers, most notably around the period preceding the Spanish-American war in 1898, some of the lore around his actions has been challenged. Kenneth Whyte (2009) disputes the often repeated statement, "you furnish the pictures and I'll furnish the war," that Hearst allegedly said to an illustrator he sent to Cuba to draw images of the desperate conditions Cubans were living in as a result of Spanish colonization. Whyte documents that the illustrator returned fifteen months before the war began and suggests the conflict would have happened regardless of what Hearst published. However, the power of the press, including Hearst's pro-war stance that was pervasive in his papers, is recognized as a force in influencing public opinion about the United States' participation in the war (Great Projects Film Company 1999).

By 1930, the Hearst empire had grown, and a quarter of Americans were reading Hearst publications (Proctor 2007). Historians describe Hearst as a hardworking, ambitious, and crusading publisher who used his paper's editorial pages to convey his viewpoints (Proctor 2007; Whyte 2009). For his part, Hearst argued that he represented the people's will and that "government by newspaper" was a way to convey what the people wanted (Proctor 2007, 6). Hearst's papers were consistently sensational in their news reporting. His approach has been described as "Gee Whiz" journalism whereby front page news should evoke a "Gee Whiz" response, second page news should prompt readers to say "Holy Moses," and third page news should prompt "God Almighty" (Proctor 2007, 5). In his quest to achieve and maintain high circulation numbers, Hearst also included both international and local news in his papers. Newspapers also featured entertainment—stories by known writers, puzzles, contests, and cartoons (Proctor 2007). Though Hearst continued to be an influential figure in the early part of the twentieth century, by 1940, he no longer controlled much of his media holdings because of financial difficulties ("William Randolph Hearst," n.d.). The film *Citizen Kane* is based on his life.

Rheta Childe Dorr (1866–1948)

Rheta Childe Dorr's career as a journalist and writer lasted over thirty years and includes her work as a newspaper and magazine staff writer, a journalist who reported on foreign affairs, a war correspondent, and an author of five books ("Rhea C. Dorr . . ." 1948). Dorr is remembered as one of the chief muckraking journalists to address women's issues (Hillstrom 2010). In order to understand and ultimately write about the working conditions women endured in factories, Dorr worked in corset, trouser, coat, and underwear factories to research how workers were treated and what the working environments were like (Gottlieb 1994). Using her extensive notes, Dorr intended to write a series of articles for *Everybody's Magazine* that exposed the factory conditions women dealt with, but the magazine's male editors wanted to frame the content in a different way and assigned Dorr a coauthor who was advertised as being the sole writer of the series (Gottlieb 1994). Dorr was ultimately given byline credit after seeking help from an attorney but was disappointed in how the articles were published, believing her "explosive information" was "whitewashed" (Gottlieb 1994).

Dorr continued her career at *Hamptons Broadway* magazine where she was given much more freedom to write the reformist articles she favored. Over her tenure there, she wrote more than twenty long, influential pieces on such topics as child labor, working conditions, and women's issues (Gottlieb 1994). As a proponent of women's rights, she was particularly interested in how problematic aspects of society impacted women. Dorr also worked as a war correspondent for the *New York Evening Mail,* as a foreign correspondent stationed in Prague, and contributed articles to magazines such as *Collier's* and *Cosmopolitan* ("Rheta C. Dorr . . ." 1948).

Henry Luce (1868–1967)

Henry Luce is considered one of the most influential figures in American journalism history because his development of such successful magazines as *Time, Fortune,* and *Life* in the twentieth century provided mass audiences with a novel way to consume news. Biographer Alan Brinkley (2010) explains that Luce entered the field of journalism after college, but he and his friend, Briton Hadden, were not satisfied with the type of work they were asked to do. Together they developed an idea for a new type of publication that would come out once a week and present a breadth of news-oriented topics—from politics to sports to crime—in short, interesting articles that would appeal to a broad audience. Though the pair initially conceived of this idea as a weekly newspaper, the work eventually debuted as *Time* magazine, a publication the pair called a "news-magazine," the first iteration of the term (Brinkley 2010, 99). The first issue of *Time* was available on newsstands on February 27, 1923 (the magazine was dated March 1923), and although initially sales weren't what Luce and Hadden projected, eventually the magazine became popular, profitable, and a long-running staple in print media. *Time* magazine mainly adhered to the formula its creators conceived—articles were short and spanned topics from world and national news to the arts to finance. The first cover of *Time* featured a drawing of the retiring Speaker of the House of Representatives, Joseph Cannon, establishing the still running tradition of featuring people on the cover (Brinkley 2010).

Hadden died in 1929, and Luce alone continued to grow his publishing company, downplaying the role Hadden played in establishing *Time* (Wilner 2006). Over the years, the company launched the magazines *Fortune, Life, House and Home,* and *Sports Illustrated* and also developed a book division. Luce, a conservative Republican, was often criticized for integrating his own views into his magazines, suggesting how readers should interpret events (Daly 2012). His publishing empire reached millions of readers, and many in the journalism and political spheres recognized, and sometimes deferred to, his power and influence (Wilner 2006). Historians recognize his creativity and business success in dominating the magazine industry in the twentieth century.

Dorothy Thompson (1893–1961)

Dorothy Thompson was an American journalist, columnist, and broadcaster who is remembered for her determination, risk taking, and use of her media platforms to warn against the emerging Nazi movement in Germany. A college-educated woman not trained as a journalist, Thompson worked for a number of organizations, including a women's suffrage organization, an advertising agency, and a social service project group, before becoming a newspaper reporter (Alexander 1940). She began her work as an international news correspondent in 1920, and from there she built a freelance career, learning from more experienced journalists and writing stories that were picked up by various publications (Alexander 1940). Thompson, whom historians describe as an intelligent hard worker, had an engaging personality that assisted her in procuring sources and story leads that informed her reporting (Sanders 1973). She worked as a correspondent throughout Europe, ultimately being hired by the *Philadelphia Public Ledger* as a full-time correspondent for Vienna (Alexander 1940).

In 1925, Thompson became the first woman to lead an American news service in Europe, working as the *New York*

Evening Post's European bureau chief (Sanders 1973). She interviewed Adolf Hitler in 1931, and her critical assessment of him resulted in her expulsion from Germany. After leaving Germany, she took a job with the *New York Herald* as a columnist, writing for the paper three times a week (Sanders 1973). Her syndicated column, called "On the Record," ran in two hundred newspapers with an estimated circulation of eight million (S.R. 1994). Thompson also advanced her ideas on the radio, sharing her perspectives on the *General Electric Hour* to an estimated five million tuned in to radio sets (Sanders 1973). She used her columns and radio program to relentlessly highlight the dangers of the Nazi regime, advocating for intervention (Sanders 1973). Her popularity and influence prompted *Time* magazine to dub her "second in power and prestige only to Eleanor Roosevelt" (S.R. 1994, 23).

Margaret Bourke-White (1904–1971)

American photographer Margaret Bourke-White contributed to establishing the field of photojournalism. She began her career in Cleveland, Ohio, where she opened a photography studio and began selling her work. Her photos of the Otis Steel Mill caught the attention of publisher Henry Luce who hired her as the first female photographer to work for him at Time, Inc. (Brinkley 2010; Oden, n.d.). Luce asked her to capture elements of "the machine age aesthetic," for *Fortune* magazine, highlighting the publication's focus on industrialization and the technology that supported it (Brinkley 2010, 157). Her photos of a steel mill, a meat packing plant, and New York's Chrysler Building while it was under construction captured aspects of this perspective, and her work for the publication contributed to public recognition of her name and work (Goldberg 1986).

Bourke-White's work contributed to the establishment of photojournalism. In 1936, Bourke-White's photographs of the Fort Peck Dam in Montana appeared on the debut cover of another Time, Inc. magazine called *Life*. The cover photo connected to what was the magazine's first photo essay, a feature that examined, through photographs and text, the Fort Peck Dam public works project and its people (Brinkley 2010). *Life* magazine presented a new form of storytelling to readers. According to Bourke-White biographer Vicki Goldberg (1986), "Before *Life* none of the illustrated periodicals in this country gave the news (or any other kind of story) principally or coherently in photographs" (172).

In addition to her tenure at Time, Inc., Bourke-White established herself as an influential photojournalist through her engagement with a number of other projects. She participated in the documentary photography movement that engaged photographers in capturing injustice through photographs (some cropped, some staged) as a way to advocate for social change (Brinkley 2010). As a photojournalist, she traveled to the Soviet Union, worked as a war correspondent, covered World War II from several countries, photographed aspects of the Korean War, and captured the violence related to the establishment of the India-Pakistan partition (Goldberg 1986). She created eleven photographic books and is remembered for her contributions to establishing photography as a means by which to tell stories.

Edward R. Murrow (1908–1965)

Edward R. Murrow was an American broadcasting pioneer who has iconic status in journalism history. The high quality of his reporting established expectations for broadcast journalism as the form was being developed. Murrow began his career on the radio and contributed to the development of broadcast journalism when he and his team reported on World War II (Edgerton 2004).

After the war, Murrow began working with radio producer Fred Friendly to create a radio documentary series called *Hear It Now* (1950–1951). *Hear It Now* used a magazine format that relied on the sound reporting Murrow utilized during his

World War II radio reporting. The premise of the program remained when the pair transitioned to television to produce *See It Now* (1951–1958), a formative television documentary series recognized as a central influence in the development of news programming (Simon 2004). Recognized for his independence and high journalistic standards, Murrow reported on topics such as the lives of soldiers in Korea during the war's stalemate, coal mining, and mental health (Barkin 2003). During the communist scare advanced by Senator Joseph McCarthy in the early 1950s, *See It Now* broadcast several stories about the impact of these allegations on U.S. citizens (Barkin 2003). These reports preceded the now famous *See It Now* episode on March 9, 1954, where Murrow used audio recordings and newsreel footage to expose the falsehoods being perpetuated by McCarthy, urging the public to act (Simon 2004).

Some viewed Murrow's activist style of reporting as controversial, wondering if he was editorializing too much, and some television advertisers became reluctant to sponsor his program (Barkin 2003). *See It Now*, however, won several awards, and historians consider Murrow's work as pivotal in the development of television (Simon 2004). Murrow also hosted a celebrity interview–driven television series called *Person to Person* (1953–1959) and moderated and produced *Small World* (1958–1960), a discussion show featuring world leaders (Simon 2004). Ultimately, however, Murrow became critical of television news. In a famous speech in 1958, he argued that commercial television was inherently flawed because the goal of television was to attract a large audience, and such a goal conflicts with the tenants of good reporting (Barkin 2003). After he left the broadcasting field, Murrow worked for the Kennedy administration at the United States Information Agency.

Walter Cronkite (1916–2009)

Walter Cronkite was an award-winning broadcast journalist most remembered for his time spent as managing editor and anchor of the *CBS Evening News*, a position he held from

1962 to 1981. Early in his career, Cronkite worked for a public relations firm, at newspapers, and at small radio stations before joining the United Press in 1939 to report on World War II (Auster 2004). His reporting as a war correspondent was notable, prompting Edward R. Murrow to recruit him to work for CBS News, an offer Cronkite initially refused, preferring to stay with the United Press and then move on to be the Washington correspondent for a number of midwestern radio stations (Martin 2009). Cronkite eventually joined CBS in 1950, beginning his career at the network in the entertainment division before moving to work on a documentary series and anchor the coverage of the 1952 party conventions (Auster 2004).

Cronkite assumed the role of CBS's television news anchor in 1962 and, in so doing, insisted he contribute as a reporter on his own show. As the newscast developed, Cronkite, who was under pressure from the network to increase viewership, became recognized for his journalistic talents, his competitive grit, and his ability to accurately predict which news stories would be successful (Brinkley 2012). In 1963, CBS announced that they were increasing their nightly newscast from fifteen minutes to thirty (which meant twenty-two minutes after commercials), and competitor NBC followed suit (Brinkley 2012). This change marked a shift in the television news landscape. Prior to the increase in the broadcast time, newscasters would read summaries of wire service reports on the air; by allotting more time for the news broadcast, "CBS News changed from *disseminating* news to *gathering* news" (Brinkley 2012, 258; italics in original). These longer broadcasts focused on stories such as the Vietnam War, the antiwar movement, and civil rights, impacting viewers' engagement with the American political process (Brinkley 2012). The longer newscast contributed to the development of television as a news medium that provided a public service to viewers. Cronkite, and many others in the television news field, worked to develop television news reporting practices that resulted in substantive journalism.

Cronkite competed for viewers primarily with Chet Huntley and David Brinkley of NBC News, and the three are known as the first celebrity anchormen. Cronkite, who eventually became known as the "most trusted man in America," garnered support from his viewers early in his anchoring career (Auster 2004). In 1964, CBS decided to pull him from anchoring the 1964 political conventions because they were worried about losing in the ratings competition to NBC's Huntley and Brinkley, a choice that resulted in eleven thousand letters sent to the network protesting this shift (Auster 2004). Cronkite's newscast eventually prevailed in the ratings battle; from 1967 until his retirement, he anchored the top-rated network newscast (Auster 2004).

During his almost twenty years as a news anchor, Cronkite led "viewers through national triumphs and tragedies alike, from moonwalks to war, in an era when network news was central to many people's lives" (Martin 2009). CBS was the first to break the story of President Kennedy's assassination. Cronkite anchored the hours and days of news coverage that followed, ending with a commentary after the reporting on Kennedy's burial that "pulled Americans together" (Brinkley 2012, 281). He also reported comprehensively on the war in Vietnam, working with his team not to glamorize or sensationalize the atrocities of the war but to show some of the "harsh realities" (Brinkley 2012, 354). Other notable reporting that Cronkite is remembered for includes stories on Apollo XI's mission, the Watergate scandal, and interviews with President Anwar el-Sadat of Egypt and Prime Minister Menachem Begin of Israel (Martin 2009). After his retirement from CBS, Cronkite engaged in documentary work for PBS, the Discovery Channel, and the Learning Channel.

In reflecting on his passing, biographer Douglas Brinkley (2012) states, "The Cronkite brand, to the very end, stood for Straight News truthfulness against the septic corruption of Vietnam and Watergate. . . . Although his trade was objective journalism, his product was fair-mindedness, judicial wisdom, and a moral compass that knew how to decipher right from wrong" (657). His accomplishments prompted an appropriation of his last name to represent the figure of a reputable and trustworthy news anchor, even internationally as seen with the use of "Kronkiters" in Sweden (Auster 2004).

John H. Johnson (1918–2005)

John H. Johnson was an American businessman who successfully integrated news about black Americans into American culture through several popular magazines including *Negro Digest*, *Ebony*, and *Jet*. Born in a poor area in Arkansas as a grandson of slaves, Johnson's city did not have a high school for black students, so he repeated eighth grade before his family moved to Chicago where he could pursue his education (Martin 2005). He worked as an editor for an internal insurance company magazine that mainly catered to black clients; it was here that Johnson got the idea for creating a magazine that featured stories of black people and culture (Gregory 2017).

Funded by a bank loan and a commitment from a large number of subscribers, in 1942, Johnson started *Negro Digest*, a magazine similar in scope to *Reader's Digest* but focused on stories of black people. The magazine's success led him to launch *Ebony* in 1945, a magazine that showed the everyday lives of black people, and *Jet* in 1951, a publication that focused on black public figures and celebrities. These magazines communicated positive imagery and stories about a demographic that often was the focus of negative news and introduced "a black aesthetic and culture to national and international audiences" (Rebuild Foundation 2018). As one writer explained, "*Ebony* and *Jet* had black photographers taking pictures of people and things that white photographers wouldn't even have thought of" (Gregory 2017). His company, Johnson Publishing, also launched magazines for kids and published books, and Johnson purchased two radio stations, becoming the first black person in Chicago to own a broadcasting company (Gregory

2017). His success earned him a place on *Forbes'* list of wealthiest Americans, an achievement not previously achieved by an African American (Martin 2005).

Helen Thomas (1920–2013)

Helen Thomas was a smart, tough, driven reporter, and later columnist, who is recognized for her talents and contributions to the advancement of women in journalism. A daughter of Lebanese immigrants, Thomas began her career at the *Washington Daily News* in 1942 and began working for United Press International (UPI) the following year, advancing in her career as she moved from reporting on women's issues and celebrities to reporting on the U.S. Justice Department, the Federal Bureau of Investigation (FBI), and other federal agencies (McGreal 2010).

Thomas is credited with challenging the status quo of journalists as white men. She first began covering presidents when John F. Kennedy was a president-elect, and she became known for her "relentless questioning that exasperated American leaders" (McGreal 2010). In 1970, she became the UPI chief White House correspondent, and in 1974, she became head of UPI's White House bureau, two positions not previously ever held by women (CNN 2013). Thomas also accompanied President Nixon on his historic trip to China in 1972, the only female print reporter to do so. She became the first woman to lead the Gridiron Club and the White House Correspondents Association, two organizations central to journalists working in Washington, DC ("Talk of the Nation" 2010). She covered every president from President Kennedy to President Barack Obama, and her tough questions became expected in the White House briefing room. Some of these questions reflected her standpoint on particular issues, especially issues connected to the Middle East (Cruickshank 2013).

After fifty-seven years working for UPI, Thomas resigned and became a Hearst newspaper columnist. She retired in

2010, at the age of eighty-nine, after the controversial comments she made about Jewish people and Palestine went viral.
Thomas apologized, but her comments, which many journalists described as "unsupportable," marked an end to her
career in Washington, DC, as a woman who had a tremendous
impact on political journalism ("Talk of the Nation" 2010).
Thomas wrote a column for the weekly newspaper the *Falls
Church News-Press* for a little over a year before her death in
2013 (CNN 2013).

Barbara Walters (1931–)

Barbara Walters is a broadcast journalist whose successful work
on American television contributed to the dismantling of
male-dominated broadcast news that was pervasive in the mid-
twentieth century. Walters is best known for her in-depth and
exclusive television interviews, "a form of television news she
perfected and personified" (Mahler 2014). Her first *Barbara
Walters Special* featured interviews with Barbra Streisand and
then president-elect Jimmy Carter and his wife, choices Walters (2008) claimed reflected her view on how she wanted these
interview specials to evolve as programs that featured at least
one celebrity and one political figure on each episode's slate
of three interviews. While the *Specials* sometimes prioritized
celebrity interviews as a response to audience's preferences,
Walters interviewed newsmakers on other programs such as
20/20 (Walters 2008). Over her fifty years working in television, Walters interviewed a long list of world leaders, American presidents, celebrities, and other notable figures. The list
includes some notable exclusives. In 1977, Cuban president
Fidel Castro agreed to his first American prime-time interview
with Walters, and she also secured the first joint interview with
president of Egypt Anwar el-Sadat and prime minister of Israel
Menachem Begin (Lipton 2001). In 1999, Monica Lewinsky
agreed to speak with Walters about her relationship with President Clinton, a show watched by an estimated 48.5 million

viewers (Carter 2004). Other interviews include conversations with Katherine Hepburn, Bing Crosby, Margaret Thatcher, Vladimir Putin, Christopher Reeve, Clint Eastwood, President Obama, Oprah Winfrey, and Hillary Clinton. Over the years, Walters has been criticized by some who suggested her work blurs the lines between journalism and entertainment, while others celebrate her achievements as a pioneering female journalist (Carter 2004; Williams 2013).

Walters began her career as a writer for CBS before moving into a producer role at NBC. She wrote for NBC's *Today Show*, beginning as a writer of features delivered by whoever was the current "Today Girl," an on-air personality whose job was to engage in simple conversation and look nice. Walters (2008) notes that at the time, television "did not include women who were doing anything with their brains" (107). Moving to challenge this status quo, Walters established herself as a talented contributor at the *Today Show*, moving from a writer to a "reporter at large," to the show's first official female cohost (McLeland 2004). Walters expanded her role as cohost from reporting on soft news features to more hard news stories and established herself as a strong interviewer (McLeland 2004; Walters 2008).

In 1976, she left the *Today Show* to coanchor the *ABC Evening News* with Harry Reasoner and became the first woman to take on the role of a network anchor. Her lucrative contract of $1 million a year was controversial, and her style was perceived as threatening to the status quo of male reporting at the time (Lipton 2001; McLeland 2004). Walters coanchored the half-hour newscast while working on developing her interview specials and later developing content for the newsmagazine program *20/20*. In 1984, she joined *20/20* as a cohost while continuing to produce her interview specials. In 1997, Walters and producer Bill Geddie developed a daytime talk show called *The View* where contemporary topics would be discussed by Walters and a group of cohosts from different generations with various backgrounds and perspectives. *The View* added a new component to the morning television lineup. Before *The View*, politics was not a topic of discussion on daytime television, and it was uncommon for those in journalistic roles to share their opinions (Setoodeh 2017). Though the program's hosts have changed over the years, the program is still a staple of ABC's daytime television lineup. Walters left *20/20* in 2004 and officially retired from *The View* in 2014.

Carole Simpson (1940–)

During a period in U.S. history when there were fewer opportunities for women in broadcasting, journalist Carole Simpson began her long career, often being the "first" to hold particular jobs. She was the first woman to work at the University of Iowa campus radio station, and when she began her professional life at a Chicago radio station in the 1960s, she was the first woman on Chicago radio (Geimann 1994). Later, she worked for a CBS radio station in Chicago as a news reporter and then at a Chicago NBC television station as a national correspondent and weekend news anchor, becoming the first black woman to anchor a news program in Chicago (Geimann 1994).

Simpson moved to Washington, DC, in 1974 to work for NBC News as a reporter and, after a few years, began working as an NBC congressional correspondent before moving to work for ABC News in 1982 (Simpson 2010). She covered Vice President George Bush, traveling all over the world, and, after he decided to run for the presidency, the country. Although she expected to become a senior White House correspondent after the election, Simpson was instead given the weekend anchor slot on ABC's *World News*, becoming the first black woman to anchor a network newscast, a position she would hold for fifteen years (Simpson 2010). At ABC she also served as a correspondent for "American Agenda," a daily segment that focused on various social issues, and worked on several prime-time specials (Geimann 1994). She also contributed to the late night news program *Nightline*, reporting on the end of apartheid in

South Africa and Nelson Mandela's release from prison in 1990 (Simpson 2010). In 1992, she became the first woman and first person of color to moderate a presidential debate, something Simpson describes as the "crowning achievement of my career" (Simpson 2010, 206). She officially retired from ABC News in 2006, moving on to become a Leader in Residence at Emerson College in 2007, where she taught journalism courses.

In her autobiography *NewsLady*, Simpson (2010) describes her experiences as a reporter as she advanced in her career, recounting exchanges with both subjects of her reporting and her news colleagues, producers, and executives. Underscoring her tale of success are stories of sexism and racism that dominated the culture of the news industry and impacted her personally. Simpson describes working at ABC with her female colleagues to address the inequities women dealt with; their actions resulted in some change. At ABC, she also mentored young journalists and often spoke to civic groups and on college campuses (Geimann 1994). In 2012, twenty years after Simpson moderated the 1992 presidential debate, CNN's Candy Crowley was invited as the second woman to take on the role, something Simpson celebrated but discussed as an example of how there are still barriers women and minorities have to overcome in the news industry (Edes and Hayes 2012).

Robert (Bob) Woodward (1943–)

Bob Woodward is an American journalist known for investigative reporting, often in the realm of politics. In the 1970s, *Washington Post* reporters Woodward and his senior colleague, Carl Bernstein, engaged in two years of investigative journalism that detailed what is now referred to as "Watergate," a political scandal involving the Nixon administration that ultimately resulted in President Nixon's resignation after a series of government investigations into ethically suspect and illegal activities. Bernstein and Woodward wrote a book about their experiences, and a film adaptation followed, solidifying cultural recognition of these journalists and their work. "Watergate" contributed to the idea that journalists could be celebrities and that the profession was comprised of "crusaders for truth" (Harris 2004). Additionally, the *Washington Post*'s unwavering support for the journalists' work established the paper as a valuable source of political reporting, challenging the then *New York Times*' dominance (Schudson 1992).

After Watergate, Bob Woodward, who began his career as a journalist after a tour in the navy where he published a ship newspaper, continued to work for the *Post*, writing numerous feature stories and top news. He has written twenty books to date. His investigative books have addressed numerous topics including the Supreme Court and the Central Intelligence Agency (CIA) and such notable figures as Alan Greenspan and John Belushi. He has also written books that have profiled aspects of the sitting U.S. presidents Bill Clinton, George W. Bush, and Barack Obama, focusing on their administrations and their policy decisions. His most current book is *Fear: Trump in the White House*, about the Trump administration. Woodward is "known as a meticulous note-taker and fact checker," and his work emerges from hours of interviews and research (Gangel and Merica 2018). The *Guardian*'s Paul Harris points out that Woodward's success has made him a member of the Washington circuit and has allowed him to practice "access journalism," a term that refers to the access Woodward has been granted to the "establishment that he chronicles so thoroughly" (Harris 2004). While Woodward has not been exempt from criticism, he is a highly regarded journalist, popular author, and recipient of many journalism awards. In considering the parallels between iconic journalist Walter Cronkite and Woodward, *Atlantic* writer James Fallows (2018) points to Woodward's goal of presenting "just the facts" and the fact that "over millions of words, and thousands of quotes and anecdotes, in 20-some books, the vast majority of what Woodward has reported has either stood unchallenged, or been acknowledged long after the fact as having been correct."

Arianna Huffington (1950–)

Arianna Huffington is an online media pioneer, entrepreneur, notable speaker, and author of fifteen books. Born in Greece as Arianna Stassinopoulos, Huffington cultivated a diverse list of professional experiences in the United Kingdom and the United States—from a radio program cohost to a conservative magazine writer to a political activist to an actress—before launching the Huffington Post, often referred to as HuffPost or HuffPo, in 2005.

The Huffington Post was cofounded by Huffington and Kenneth Lerer as a news aggregator and group blog with a political focus (Nieman Journalism Lab 2014). This "internet newspaper" ultimately shaped the direction of how online news was produced, and some credit Huffington with "inventing the internet news business" (Collins 2008; Segal 2015). When the site began in 2005, it used its news aggregator to organize stories and published a blogging section that featured posts from about two thousand contributors, many of whom were famous people in Huffington's network such as Nora Ephron and Alex Baldwin (Collins 2008). The Huffington Post presented a liberal counterpoint to the online Drudge Report, a news aggregator site with a conservative point of view, and as HuffPost's popularity increased, its reported 3.7 million visitors surpassed the visitor numbers the Drudge Report was seeing within a few years (Collins 2008).

Huffington and her team pioneered numerous successful strategies that served as primers for the developing internet news market. First, writers summarized other news agencies' stories and posted these summaries with provocative, clickbait headlines (Yu 2016). This was part of a strategy to provide as much content as possible on the site, and although the practice was criticized, it was soon imitated, leading to what one *New York Times* writer called "the birth of the industrial aggregation" (Segal 2015; Yu 2016). Second, Huffington advocated strongly for blogging, and in establishing the blog component of the site, the company provided a writing space for contributors who were unpaid; their potentially large reading audience was considered payment enough (Segal 2015). Third, the company collected and analyzed data to inform strategies used to increase readership such as testing headlines and placing popular stories in key places on the website (Segal 2015). The site also initially engaged readers by using "entertaining, if inelegant categories" to organize links and posts (Collins 2008). Finally, native advertising, paid-for material that is designed to blend in with editorial content, provided revenue to Huffington Post; the company clearly labeled it as sponsored content but also worked with advertisers to develop it (Segal 2015).

Since its beginning, HuffPost also engaged in providing original reporting, and its staff has increased over the years. In 2008, the organization was a prominent source of news during the election season, scooping the mainstream media on some stories via its Off the Bus initiative that engaged eleven thousand citizen journalists in election coverage (Collins 2008). Under Huffington's leadership, the site continued to develop its content, engage readers, and host an active community of bloggers and commentators. In 2009, a partnership with Facebook resulted in opportunities for readers to share stories with friends (Nieman Journalism Lab 2014).

In 2011, America Online (AOL) bought the Huffington Post for $315 million, and Arianna Huffington was named president and editor in chief of the Huffington Post Media Group, a company that oversees HuffPost, other digital news sites, and additional digital media companies (Yu 2016). After the AOL purchase, HuffPost continued to expand, developing international sites and streaming videos (Nieman Journalism Lab 2014). In her new role, Huffington presided over digital companies that counted 117 million visitors a month in the United States and 270 million visitors a month from outside the United States (Segal 2015). Huffington left the Huffington Post Media Group in 2016, shortly after Verizon's acquisition of AOL was finalized, to create a new venture called Thrive Global, a company that focuses on health and wellness.

Oprah Winfrey (1954–)

In 2018, the Smithsonian's National Museum of African American History and Culture opened an exhibit called Watching Oprah: The Oprah Winfrey Show and American Culture, which is described as work that "considers the story and impact of Oprah Winfrey in her many roles: as host of a world-famous television show; as an actress, film producer and media mogul; as a philanthropist and educator; and as a daughter of the civil rights generation whose phenomenal story of success illustrates the struggles and achievements of African women throughout history." The existence of this exhibit points to the lasting impact the former "queen of daytime" and often called "queen of all media" has had over the course of her career. Currently, Winfrey runs her company, Harpo, Inc. and oversees her *O Magazine* and cable television channel OWN: Oprah Winfrey Network. In 2018, she partnered with Apple, striking a deal to create original programs for the company, and also began working as a contributor to *60 Minutes*. Winfrey's work as a philanthropist includes donating over $100 million for girls' education opportunities (Otterson 2018).

Winfrey began her career at a Nashville, Tennessee, television station as a reporter and news anchor in the 1970s before moving to Baltimore, Maryland, to coanchor an evening news program (Byrne 2011). There she also hosted a local talk show before moving to Chicago in 1984 to host a morning television talk show called *AM Chicago* (Kelly 2010). Her success in this work led to the development of an hour-long, nationally syndicated program called *The Oprah Winfrey Show* that aired from 1986 to 2011. Winfrey initially established herself as a talk show host who would embrace guests and topics that were taboo and sensational, such as nudist colonies, women's sexual satisfaction, the Ku Klux Klan, and sex crimes (Kelly 2010). Although her show sometimes replicated elements of the "trash" TV programs that were dominant at the time, Winfrey also elevated discussions of sensitive topics with her direct questions, warmth, and, at times, humor. Biographer Kitty Kelly (2010) points out that she focused on many worthy topics during the show's first years including education, drunk driving, AIDS, and date rape. Later, in the 1990s, she rebranded the show to adhere to a more spiritual, wellness, self-improvement–oriented perspective. As the show continued to prosper, Winfrey welcomed a diverse slate of guests—from experts to celebrities to politicians—to educate and engage her viewers and launched the television careers of many of her reoccurring guests including Dr. Phil, Rachael Ray, and Dr. Oz.

Winfrey's influence on public opinion and commerce has been called "The Oprah Effect," and products endorsed by her have enjoyed lucrative profits (Quintanilla 2013). Her book club, which began in 1996, resulted in chosen authors seeing their books sell millions of copies (Kelly 2010). One writer notes that some guests tried to appropriate Winfrey's "effect" for their own benefit observing "it was this quality of being loving and giving that also led so many celebrities to Oprah's to sit on her couch over the years, in hopes that this perceived warmth could potentially help them spin various public relations disasters into something manageable" (Stafford 2016). Her popularity, however, mainly emerged from her ability to connect with others, make topics accessible and personal, and highlight common aspects of the human experience (Kelly 2010; Stafford 2016).

Amy Goodman (1957–)

Amy Goodman is a journalist, book author, and columnist. She is best known for her work as the host and producer of *Democracy Now!*, a long-running, independent public media news organization. Goodman began her career as a news producer and director at Pacifica Radio. In 1996, she cofounded *Democracy Now!*, a daily radio news program she hoped would be an alternative to what she viewed as ineffective, corporate-driven mainstream media. At the time, the program was focused on covering the 1996 presidential election as an independent news source; the program then evolved as a news and public affairs program. Goodman has reported from numerous countries and has been the recipient of several journalism awards. Under her leadership, *Democracy Now!* has focused on social movements, issues of social justice, and American foreign policy in addition to daily news events (Stelter 2011). Goodman and her team have reported on some stories that mainstream media ignore or are slow to pick up on. For example, *Democracy Now!* reported on protests against the war in Iraq more so than mainstream media, and Goodman claims their organization was one of the first to hone in on the Occupy Wall Street movement (Stelter 2011). As an advocate for independent media, Goodman often argues that mainstream media reporting is incomplete and sometimes incorrect, often influenced by larger, corporate forces (Kainth 2010).

Democracy Now! adheres to the principle of remaining independent from any editorial influence. Its website states that the news organization is supported by members and does not accept "government funding, corporate sponsorship, underwriting or advertising revenue." There are no commercials during the newscast, and the organization relies on volunteers as well as paid staff (Stelter 2001). In an interview with C-SPAN (2016) that marked the twentieth anniversary of the program, Goodman pointed out that their member-supported approach has informed their success because independent media "allows people to speak for themselves" and prevents elite groups of pundits from describing situations they know little about. In criticizing corporate media, or mainstream news organizations owned by large corporations, Goodman argues that there is a "hunger for independent voices," suggesting that *Democracy Now!*'s growth from nine radio stations in 1996 to over fourteen hundred radio, television, internet, and global outlets is evidence that many consumers are looking for independent news reporting. Goodman also dismisses the idea that *Democracy Now!* is what some call "progressive," noting that their goal is to give people a platform to express their ideas and voices (Stelter 2001).

Christiane Amanpour (1958–)

Christiane Amanpour is the chief international anchor for CNN and the host of the public affairs program *Amanpour*, which airs on PBS. Amanpour was born in London to a British mother and Iranian father, spent her formative years in Iran, and attended college at the University of Rhode Island. After college, in 1983, she began to work at the newly established CNN in Atlanta and advanced her career, working for a while at CNN's New York bureau, in Frankfurt, Germany, and volunteering to cover the Gulf War in 1990 (Kinzer 1994).

Amanpour established herself as a recognizable international war reporter during her coverage of the conflict in Bosnia in the early 1990s. Like many CNN reporters, Amanpour was allowed to choose what stories to report on and how to report on them; she chose to focus on the situation in Bosnia, a story that was not on the mainstream media's radar (Kinzer 1994). From Bosnia, Amanpour showed the suffering that resulted from what she described as ethnic cleansing at the hands of the Serbs, suggesting that it was important to relentlessly highlight this suffering for others to see (Peretz 2002). CNN (n.d.a) described her "outspoken reporting" as focused on human rights and the plight of Bosnian citizens. Although Amanpour insists she placed her reporting of the violence in Bosnia in appropriate context, some questioned whether she adhered to objective journalistic standards in her reporting, suggesting she was practicing advocacy journalism, while others dismissed this idea, pointing out that while Amanpour highlighted human suffering, she was not advocating for a particular solution (Kinzer 1994; Peretz 2002). Amanpour (2017) argues that reporters should not adhere to standards of objectivity to the point where they create a false equivalence, because in doing so, truthfulness in reporting is compromised.

After Bosnia, Amanpour continued her international report-ing by interviewing a diverse slate of world leaders and bring-ing viewers stories from countries such as Haiti, Chechnya, Afghanistan, Israel's West Bank, and Rwanda. A *New York Times* reporter commented, "Her success in bringing stories of carnage and conflict into living rooms around the world has made her one of the most visible war correspondents of her generation" (Kinzer 1994). Recently, Amanpour (2017) has spoken out about the dangers of so-called fake news from national and international reporting perspectives, explain-ing how, in addition to the problems that emerge when bad information spreads quickly, President Trump's use of this term "chips away" at journalists' "credibility" and gives autocratic leaders implicit permission to disparage journalism.

Jorge Ramos (1958–)

Jorge Ramos is an award-winning journalist and television broadcaster for Univision, the largest Spanish language tele-vision network in the United States. Born in Mexico City, Mexico, Ramos began his career as a news writer and on-air reporter for Televisa in Mexico, later making his way to the United States in 1983 at age twenty-four (he became a natural-ized U.S. citizen in 2008) (Finnegan 2015). In the country on a student visa, Ramos attended school and began working for a Spanish-language television station that eventually became Univision (Connery 2017). After working for Univision's news department, in 1986, Ramos was hired to coanchor the eve-ning news, first with Teresa Rodriguez and then with Maria Elena Salinas. Ramos and Salinas are "the best-known news people, perhaps the best known faces, among the fifty-five mil-lion Latinos now in the United States" (Finnegan 2015). Over the years, Ramos has interviewed international heads of state, American presidents and politicians, and he has covered many national and international news events. For its part, Univi-sion began expanding its news operations in 2010 with new investigative and documentary departments, a fact-checking team, and resources dedicated to digital journalism, adding to what the network already provided for its audience (Rutenberg 2017). Univision is widely viewed; its evening newscasts regularly top other networks in the ratings in the United States, and the station is popular in several Latin American countries (Connery 2017).

Ramos is sometimes referred to as the Latino Walter Cronkite (and was the recipient of the Walter Cronkite Award for Excellence in Political Journalism in 2017) and envisions part of his role as one that gives voice to Latino and immigrant communities (Connery 2017). His influence is hard to dispute. Academic Sergio Garcia-Rios (2015) points out that his research suggests that "Spanish-language media plays an important role in socializing and mobilizing Latinos to vote, and that exposure to Spanish TV news significantly increases interest in voting and campaign involvement." Because Ramos is a central figure in the Spanish-speaking news media, Garcia-Rios calls this impact the "Jorge Ramos effect." *Time* dubbed him one of the "100 Most Influential People" in 2015, and *Fortune* named him one of the "World's 50 Greatest Leaders" in 2016.

Ramos also writes a syndicated column, hosts a public affairs television show called *Al Punto*, and has worked on projects in English for the ABC-Univision network Fusion, including *Real America with Jorge Ramos*, the documentary *Hate Rising*, and the interview program *Show Me Something*. He is also the author of thirteen books and maintains a popular Twitter feed and website, jorgeramos.com, that features his columns and *Real America with Jorge Ramos* podcast episodes and videos.

Ira Glass (1959–)

Ira Glass is a public radio broadcaster and producer. He is also a stage performer, a producer of two films, and the editor of the book *The New Kings of Nonfiction*. Glass began his career at National Public Radio (NPR) in 1978 as an intern and was hired by NPR in 1982. While at NPR, he sometimes hosted *Talk of the Nation* and *Weekend All Things Considered* and was a writer, editor, associate producer, and producer (Phillips 2006). In 1989, he moved to Chicago to work as a reporter for the public radio station WBEZ where he developed a program called *Your Radio Playhouse* that eventually became the nationally syndicated, immensely popular, and award-winning *This American Life* (Augustyn 2017). Glass's initial idea for *This American Life* was to "apply novelistic techniques to radio reporting" and focus on "everyday life, with fiction or poems sandwiched between strangely ordinary people telling strange stories" (Coburn 2007). This premise shifted as Glass developed his storytelling style and discovered that he and his team wanted to "take that style and apply it to the news," reporting on people's stories (Coburn 2007). The popularity of the program prompted affiliate stations to air it and Public Radio International (PRI) to distribute it (Phillips 2006). *This American Life* cultivated a large following, unusual for a public radio program, and in 2007, Glass moved from Chicago to New York to produce a television version of the program, a venture he could only sustain for two seasons given the demands of producing both a radio and television program (Augustyn 2017; Coburn 2007). The radio version continued to succeed and eventually would regularly become the number one podcast downloaded from iTunes each week (Buckley 2014). Its success informed subsequent radio programs and podcasts.

In 2014, Glass and *This American Life* parted ways with its distributor, PRI, to become an independent entity. The program could be distributed through an online platform, and Glass assumed the role of securing funding, distributing the show, and marketing (Buckley 2014). So far, this move has been successful, and Glass and his team have also established themselves as leaders in the podcast market. According to the *This American Life* website, the show is heard on five hundred public radio stations by 2.2 million listeners a week. The website also claims 2.5 million podcast listeners. In the fall of 2014,

Glass, along with producers Julie Snyder and Sarah Koenig, debuted an *American Life* "spin off," called *Serial*, whose first season broke records in podcast listening and received numerous awards (Spangler 2017). *Serial* launched its third season in 2018. It established its own podcast production company in 2017 "to develop new shows using the reporting and editorial talent at *This American Life*" (This American Life, n.d.). The company's first podcast, *S-Town*, was downloaded ten million times after it had been released just four days, breaking another podcast record (Spangler 2017).

Nonny de la Peña

Sometimes referred to as the "godmother of virtual reality," Nonny de la Peña is a pioneer and developer of immersive journalism, a storytelling technique that uses virtual reality technology to "place viewers within news stories" (Volpe 2015). de la Peña began her career as a journalist working as a correspondent for *Newsweek* before expanding her professional experience to include documentary and television work. As part of her fellowship work at USC Annenberg School of Communication and Journalism, de la Peña developed prototypes of immersive journalism, one on Guantanamo Bay prison and the other on the carbon business market, which demonstrated ways this reporting technique might work (Parker 2011). She also published an article with her colleagues that introduces and advocates for the development of immersive journalism, defining it as a space where "people can gain first person experiences of the events or situations described in news stories" and, like quality journalism, is a practice that "aims to elicit a connection between the audience and the news story" (de la Peña et al. 2010, 291). Immersive journalism, the authors write, "does not aim solely to present the facts, but rather the opportunity to experience the facts" (299).

In 2012, de la Peña's *Hunger in LA*, the first virtual reality film ever made, debuted at the Sundance Film Festival. *Hunger in LA* told the story of a diabetic in a food line who collapses because he cannot get food in time; viewers experience this story as they virtually wait in line with others and witness the collapse. In a TED Talk, de la Peña (2015) describes the emotional reactions people had to *Hunger in LA*—walking around the virtual characters and crying. The success of *Hunger in LA* prompted the launch of additional immersive journalism projects by others (Volpe 2015).

de la Peña was commissioned to produce *Project Syria,* an immersive experience that takes place in Aleppo and in a refugee camp, after the success of *Hunger in LA* (de la Peña 2015). In a 2015 interview with NPR's Robert Segal about *Project Syria,* de la Peña addressed how virtual reality offers a different experience for understanding news even if it doesn't quite match up with current understandings of journalism. She noted, "I would say that we know that each platform has a different—conveys a different feeling. Newspapers differ from radio, radios differ from television. This is just a brand new platform, and the experience is going to offer different affordances. This is going to have different things that perhaps might not be considered as acceptable by today's standards, but later on we'll understand that there's a real value to telling stories in this way."

de la Peña has continued to work on developing this medium as a journalistic storytelling method using real-life accounts and "captured audio and video footage from real events" to inform the environments created in the virtual reality (Goldman 2018). She founded and is the CEO of Emblematic Group, a company that uses virtual reality in storytelling to produce projects (Volpe 2015). She has also worked with PBS, the *New York Times,* the *Wall Street Journal,* and others to create immersive experiences of real events (Goldman 2018). For example, de la Peña worked with PBS's *Frontline* and *Nova* to create the project Greenland Melting where people feel like they are in a helicopter while they examine how Greenland is being impacted by climate change. She also partnered with Planned Parenthood to engage people in understanding how some women face challenges in obtaining reproductive health services (Goldman 2018). As a leader and pioneer in this field, de la Peña is working with the Aspen Institute and the Knight Foundation Commission on Trust, Media and Democracy to discuss the integrity of, and best practices related to, immersive journalism given its inherent subjective nature (Goldman 2018).

Jodi Rave-Spotted Bear (1964–)

Jodi Rave-Spotted Bear is a Mandan, Hidatsa, and Minneconjou Lakota journalist, opinion writer, and executive director of the Indigenous Media Freedom Alliance (IMFA), an organization whose goal is to provide news for the American Indian community in the Great Plains region of the United States. The organization is the publisher of Buffalo's Fire, a digital news site dedicated to issues related to tribal communities, and, according to its website, IMFA aims to "advocate for independent native news, campaign for tribal media literacy, revitalize indigenous languages and culture, and promote [an] American Indian broadcast network." Rave has written feature stories on Indian land management, Native American grave site protections, domestic violence, education, renewable energy in Indian communities, and tribal affairs. She is the recipient of numerous national journalism awards.

Siobhan Benet (2001) writes that her experiences as the sole Native American in her North Dakota school prompted Rave to reflect upon and write about the differences between her school community and her childhood experiences on the Fort Berthold reservation in the northwestern part of the state. After high school, Rave took a job reporting and writing for a tribal newspaper before going to technical school and working at a power plant. Later she joined the National Guard, spent a year in the army, and worked as a journalist for the National Guard before enrolling in an undergraduate journalism program. After a couple of post-college reporting jobs, Rave was hired by the *Lincoln Star Journal* to report on Native American issues. The role evolved into one where Rave became a national correspondent, based at the *Missoulian* newspaper, for Lee Enterprises, an organization that publishes fifty-eight newspapers in twenty-three states (Rave 2005).

Rave has been recognized for her work in reporting on complicated Native American stories. Her Broken Trust series was acknowledged in *The Authentic Voice: The Best Reporting on Race and Ethnicity*, published by Columbia University Press. The Broken Trust series of articles explores the complex and problematic system of Native American land ownership and management by the U.S. government, a story Rave did not see being covered in the mainstream media. Rave was praised for her fact-based reporting that was informed by her understanding of Native American culture (Morgan, Pifer, and Woods 2006). In the series, "Rave discusses how she used deep cultural knowledge to advance her reporting but also challenges the notion that there is an automatic advantage of being Indian when covering Indians" (Morgan, Pifer, and Woods 2006, 132). Connected to her work as a Nieman fellow, Rave wrote about the need for an increase in Native American reporters in newsrooms, stating, "It largely falls on mainstream news outlets to explain what's happening on tribal lands and in urban Indian settings. That means it is often non-Natives who are telling Native stories, since only 295 self-identified Native journalists work at daily newspapers . . . and they are even more nonexistent in broadcast news divisions" (Rave 2005, 8). She additionally has pointed out that tribal newspapers are often problematically viewed by tribes as public relations vehicles rather than as independent sources of news for communities that operate as a watchdog over tribal government (Rave 2005).

Soledad O'Brien (1966–)

Maria de la Soledad Teresa O'Brien is an experienced and award-winning journalist and producer who has contributed as a reporter and producer at NBC, CNN, PBS *NewsHour*,

HBO, and Al Jazeera America. She is the current CEO of Star-fish Media Group, a media production and distribution company she established in 2013. According to the Starfish Media Group's website, part of the mission of the company is to "look at often divisive issues of race, class, wealth, poverty and opportunity through personal narratives." O'Brien is the host of the syndicated political magazine program, *Matter of Fact*, a show that examines diverse topics such as health care, tariffs, artificial intelligence, climate science, and upcoming elections.

O'Brien began her career as a reporter for a radio medical talk show and later spent many years working for NBC in various roles. She left NBC in 2003 to work as a coanchor for CNN's *American Morning*. At CNN, O'Brien reported on stories ranging from the tsunami in Thailand to Hurricane Katrina to the 2005 terrorist attacks in London before moving to CNN's documentary division where she worked on two notable projects, *Black in America* and *Latino in America* (The History Makers 2014). Both documentary programs focus on the complex lives and wide range of experiences members of each demographic group experience. As the daughter of a black and Cuban mother and a father with Irish and Scottish roots who is from Australia, O'Brien describes herself as "a mixed race, first generation American" (O'Brien 2009). When discussing her work on *Latino in America*, she points out that "her ethnic roots are relevant" when considering just how few journalists are Latino despite the growing population of Latinos in America, suggesting that a lack of understanding about the Latino community may be a contributor to a dominant news focus on Latinos that prioritizes immigration, crime, and drugs (O'Brien 2009).

O'Brien is active on Twitter and uses the platform to weigh in on aspects of race, diversity, and politics in American culture. She made news headlines when she criticized CNN, her former employer, for their lack of diversity in senior staffing after the network pointed out that the Trump administration did not have any black senior staff members in a tweet (O'Brien 2018).

She regularly challenges elements of news reporting and political commentary on Twitter, directly addressing a racial element of a reported story or the author of another tweet. In a video posted on the the *Root*'s YouTube channel, O'Brien stated that she has "assigned herself the job of the Twitter race correspondent," pointing out racist language and asking that journalists become more honest and accountable in their reporting by more straightforwardly noting when public officials and others make racist comments rather than using euphemisms to soften the rhetoric (Root 2018). Her investment in this topic extends beyond Twitter; O'Brien has toured college campuses nationwide to engage students in conversations about race (Trent 2015). She also runs PowHERful, a nonprofit organization that supports women of color in their quest to earn an undergraduate degree.

Lisa Ling (1973–)

Lisa Ling is a television broadcaster and journalist. She began her career at the age of sixteen as the host of a newsmagazine program for kids called *Scratch*. A couple of years later, she took a job as a *Channel One News* reporter (*Channel One News* was delivered to middle and high schools in the United States), staying with Channel One for seven years and becoming their war correspondent (Champagne 2014). In 1999, Ling became a cohost of *The View* until 2002, leaving because she wished to pursue international journalistic work (Champagne 2014). She moved on to host and report for *National Geographic Explorer*, work as a correspondent for the *Oprah Winfrey Show*, and contribute reporting to CNN's *Planet in Peril: Battle Lines* documentary.

As a Chinese American, Ling (2011) has written about the need for diversity on television, both in its broadcasters and production staff and in the stories reported to the country. She reflects that when she was growing up, TV journalist Connie Chung was her hero and inspired her to pursue a television career. Ling acknowledges that the television landscape has changed in the twenty-first century but argues that the over-all image television provides of the country does not reflect the nation's diversity. Some of her recent work addresses this disconnect. From 2011 to 2014, she worked on *Our America with Lisa Ling*, a television series for OWN (the Oprah Win-frey Network). On *Our America*, Ling explored such topics as transgender communities, aspects of faith healing, domestic sex trafficking, black American incarceration, and drug addic-tion. Later in 2014, Ling joined CNN to work on the docu-mentary TV series *This Is Life with Lisa Ling*. Here, she and her team have examined stripper culture, genetic engineering, oil rig communities, gender fluidity, gangs, and screen addiction.

Ezra Klein (1984–)

In 2013, *Time* magazine described Ezra Klein as "one of cyberspace's most popular self-made bloggers" and gave him the moniker of "the explainer" in a feature about the thirty people under age thirty who are changing the world (Nicks 2013). Klein has written for the *Washington Post* and the *New Yorker* and contributes to several television news and business-oriented programs. He is a cofounder (with Melissa Bell and Matthew Yglesias) of Vox, a news website that describes itself by stating "Vox explains the news."

Klein began his professional career as a blogger. His success earned him a position at the *Washington Post* where he founded Wonkblog, a site that offers reports, analysis, and perspectives on economic and political topics. Wonkblog became incred-ibly popular, and readers appreciated the explanatory methods Klein used in presenting and discussing policy (Wallace 2014). Although he was successful in managing Wonkblog, Klein left to develop Vox, a news site he hoped would contribute to improving internet news. He believed that despite the internet's capabilities, journalistic reporting continued to reflect produc-tion patterns seen in journalism before the digital revolution where a priority was placed on what stories were new rather than what stories were important (Wallace 2014). Additionally, Klein criticized journalists for not providing the relevant context needed to understand any given story, telling *New York Magazine*, "There is little allowance made for readers coming to the story late and an assumption that anyone who's been following a story over time will remember the textual details" (Wallace 2014).

Klein explained that he hoped the news site Vox, with an emphasis on explanatory journalism, would be a step in "improving the technology of news" to produce web journalism that "helps people understand the news better" (Carr 2014). Initial reviews of the site after its launch were mixed. Some critics wondered how Vox is reinventing journalism when it has similar features as Wonkblog and Wikipedia, while others celebrated the site's explanatory features that provide detailed context (Beyers 2014). Vox contains a variety of elements for users to engage with. In addition to the written stories, there are "Explainers," where topics are unpacked with context in text and video form, live StoryStream updates, and podcasts.

Organizations

CNN (Cable News Network) (1980–)

Cable News Network, most commonly referred to as CNN, was developed by Ted Turner, a businessman from the southeastern part of the United States, in 1980. Turner was interested in participating in the fragmented cable channel landscape by creating a 24-hour news channel (Barkin 2003). Turner described his idea as a channel as providing news "when people had a chance to watch it, rather than when the networks wanted people to watch it" as well as offering debate, financial, and expanded sports reporting (Byrne 2011, 164). Turner and his channel were initially poked fun at by others in the news business (calling CNN "Chicken Noodle Network"), but their jabs were unfounded as CNN quickly grew to establish itself as a prominent component of the news landscape. In 1982, CNN debuted Headline News, a second channel, which provided thirty-minute news broadcasts, audio of which was sold to radio stations (Krumsvik 2013). The company also established CNN International and a little over a decade later was the first television enterprise to invest in online news; in 1993, CNN established itself online through CompuServe and, by 1995, launched CNN.com (Krumsvik 2013). CNN's web presence expanded internationally, providing local language versions of their news. According to their online Worldwide Fact Sheet, CNN notes "two dozen branded networks and services are available to more than 2 billion people in more than 200 countries and territories," employs over three thousand people at thirty-six editorial sites around the world, and claims "CNN Digital is the number one online news destination, routinely registering nearly 200 million unique visitors globally each month."

The multiple CNN networks had a tremendous impact on the reporting and dissemination of news and information. Joe Foote (1998) discusses the impact CNN had on news correspondents and network news. CNN debuted at a time when network news was feeling the pressure to become profitable and news correspondents were being cut from network news budgets. CNN's news model focused on prioritizing correspondents over news anchors and hired a new generation of professionals who were expected to report with smaller than typical news crews and modest budgets. While network news producers were cutting international stories that were not explicitly relevant to the United States, CNN embraced these stories and others. Given the pressures of the 24-hour news cycle, correspondents were often forced to report live on a scene before they were ready and had the substance of the news story, prompting their competitors to do the same. Additionally, Foote points out, CNN's presence impacted the network newscast that aired each evening. ABC, CBS, and NBC assumed that people were already aware of each day's major stories before the evening newscast, so the "networks opted for more reflection, stylized reporting, longer trend stories and a hint of 'infotainment' " (12).

CNN's ratings grew steadily as the network developed. It covered the 1991 war in the Persian Gulf extensively. At this time, the cable network became a source of information for the country's leaders and policy makers, reversing the traditional dynamic where leaders and policy makers are the sources for news reporters, and often information from the media was used in governmental decision-making processes (Ammon 2001). CNN was also relied on as a "diplomatic channel" during the conflict in the Persian Gulf. Secretary of State James Baker communicated information by appearing on the network; Baker noted it was faster to "get out there on CNN" because "we knew Saddam Hussein watched CNN" (Ammon 2001, 74). Other CNN reporting, particularly on areas of the world where people were struggling, was thought to have an impact on public policy making, known as the "CNN effect," where public reactions to particularly intense or emotional CNN reporting prompted government officials to respond (Ammon 2001; Daly 2012). In a more sensational vein, CNN provided around-the-clock coverage of the O.J. Simpson (a former sports star accused of murder) case, prompting some to criticize the spectacle of media coverage that CNN spearheaded (Rosenberg and Feldman 2008).

Journalist and scholar Christopher Daly (2012) describes CNN's impact on reporting in this way.

> Before CNN, news was almost always presented to the audience as a finished product. . . . The story was the results of certain steps taken by a journalist, usually with help from an editor. Someone had to make inquiries, gather the results, distill them into a familiar format, double-check the facts and spelling and put them before an audience. . . . CNN changed the basic premise of journalism by presenting it as a *process* rather than a product. In a live, twenty-four hour format, news is

whatever information or pictures you have right now. If the information is incomplete, so what? You can always come back on the air in a few minutes or hours with an "update" to supply the missing denial, counterpoint or fact. (408)

Bill Kovach and Tom Rosenstiel (2010) point out that in the "continuous news culture" that began with CNN, technology allows for the fast breaking of and distribution of news. The 24-hour news cycle on television, they argue, has resulted in less vetting and filtering of information, and when television news is packaged and edited, there is more time to vet and verify facts (40). Television critic Howard Rosenberg and journalist Charles Feldman (2008) suggest that CNN changed the definition of what news is for the worse by featuring "filler" segments, broadcasting live when there was little to report, celebrating its own journalists' work, and providing space for lots of analysis and opinion sharing among experts. Despite these critiques, CNN is relied on by many Americans for news. Though the company is not alone in providing around-the-clock news, information, analysis, and opinion sharing, its invention of the around-the-clock news concept changed the way news is produced and consumed.

USA Today (1982–)

USA Today, the country's first daily newspaper to solely report national news, was first published on September 15, 1982. Its circulation reached over a million in less than one year and over two million in the 1990s (USAtoday.com, n.d.). Founder Al Neuharth designed USA Today to be a visually oriented paper that adhered to a consistent structure each day and included short stories that were easy to read and photos, charts, and graphics that are visually appealing.

Although the paper was initially criticized and called "McPaper," suggesting that its content was not substantial, its impact on other newspapers cannot be disregarded given their eventual incorporation of their own use of color, maps, and infographics (Daly 2012). The paper has, over time, established itself as a substantial publication that publishes quality journalism as many of its writers have been recognized with prizes and other recognitions. In 2014, Gannett, *USA Today*'s parent company, began inserting some of the national paper's international and national news sections into its local daily papers (Johnston 2014). According to *Columbia Journalism Review*'s David Cay Johnston, "The national-local model is designed to free up, and generate, resources for more and better local news reporting and is part of a larger move underway at Gannett to invest in the quality of its journalism. This would represent a fundamental shift for a chain long known less for the quality of its news than for its ruthless focus on the bottom line." More recently, the paper and its network of journalists from local papers have been recognized for their goal of prioritizing investigative journalism, increasing national staff numbers of investigative journalists, and partnering with local news organizations to produce substantive work (Hare 2019).

The Daily Show (1996–)

The Daily Show is a "fake news" show on the cable television network Comedy Central. The comedic program debuted in 1996 and was hosted by Craig Kilborn until the end of 1998. In early 1999, Jon Stewart took over as host and changed the direction of the program to be more politically oriented. He hosted the show until 2015, succeeded by the current host, Trevor Noah. Stewart's leadership in changing the direction of *The Daily Show* resulted in the comedy show becoming both a source of news and of media criticism.

Chris Smith (2016) points out that Stewart and his team "arrived at the perfect moment, with the media and political worlds on the cusp of upheaval," noting that the expansion of cable news and the 24-hour news cycle, stylized newsmagazine programming, and the internet would shortly change the American news landscape and alter television network news' dominance. Stewart wanted *The Daily Show* to target "the people who have a voice, and that's politicians, and that's the media" (Smith 2016). To do this, Stewart and his comedic team took on satiric reporter roles, Stewart at the anchor desk and his colleagues as fake news *Daily Show* correspondents, who assumed the role of reporters working for a news organization. The show evolved to be one that used news satire to both highlight questions the mainstream media was not asking public figures and one that humorously pointed out the reluctance of mainstream television news, particularly cable news programming, to ask questions Stewart and his colleagues believed important to be asked. This tactic worked; *The Daily Show* rose in popularity, implying that citizens responded to the program's critique of the mainstream reporting that allowed for officials to spin versions of events that didn't line up with known evidence (Bennett 2016). The program's success led to the development of news satire as a contemporary television program genre that inspired the launch of such shows as *The Colbert Report, Late Night with Larry Wilmore, Last Week Tonight with John Oliver,* and *Full Frontal with Samantha Bee.*

Given its popularity with millions of viewers, *The Daily Show's* influence on the culture has been widely studied. During the 2004 presidential campaign, the Pew Research Center for People and the Press found that many younger viewers were obtaining their news from *The Daily Show,* while other publications noted that Stewart was a top media figure who would influence the election (Cosgrove-Mather 2004). Other research suggests that *The Daily Show* and other news satire programs such as *The Colbert Report* were associated with increased political participation among their viewers when contrasted to viewers of late night programs that didn't solely consist of news satire (Baumgartner and Lockerbie 2018). At the time of Stewart's retirement from *The Daily Show,* Pew Research compiled a report that summarized some research on the show and its viewers, including information that 12 percent of Americans who are online consider *The Daily Show* a news source but that regular viewers of the program look elsewhere for in-depth reporting and watch the program primarily for entertainment (Gottfried, Matsa, and Barthel 2015).

Fox News/The Fox News Channel (1996–)

Fox News was established by Australian and naturalized U.S. citizen Rupert Murdoch in 1996. Murdoch's company News Corp had newspaper, book publisher, magazine publisher, and movies and television stations in multiple countries, and the politically conservative-minded Murdoch was interested in expanding his holdings in the United States. Initially he tried to acquire CNN, but when that did not work out, Murdoch set about establishing his own news channel (Sherman 2014). Fox News began with the former aggressive republican campaign operative Roger Ailes as the CEO and chairperson (Sherman 2014). Ailes, who previously opined mainstream media operated with a liberal bias, claimed that he anticipated Fox would "do fine, balanced journalism" (Hall 1996).

In comparison to its competitors, CNN and MSNBC, which also launched in 1996, Fox News had a small news department, and Ailes grew the channel by developing opinion programming. Gabriel Sherman (2014), in his book about the development of Fox News under the direction of Ailes, points out that Ailes aimed to build a talk-oriented network rather than a hard news network. Ailes was guided by television advisor Chet Collier who often stated, "Viewers don't want to be informed; they want to feel informed" (Sherman 2014, 191). Though the network's slogans eventually emerged as "fair and balanced" and "we report, you decide," the talkers who were hired were decidedly partisan and included a slate of provocative pundits who would become the network's early stars, including Bill O'Reilly, Sean Hannity, and Glen Beck. The content discussed on opinion programming overshadowed the straightforward journalism that emerged from the conservatively oriented news division. Under Ailes, this tactic, which some describe as taking the success of political talk radio to the television format, worked as Fox emerged as a lucrative and powerful force in the news landscape. Sherman writes, "Ailes had fundamentally altered the basic idea of news on television as it was historically understood. While millions continued to watch the Big Three nightly newscasts, partisan cable news drove politics. And CNN, lacking a partisan brand, was left out of the conversation" (338).

The network's tactics have been largely criticized by academics, public officials, and other news organizations for advancing false information, perpetuating fear campaigns, and for smearing people who do not advance the proper conservative ideology. The authors of *The Fox Effect: How Roger Ailes Turned a Network into a Propaganda Machine* document many of the network's choices including how Fox perpetuated multiple falsehoods about President Obama, how on-air talent was required to use republican endorsed phrases when discussing topics such as health care, and how the network encouraged and gave voice to the Tea Party. They claim that Ailes "ushered in the era of post-truth politics. The facts no longer matter, only what is politically expedient, sensationalistic and designed to confirm the pre-existing opinions of a large audience" (Brock, Rabin-Havt, and Media Matters for America 2012, 283). Others argue that Ailes "reshaped a television network as a force for Republican politics" and, as a result, has had an impact on its audience members' perceptions due to its blurred presentation of news and opinion (Dickenson 2011). Research studies have tried to determine the effect of Fox programming on viewers, sometimes finding that Fox News viewers are less informed than other news consumers (Adler 2011; Cassino, Woolley, and Jenkins, 2012). Some argue the partisan nature of Fox News prompted other cable networks to become more liberal, contributing to the current partisan culture and inherently justifying Ailes's choices (Dickenson

2011). Ailes left Fox in 2016 after multiple charges of sexual harassment surfaced, and he died in 2017.

After the 2018 presidential election, explicitly pro-Trump programming dominated the network, and President Trump has complemented Fox television personalities for their framing of information and support of him. Currently, some at the network struggle with asserting that its news division relies on journalistic principles. A *Washington Post* report claims that the network is "in the midst of its own version of a civil war, pitting its news anchors against its big-name pundits, who are avid promoters of President Trump" (Ellison 2018). This disconnect between the pro-Trump opinion show personalities and news contributors has prompted some to leave Fox because they are uncomfortable with the pervasive pro-Trump stance and the direction of the network (Peters, R. 2018; Schwartz 2018). Additionally, such journalists as Bret Baier and Shepard Smith have had to respond to the false conspiracies perpetuated by their colleagues (Ellison 2018). During a final rally of the 2018 midterm election season, Fox pundits Hannity and Jeanine Pirro joined President Trump on stage. Hannity hugged him and gave a high five to White House deputy chief of staff Bill Shine (a former Fox News executive). In response, the network issued a statement of disapproval, noting, "Fox News does not condone any talent participating in campaign events. We have an extraordinary team of journalists helming our coverage tonight and we are extremely proud of their work. This was an unfortunate distraction and has been addressed" (Fredericks 2018). Concerns about the relationship between some at the news network and the administration continue, however. A recent investigative article by the *New Yorker*'s Jane Mayer (2019) details the close ties the news organization has with the White House and President Trump, raising concerns that Fox News is distributing more propaganda than partisan news and news commentary. Despite concerns about Fox's practices articulated by both conservatives and liberals, the network remains successful in its ratings and its audience's approval.

Google News (2002–)

The technology company Google revolutionized the way people research and obtain information. As a company that marked its twenty-year anniversary on September 4, 2018, Google is credited with shaping the twenty-first-century internet and people's use of it (Verge Staff 2018). The search engine Google, developed by Larry Page and Sergey Brin, was created to provide results based on the way web pages were linked, an algorithmic invention that led to accurate search results (Verge Staff 2018). Google the company was established in 1998 and, over the decades, has grown in its popularity, product offerings, and experimentation with new initiatives. The pervasiveness of Google products and acquisitions—Google Docs, Gmail, YouTube, Google Glass, Chromebooks, Android, and many more—has established the company as having a transformative impact on the culture. In 2015, Page reorganized his giant company; currently Google is a branch of a holding company called Alphabet and has a $850 million market value (Fleishman 2018).

Google News was developed by Krishna Bharat and was launched in 2002. This service began by aggregating news reports from across the web to present users with a selection of linked stories. Google News does this by employing a complicated algorithm that "harvests" stories that present a range of perspectives on any given event (Garber 2012). Initially, some journalists and news leaders were critical of Google News but later realized that the service prompted increased traffic, via billions of clicks, to their news sites (Garber 2012). The popularity and use of Google News shifted previously held ideas about what companies could distribute the news (Verge Staff 2018). As Google News developed, its engineers worked with news producers so their preferences over what articles appeared on the Google News home page were adhered to, and they established an Editor's Picks section of the site where news organizations may feature content of their choice (Garber 2012). The company also continued to develop stories on the Google

News home page that appealed to users like breaking news, location-targeted local news, and video and Wikipedia links relevant to a news report's context (Garber 2012).

In May 2018, Google News launched a redesign of its platform. The company describes the new "A/I meets human intelligence" Google News in the following way: "When we created the original Google News 15 years ago, we simply organized news articles to make it easier to see a range of sources on the same topic. The reimagined Google News uses a new set of AI techniques to take a constant flow of information as it hits the web, analyze it in real time and organize it into storylines" (Upstill 2018). The redesign emphasizes the service's quest to identify quality journalism and provide context for aggregated stories. It also includes a fact-checking section and the ability to subscribe to news services through a Google account (Upstill 2018). The company's stated mission to support quality journalism is additionally funded through its Google News Initiative, a project where the company has committed $300 million over three years to programs that support news publishers and the challenges they, and news consumers, face (Wang 2018).

Facebook (2004–)

The social media platform Facebook began in 2004, created by Harvard University student Mark Zuckerberg and his classmates. Though it initially began as a closed platform, by 2006, the site was available for use by the general public. Zuckerberg has consistently described the purpose of his company is to "make the world more open and connected" while adhering to the tag line "move fast and break things" so as to keep up with, and ahead of, the culture (Byrne 2011, 256–257). While many users of the platform engage with it to share photos, communicate updates, and message friends, the site has become a key player in the news and information landscape.

In 2006, Facebook debuted its News Feed, a service that provides Facebook users with an ongoing stream of updates about people in their network. The News Feed eventually evolved to feature news from news websites and advertising in addition to friend updates. News Feeds are customized to the user; the company's algorithms analyze people's activity on Facebook and preferred content to determine what information to then prioritize in an individual feed, resulting in a personalized stream of information (Bourg and Jacoby 2018). Pew Research found that in 2012, 54 percent of adults in the United States used Facebook and, in 2018, 68 percent of adults used the platform, with 43 percent noting that they obtain news from the platform (Gramlich 2018). As Facebook's popularity increased to two billion users a month as of the fall of 2018, so did its standing as a place where people obtained their news of the day via the customized News Feed (Bourg and Jacoby 2018). Despite using the Facebook News Feed as a "pathway" to news, more than half of those surveyed by Pew did not clearly understand how the Facebook News Feed worked (Gramlich 2018).

The immense reach and power of Facebook has been discussed as a tool for activism, and many point to the use of Facebook in the political uprisings in the Middle East, collectively called the "Arab Spring." After the celebrations around how Facebook supported liberation movements in the Middle East subsided, however, some noted in 2011 that "fake news," or misinformation, was spreading on Facebook in Egypt, and while the company was aware of this, they did not have a solution (Bourg and Jacoby 2018). Since 2011, researchers and journalists have documented multiple instances of Facebook being used as a platform to support and spread propaganda and disinformation; one key example is the findings of the U.S. intelligence determining that a Russian-sponsored disinformation campaign was implemented to interfere with the 2016 presidential election (Bourg and Jacoby 2018). Although a news verification program was implemented by Facebook in 2018, the company's practices around information screening and sharing, in addition to other issues about how the company uses customers' private information, remain under investigation.

Twitter (2006–)

The social media platform Twitter was created by a team of innovators including Noah Glass, Evan Williams, Jack Dorsey, Florian Weber, and Biz Stone in 2006 as part of a start-up company (Casti 2013). The idea was to develop a way to send a short message to a group of people publicly; initially these "tweets" were limited to 140 characters (today the limit is 280 characters). In 2007, Twitter became its own company and, after being used at a prominent interactive media conference, became established in the culture, growing at a fast rate (Casti 2013). In 2007, the platform claimed four hundred tweets per quarter; by 2008, the company noted one hundred million tweets per quarter, and since then the platform has continued to grow with increased users and various feature options (Casti 2013). There are a couple of central features that distinguish Twitter from other social media sites. The open nature of the platform allows for any user to "follow" the tweets of anyone else. Additionally, Twitter popularized the use of a tool called a hashtag, a searchable phrase that identifies tweets about the topic noted. Users can engage in conversation on Twitter and use it as a tool to engage in social media activism. The platform is famously used by President Donald Trump to communicate directly with the American people; his frequent tweets are currently being logged in the Trump Twitter Archive. The company was number 21 on *Forbes* magazine's list of top digital companies in 2018 with a $24.7 billion value (Forbes 2018).

As Twitter grew in popularity, it became a platform for quickly sharing information, breaking news, and social interactions. A report in 2015 indicated that journalists made up a quarter of the site's verified accounts, accounts determined to be central to the public interest by Twitter, demonstrating the news industry's embrace of the platform (Kamps 2015). Twitter has been credited with "changing the way news is gathered, disseminated and consumed" and has contributed to shifts in the digital news space because tweets direct users to visit news organizations they may not have thought to look at (Jewell 2013). Breaking news can occur faster on Twitter than in newsrooms. This can provide journalists and news organizations with content quickly but can also pose issues if information cannot be appropriately confirmed or fact-checked. Journalists' use of Twitter has evolved as the platform gained a prominent place in the digital sphere.

Journalists' use of Twitter is not without controversy. To guard against credibility challenges, some news organizations require their staff adhere to professional news reporting standards on professional and personal Twitter accounts (Byers 2018). Some have advocated for journalists to do nothing on Twitter but share stories to avoid being accused of partisan bias if a comment, quip, or joke suggests an opinion, while others argue that it is ridiculous to think that the public does not believe journalists have opinions (Byers 2018). One recent study points to the complexity of journalists' use of Twitter. On the one hand, journalists may miss newsworthy information if they are not active Twitter users, while on the other hand, some journalists who rely on Twitter might be less able to evaluate the newsworthy nature of tweeted information (McGregor and Molyneux 2018). The News Media Alliance, a nonprofit news industry group, suggests that journalists should use Twitter to share stories reported on by themselves and their colleagues, provide expert commentary on appropriate news development, engage with followers, ignore or block trolls, and selectively use the platform to crowdsource stories (Peters, J. 2018).

Twitter has also emerged as a platform for those who feel marginalized. A study that examined communities, subcultures, and journalists who are on Twitter found that the platform is used by different constituencies in different ways. Users in particular Twitter subcultures like Black Twitter, Feminist Twitter, and Asian American Twitter use the platform to call attention to issues they don't see reported in mainstream media and to challenge the framing of particular news reports (Freelon et al. 2018). Twitter is often used as an activist platform where social justice–oriented issues are highlighted. Because members of Twitter subgroups indicate low trust in the mainstream media, they use Twitter to communicate with leaders and politicians more so than news organizations (Freelon et al. 2018).

Additionally, as with Facebook, Twitter has had to deal with a proliferation of fake accounts and the spreading of disinformation, particularly during the 2016 presidential election campaign, via its platform. The company has tools in place to combat misleading and false information. It is working with the Department of Homeland Security and the FBI, has created a "data science team" to address the issue, and has instituted a reporting tool for users to report inaccurate tweets (Conger and Satariano 2018). Despite these efforts, fake accounts persist on the platform. Prior to the 2018 midterm election, Twitter pulled chunks of misinformation from their platform, including fifty fake accounts alleging they were Republican officials, ten thousand accounts with anti-voting messages coming from alleged Democrats, and a series of memes that falsely claimed that Immigrations and Customs Enforcement (ICE) would be at voting sites (Conger and Satariano 2018).

Breitbart News Network (2007–)

Breitbart News Network, usually called Breitbart News, is a news and information site that was founded in 2007 by Andrew Breitbart in Los Angeles, California. Breitbart had worked at both the Drudge Report and at the Huffington Post when bloggers and their respective sites were emerging as powerful voices on the internet, and he was an early adopter of the idea that ideas shared online could both be influential and challenge the mainstream media (Carr 2012). He founded the Breitbart News Network to provide news and commentary that were antiestablishment in nature and aligned with the ideas of the political right, claiming that the mainstream media perpetuated a liberal bias (Mark 2016). The news site provides both news coverage and news commentary and is designed to antagonize and provoke, a tactic often criticized as problematic because information on the site is often misleading or presented without appropriate context (Bromwich 2016). Breitbart News' profile was raised as it defended the Tea Party movement; distributed a misleading video featuring Shirley Sherrod, an official from the U.S. Department of Agriculture that resulted in her termination; and broke the story about Democrat Anthony Weiner's use of sexually explicit photos and text messages (Bromwich 2016; Mark 2016).

While some of the news stories Breitbart News published were accurate under Andrew Breitbart's leadership, others were not, and all stories adhered to the perspective that the news site would engage in a culture war against Democrats by "depicting the left as morally wrong, inherently dangerous and also deeply foolish" (Coaston 2018). Some of the site's bloggers advance arguments that represent the far right side of the political spectrum. Many have dismissed the site as divisive; "the website is loathed by many liberals, moderates and establishment republicans who say it stokes a partisan atmosphere and misleads readers in order to escalate what they see as nonissues" (Bromwich 2016). Others view the site as representative of conservative views that are not present in the mainstream media.

Andrew Breitbart died in 2012, and after his death Steve Bannon, then a colleague who had been involved periodically with Breitbart News from its beginning, assumed the role of executive chairperson. Bannon has described Breitbart News as a "platform of the alt-right," a perspective that "aims to re-emphasize the value of Western European culture," and is seen by many as adhering to the ideas of white nationalism and bigotry (Mark 2016). Under Bannon, Breitbart focused more on politics than the culture wars, with a particular interest in challenging the mainstream Republican Party, something not all conservatives and Breitbart employees were on board with (Coaston 2018). Breitbart News positively reported on Donald Trump during the primary elections and supported Trump's campaign manager against claims of assault against a Breitbart staff member, resulting in the resignations of several Breitbart employees

(Mark 2016). Breitbart's popularity increased in the fall of 2016, noting high web traffic, as Trump praised the site for its support of him and for Breitbart's criticism of mainstream media (Mark 2016). Bannon left Breitbart to work for the Trump administration in 2016, returned to the news site in 2017, and left Breitbart again in early 2018. Today, Breitbart News remains a provocative news site aligned with the political right.

Bibliography

Adler, Ben. 2011 "The Real Problem with Fox News." *Columbia Journalism Review*, March 25. https://archives.cjr .org/campaign_desk/the_real_problem_with_fox_news.php.

Alexander, Jack. 1940. "Rover Girl in Europe." *Saturday Evening Post* 212, no. 48: 20–116.

Amanpour, Christiane. 2017. "How to Seek Truth in the Era of Fake News." TedGlobal. September 2017. Accessed January 1, 2019. https://www.ted.com/talks/christiane_ amanpour_how_to_seek_truth_in_the_era_of_fake_ news#t-790043.

Ammon, Royce. 2001. *Global Television and the Shaping of World Politics: CNN, Telediplomacy and Foreign Policy.* Jefferson, NC: McFarland & Company.

Augustyn, Adam. 2017. "Ira Glass." Britannica.com. Updated March 30, 2017. Accessed January 4, 2019. https://www .britannica.com/biography/Ira-Glass.

Auster, Albert. 2004. "Cronkite, Walter." In *The Encyclopedia of Television*, edited by Horace Newcomb, 2nd ed., 631–633. New York, NY: Routledge.

Barkin, Steve. 2003. *American Television News: The Media Marketplace and the Public Interest.* Armonk, NY: M.E. Sharpe.

Baumgartner, Jody C., and Brad Lockerbie. 2018. "Maybe It Is More Than a Joke: Satire, Mobilization, and Political Participation." *Social Science Quarterly* 99, no. 3: 1060–1074. doi:10.1111/ssqu.12501.

Benet, Siobhan. 2001. "Rave's Unique Beat Covers an Ignored Community." Women's eNews, October 21. https://womensenews.org/2001/10/raves-unique-beat-covers-ignored-community/.

Bennett, W. Lance. 2016. *News: The Politics of Illusion, 10th ed.* Chicago, IL: University of Chicago Press.

Beyers, Dylan. 2014. "Vox Not Living Up to Hype, Explained." *Politico*, August 23. https://www.politico.com/story/2014/08/vox-ezra-klein-110276.

Bourg, Anya, and James Jacoby. 2018. "The Facebook Dilemma, Parts One and Two." *Frontline.* PBS. Boston: WGBH, October 29; October 30, 2018. https://www.pbs.org/wgbh/frontline/film/facebook-dilemma/.

Brady, Kathleen. 1989. *Ida Tarbell: Portrait of a Muckraker.* Pittsburgh, PA: University of Pittsburgh Press.

Brinkley, Alan. 2010. *The Publisher: Henry Luce and His American Century.* New York: Alfred A. Knopf.

Brinkley, Douglas. 2012. *Cronkite.* New York: Harper Collins.

Brock, David, Ari Rabin-Havt, and Media Matters for America. 2012. *The Fox Effect: How Roger Ailes Turned a Network into a Propaganda Machine.* New York: Anchor Books.

Bromwich, Jonah. 2016. "What Is Breitbart News?" *New York Times*, August 17. https://www.nytimes.com/2016/08/18/business/media/what-is-breitbart-news.html.

Buckley, Cara. 2014. "Ira Glass's 'This American Life' Leaves PRI." *New York Times*, July 2. https://www.nytimes.com/2014/07/06/arts/ira-glasss-this-american-life-leaves-pri.html.

Byers, Dylan. 2018. "The Temptations of Twitter: Why Social Media Is Still and Minefield for Journalists." NBCnews.com, October 22. https://www.nbcnews.com/news/all/temptations-twitter-why-social-media-still-minefield-journalists-n922786.

Byrne, John. 2011. *World Changers.* New York: Penguin.

Carr, David. 2012. "The Provocateur." *New York Times*, April 13. https://www.nytimes.com/2012/04/15/business/media/the-life-and-death-of-andrew-breitbart.html?_r=0.

Carr, David. 2014. "Ezra Klein Joining Vox Media as Web Journalism Asserts Itself." *New York Times*, January 27. https://www.nytimes.com/2014/01/27/business/media/ezra-klein-joining-vox-media-as-web-journalism-asserts-itself.html.

Carter, Bill. 2004. "Barbara Walters to Leave 20/20 after 25 Years, Show's Last Season of Emotion Laden Interviews." *New York Times*, January 26. https://www.nytimes.com/2004/01/26/business/barbara-walters-leave-20-20-after-25-years-show-s-last-season-emotion-laden.html.

Cassino, Dan, Peter Woolley, and Krista Jenkins. 2012. "What You Know Depends on What You Watch: Current Events Knowledge across Popular News Sources." Public Mind Poll Study, Fairleigh Dickenson University, May 3. Accessed June 28, 2018. http://publicmind.fdu.edu/2012/confirmed/.

Casti, Taylor. 2013. "Everything You Need to Know about Twitter." Mashable.com, September 20. https://mashable.com/2013/09/20/twitter-history/#8HM1XIm2Kaq3.

Champagne, Christine. 2014. "How Lisa Ling Gets to Tell the Kinds of Stories She Wants to Tell On TV." *Fast Company*, October 24. https://www.fastcompany.com/3037275/how-lisa-ling-gets-to-tell-the-kinds-of-stories-she-wants-to-tell-on-tv.

CBS News. n.d. "Watch Oprah's Work on 60 Minutes." CBSnews.com. Accessed January 9, 2019. https://www.cbsnews.com/news/watch-oprahs-work-on-60-minutes/

CNN. n.d.a. "Christiane Amanpour." CNN.com. Accessed August 25, 2018. https://www.cnn.com/profiles/christiane-amanpour-profile.

CNN. n.d.b. "CNN Worldwide Fact Sheet." Accessed November 19, 2018. http://cnnpressroom.blogs.cnn.com/cnn-fact-sheet/.

CNN. 2013. "Helen Thomas Fast Facts." CNN.com, January 29. https://www.cnn.com/2013/01/29/us/helen-thomas-fast-facts/index.html.

Coaston, Jane. 2018. "Bannon's Breitbart Is Dead. But Breitbart Will Live On." Vox, January 14. https://www.vox.com/2018/1/14/16875288/bannon-breitbart-conservative-media.

Coburn, Marcia. 2007. "His American Life: A Look at Ira Glass." *Chicago Magazine*, June 25. https://www.chicagomag.com/Chicago-Magazine/March-2006/His-American-Life/.

Collins, Lauren. 2008. "The Oracle: The Many Lives of Arianna Huffington." *New Yorker*, October 13.

Conger, Kate, and Adam Satariano. 2018. "Twitter Says It Is Ready for the Midterms but Rogue Accounts Aren't Letting Up." *New York Times*, November 5. https://www.nytimes.com/2018/11/05/technology/twitter-fake-news-midterm-elections.html.

Connery, Anna. 2017. "Jorge Ramos Proudly Represents the Latino Community." *USA Today, Hispanic Living Magazine*, September 16, 2017. https://www.usatoday.com/story/life/2017/09/16/jorge-ramos-proudly-represents-latino-community/636630001/.

Cosgrove-Mather, Bootie. 2004. "Young Get News from Comedy Central." CBS.com, March 1. https://www.cbsnews.com/news/young-get-news-from-comedy-central/.

Cruickshank, Paula. 2010. "42 Seconds That Sullied Helen Thomas—and New Media." Realclearpolitics.com, July 31. https://www.realclearpolitics.com/articles/2013/07/31/42_seconds_that_sullied_helen_thomas_--_and_new_media_119431.html.

C-SPAN. 2016. "Q&A with Amy Goodman." C-SPAN, March 25. https://www.c-span.org/video/?407176-1/qa-amy-goodman.

Daly, Christopher. 2012. *Covering America: A Narrative History of a Nation's Journalism*. Amherst: University of Massachusetts Press.

de la Peña, Nonny. 2015. "The Future of News? Virtual Reality." TEDWomen. Accessed January 1, 2019. https://www.ted.com/talks/nonny_de_la_pena_the_future_of_news_virtual_reality?language=en.

de la Peña, Nonny, Peggy Weil, Joan Liobera, Bernhard Spanlange, Doron Friedman, Maria Sanchez-Vives, and Mel Slater. 2010. "Immersive Journalism: Immersive Virtual Reality for the First-Person Experience of News." *Presence* 19, no. 4: 291–301.

Dickenson, Tim. 2011. "How Roger Ailes Built the Fox News Fear Factory." *Rolling Stone*, May 25. https://www.rollingstone.com/politics/politics-news/how-roger-ailes-built-the-fox-news-fear-factory-244652/.

Edes, Alyssa, and Christine Hayes. 2012. "Former ABC Anchor Carole Simpson Finds Herself Back in the News." Boston.com, October 15. http://archive.boston.com/yourcampus/news/emerson/2012/10/former_abc_anchor_carole_simpson_finds_herself_back_in_the_news.html.

Edgerton, Gary. 2004. "Murrow, Edward R." In *The Encyclopedia of Television*, edited by Horace Newcomb, 2nd ed., 1564–1567. New York, NY: Routledge.

Ellison, Sarah. 2018. "Will Fox News Survive as a House United? A Look at the Cable Network's Ongoing Drama in the Trump Era." *Washington Post*, November 9. https://www.washingtonpost.com/lifestyle/style/will-fox-news-survive-as-a-house-united-a-look-at-the-cable-networks-ongoing-drama-in-the-trump-era/2018/11/09/1a9017d8-e3e7-11e8-b759-3d88a5ce9e19_story.html

Ezzel, Timothy. 2017. "Aldoph Simon Ochs." *The Tennessee Encyclopedia*. Accessed September 23, 2018. https://tennesseeencyclopedia.net/entries/adolph-simon-ochs/.

Fallows, James. 2018. "Is Bob Woodward Like Walter Cronkite?" Notes blog. *Atlantic*, September 11. https://www.theatlantic.com/notes/2018/09/is-bob-woodward-like-walter-cronkite/569938/.

Finnegan, William. 2015. "The Man Who Wouldn't Sit Down." *New Yorker*, October 5. https://www.newyorker.com/magazine/2015/10/05/the-man-who-wouldnt-sit-down.

Fleishman, Glenn. 2018. "Google's 20th Anniversary: How the Search Giant Went from a Stanford Dorm to the Top of Tech." *Fortune*, September 4. http://fortune.com/2018/09/04/google-20th-anniversary-history/.

Foote, Joe S. 1998. *Live from the Trenches: The Changing Role of the Television News Correspondent*. Carbondale: Southern Illinois University Press.

Forbes. 2018. "#21 Twitter." Forbes.com. Accessed January 7, 2019. https://www.forbes.com/companies/twitter/#cca 269722a3b.

Fredericks, Bob. 2018. "Fox Rebukes Hannity and Pirro for Trump Rally Appearance." *New York Post*, November 6. https://nypost.com/2018/11/06/fox-news-rebukes-hannity-and-pirro-for-trump-rally-appearance/.

Freelon, Deen, Lori Lopez, Meredith Clark, and Sarah Jackson. 2018. "How Black Twitter and Other Social Media Communities Interact with Mainstream News." The Knight Foundation. Accessed March 31, 2019. https://knightfoundation.org/features/twittermedia.

Gangel, Jamie, and Dan Merica. 2018. "Bob Woodward's New Book Puts Readers Face to Face with Trump." CNN.com, July 30. https://www.cnn.com/2018/07/30/politics/woodward-new-book-trump/index.html.

Garber, Megan. 2012. "Google News at 10: How the Algorithm Won over the News Industry." *Atlantic*, September 20. https://www.theatlantic.com/technology/

archive/2012/09/google-news-at-10-how-the-algorithm-won-over-the-news-industry/262641/.

Garcia-Rios, Sergio. 2015. "The 'Jorge Ramos Effect' Could Hurt Donald Trump." Time.com, August 28. http://time.com/4013713/donald-trump-and-the-jorge-ramos-effect/.

Geimann, Steve. 1994. "Sacrifice & Commitment: Making a Difference Matters for ABC's Carole Simpson." *Quill* 82, no. 5: 25.

Goldberg, Vicki. 1986. *Margaret Bourke-White: A Biography.* New York: Harper and Row Publishers.

Goldman, Naomi. 2018. "Nonny de la Peña: Pioneering VR and Immersive Journalism." VFX Voice, April 3. http://vfxvoice.com/nonny-de-la-pena-pioneering-vr-and-immersive-journalism/.

Gottfried, Jeffrey, Katerina E. Matsa, and Michael Barthel. 2015 "As Jon Stewart Steps Down, 5 Facts about The Daily Show." Pew Research Center, August 6. http://www.pewresearch.org/fact-tank/2015/08/06/5-facts-daily-show/.

Gottlieb, Agnes. 1994. "The Reform Years at 'Hamptons': The Magazine Journalism of Rheta Childe Dorr 1909–1912." *Electronic Journal of Communication* 4: 2–4. Accessed August 1, 2018. http://www.cios.org/EJCPUBLIC/004/2/00429.html.

Gramlich, John. 2018. "8 Facts about Americans and Facebook." Pew Research Center, October 24. http://www.pewresearch.org/fact-tank/2018/10/24/facts-about-americans-and-facebook/.

Great Projects Film Company. 1999. "Crucible of Empire, The Spanish-American War. Yellow Journalism." PBS.org. Accessed July 1, 2018. http://www.pbs.org/crucible/frames/_journalism.html.

Gregory, Dick. 2017. "John H. Johnson and the Black Magazine." *Paris Review*, September 26. https://www.theparisreview.org/blog/2017/09/26/john-h-johnson-black-magazine/.

Hall, Jane. 1996. "Murdoch Will Launch 24-Hour News Channel." *Los Angeles Times*, January 31. http://articles .latimes.com/1996-01-31/business/fi-30597_1_ news-network.

Hare, Kristen. 2019. "How *USA Today* and Its Network of Local Papers Prioritized Investigative Journalism." Poynter, April 24. https://www.poynter.org/reporting-editing/2019/ how-usa-today-and-its-network-of-local-papers-prioritized-investigative-journalism/.

Harris, Paul. 2004. "President's Man." *Guardian*, April 24. https://www.theguardian.com/books/2004/apr/25/media .pressandpublishing.

Hillstrom, Laurie Collier. 2010. *Defining Moments: The Muckrakers and the Progressive Era.* Detroit, MI: Omnigraphics, Inc.

The History Makers. 2014. "Soledad O'Brien." The History Makers.org, February 22. http://www.thehistorymakers .org/biography/soledad-obrien.

Jewell, John. 2013. "How Twitter Has Helped the Emergence of a New Journalism." *Conversation*, November 4. https:// theconversation.com/how-twitter-has-helped-the-emergence-of-a-new-journalism-19841.

Johnston, David C. 2014. *Placing a Bet on USA Today.* Columbia Journalism Review, March/April. https://archives .cjr.org/reports/placing_a_bet_on_usa_today.php.

"Joseph Pulitzer Dies Suddenly." 1911. *New York Times*, October 30. https://archive.nytimes.com/www.nytimes .com/learning/general/onthisday/bday/0410.html.

Juergens, George. 1966. *Joseph Pulitzer and the New York World.* Princeton, NJ: Princeton University Press.

Kainth, Karina. 2010. "Amy Goodman Discusses Mainstream Media." *Washington Report on Middle East Affairs* 29, no. 6: 56.

Kamps, Haje J. 2015. "Who Are Twitter's Verified Users?" Medium, May 25. https://medium.com/@Haje/ who-are-twitter-s-verified-users-af976fc1b032.

Kelly, Kitty. 2010. *Oprah: A Biography*. New York: Crown Publishers.

King, Gilbert. 2012. "The Woman Who Took on the Tycoon." *Smithsonian Magazine*, July 5. https://www.smithsonianmag.com/history/the-woman-who-took-on-the-tycoon-651396/.

Kinzer, Stephen. 1994. "Where There's War, There's Amanpour." *New York Times*, October 9. https://www.nytimes.com/1994/10/09/magazine/where-there-s-war-there-s-amanpour.html.

Kovach, Bill, and Tom Rosenstiel. 2010. *Blur: How to Know What's True in the Age of Information Overload*. New York: Bloomsbury.

Krumsvik, Arne. 2013. "From Creator of Change to Supporter of the Traditional: The Changing Role of CNN .com." *Journal of Applied Journalism & Media Studies* 2, no. 3: 397–415. doi:10.1386lajms.2.3.397_1.

Ling, Lisa. 2011. "Use Cable to Open a Window on America." *Multichannel News*, June 20.

Lipton, Joshua. 2001. "Barbara Walters." *Columbia Journalism Review* 40, no. 4: 80.

Mahler, Jonathan. 2014. "As Barbara Walters Retires, the Big TV Interview Signs Off, Too." *New York Times*, May 15. https://nyti.ms/1nSQRVm.

Mark, Michelle. 2016. "A Brief History of Breitbart News, the Controversial Website Run by Trump's Chief Advisor." *Business Insider*, November 17. https://www.businessinsider.com/what-is-breitbart-news-steve-bannon.

Martin, Douglas. 2005. "John H. Johnson, 87, Founder of Ebony, Dies." *New York Times*, August 9. https://www.nytimes.com/2005/08/09/business/media/john-h-johnson-87-founder-of-ebony-dies.html.

Martin, Douglas. 2009. "Walter Cronkite, 92, Dies; Trusted Voice of TV News." *New York Times*, July 17. https://www.nytimes.com/2009/07/18/us/18cronkite.html.

Mayer, Jane. 2019. "Trump TV." *New Yorker*, March 11, 40–53.

McGreal, Chris. 2010. "Helen Thomas, Veteran Reporter: Why She Had to Resign." *Guardian*, June 8. https://www.theguardian.com/world/2010/jun/08/helen-thomas-reporter-why-resign.

McGregor, Shannon C, and Logan Molyneux. 2018. "Twitter's Influence on News Judgment: An Experiment among Journalists." *Journalism*, 1–17. doi: 10.1177/1464884918802975.

McLeland, Susan. 2004. "Walters, Barbara." In *The Encyclopedia of Television*, edited by Horace Newcomb, 2nd ed., 2473–2475. New York, NY: Routledge.

Morgan, Arlene N., Irene Pifer, and Keith Woods. 2006. *The Authentic Voice: The Best Reporting on Race and Ethnicity.* New York: Columbia University Press.

National Museum of African American History and Culture. 2018. "Watching Oprah." Accessed January 9, 2019. https://nmaahc.si.edu/explore/exhibitions/watchingoprah.

National Public Radio. 2015. "At Sundance 'Project Syria' Puts Viewers in Center of Conflict." *All Things Considered*, January 26. https://www.npr.org/2015/01/26/381647459/at-sundance-project-syria-puts-viewers-in-center-of-conflict.

Nicks, Denver. 2013. "These Are the 30 People under 30 Changing the World." Time.com, December 5. http://ideas.time.com/2013/12/06/these-are-the-30-people-under-30-changing-the-world/slide/ezra-klein/.

Nieman Journalism Lab. 2014. "The Huffington Post." Nieman Lab Encyclo. Accessed January 1, 2019. http://www.niemanlab.org/encyclo/huffington-post/.

O'Brien, Soledad. 2009. "Soledad O'Brien Explores Latino Experience, Mixed-Race Heritage." CNN.com, October 6. http://www.cnn.com/2009/LIVING/personal/10/06/lia.soledad.obrien.excerpt/index.html.

O'Brien, Soledad. 2018. Tweet. August 13. https://twitter.com/soledadobrien/status/1029176597780328448?lang=en.

Oden, Lori. n.d. "Margaret Bourke." International Photography Hall of Fame. Iphf.org. Accessed September 1, 2019. http://iphf.org/inductees/margaret-bourke/.

Otterson, Joe. 2018. "Oprah Winfrey, Apple Sign Multi-Year Content Partnership." *Variety*, June 15. https://variety.com/2018/tv/news/oprah-winfrey-apple-content-partnership-1202848061/.

Parker, Gretchen. 2011. "Nonny de la Peña Introduces Immersive Journalism with Paper in MIT Journal." USC Annenberg School for Communication and Journalism, February 25. https://annenberg.usc.edu/nonny-de-la-pe%C3%B1a-introduces-immersive-journalism-paper-mit-journal.

Peretz, Evgenia. 2002. "The Girls at the Front." *Vanity Fair*, June. https://www.vanityfair.com/culture/2002/06/female-war-correspondents-200206.

Peters, Jennifer. 2018. "How To: Use Twitter to Your Advantage as a Journalist." News Media Alliance.org, April 25. https://www.newsmediaalliance.org/how-to-twitter-for-journalists/.

Peters, Ralph. 2018. "Why I Left Fox News." *Washington Post*, March 30. https://www.washingtonpost.com/outlook/why-i-left-fox-news/2018/03/30/d1224648-32bb-11e8-8bdd-cdb33a5eef83_story.html?utm_term=.53f029926934.

Phillips, Lisa. 2006. *Public Radio*. New York: CDS Books.

Proctor, Ben. 2007. *William Randolph Hearst: The Later Years 1911–1951*. Oxford: Oxford University Press.

Quintanilla, Carl. 2013. "The Oprah Effect." CNBC.com, June 21. https://www.cnbc.com/the-oprah-effect/.

Rave, Jodi. 2005. "Challenges Native and Non-Native Journalists Confront." *Nieman Reports* 59, no. 3: 7–9.

Rebuild Foundation. 2018. "A Johnson Publishing Story." Accessed September 23, 2018. https://rebuild-foundation.org/exhibition/a-johnson-publishing-story/.

"Rheta C. Dorr, 82, Author, Feminist." 1948. *New York Times*, August 9. https://nyti.ms/2OCojm3.

The Root. 2018. "Soledad O'Brien Is Tired of Journalists Sugar Coating Racism." YouTube video, 0:2:48. August 10. https://www.youtube.com/watch?v=upLQiD9tnZs.

Rosenberg, Howard, and Charles Feldman. 2008. *No Time to Think: The Menace of Media Speed and the 24-Hour News Cycle*. New York: Continuum International Publishing Group.

Rutenberg, Jim. 2017. "Univision's Urgent Sense of Purpose: A Newsroom and a Lifeline." *New York Times*, June 18. https://www.nytimes.com/2017/06/18/business/media/a-newsroom-and-a-lifeline-univisions-urgent-sense-of-purpose.html.

Sanders, Marion. 1973. *Dorothy Thompson: A Legend in Her Time*. Boston, MA: Houghton Mifflin.

Schudson, Michael. 1978. *Discovering the News: A Social History of Newspapers*. New York: Basic Books.

Schudson, Michael. 1992. *Watergate in American Memory*. New York: Basic Books.

Schwartz, Jason. 2018. "Second Fox News Reporter Leaves amid Objections to the Network." *Politico*, August 23. https://www.politico.com/story/2018/08/23/fox-news-reporters-opinion-network-adam-housley-795278.

Segal, David. 2015. "Arianna Huffington's Improbably, Insatiable, Content Machine." *New York Times*, June 30. https://www.nytimes.com/2015/07/05/magazine/arianna-huffingtons-improbable-insatiable-content-machine.html.

Setoodeh, Ramin. 2017. " 'The View' Turns 20: ABC to Air First Episode with Barbara Walters." *Variety*, August 7. https://variety.com/2017/tv/news/the-view-20-anniversary-barbara-walters-meredith-vieira-joy-behar-rosie-o-donnell-whoopi-goldberg-1202517303/.

Sherman, Gabriel. 2014. *The Loudest Voice in the Room: How the Brilliant, Bombastic Roger Ailes Built Fox News—And Divided a Country.* New York: Random House.

Simon, Ron. 2004. "See It Now." In *The Encyclopedia of Television*, edited by Horace Newcomb, 2nd ed., 2041–2044. New York: Routledge.

Simpson, Carole. 2010. *Newslady.* Bloomington, IN: AuthorHouse.

Smith, Chris. 2016. "How John Stewart Took over *The Daily Show* and Revolutionized Late Night TV: An Oral History." *Vanity Fair*, December. https://www.vanityfair.com/hollywood/2016/11/how-jon-stewart-took-over-the-daily-show-late-night-tv.

Spangler, Todd. 2017. "The Serial Team's New Podcast, S-Town, Tops 10 Million Downloads in Four Days." *Variety*, March 31. https://variety.com/2017/digital/news/s-town-podcast-10-million-downloads-serial-productions-1202020302/.

S.R. 1994. "The Women Who Paved the Way. (Cover Story)." *American Journalism Review* 16, no. 2: 23.

Stafford, Zach. 2016. "The Oprah Winfrey Show: 'Hour-Long Life Lessons' That Changed TV Forever." *Guardian*, September 8. https://www.theguardian.com/tv-and-radio/2016/sep/08/oprah-winfrey-show-30-year-anniversary-daytime-tv.

Stelter, Brian. 2011. "A Grass Roots Newscast Gives Voice to Struggles." *New York Times*, October 24. https://www.nytimes.com/2011/10/24/business/media/a-grass-roots-newscast-gives-a-voice-to-struggles.html?searchResultPosition=1.

Talk of the Nation. 2010. "Helen Thomas Retires after Controversial Remark" [transcript]. National Public Radio, June 7. https://www.npr.org/templates/story/story.php?storyId=127538667.

This American Life. n.d. "Our Other Shows." Accessed January 4, 2019. https://www.thisamericanlife.org/about/our-other-shows.

Topping, Seymour. 1999. "Biography of Joseph Pulitzer." Pulitzer.org. Accessed August 13, 2018. http://www.pulitzer.org/page/biography-joseph-pulitzer.

Trent, Sydney. 2015. "Soledad O'Brien on Starbucks and Race: It's Okay to Ask and It's Okay to Answer." *Washington Post*, March 3. https://www.washingtonpost.com/news/inspired-life/wp/2015/03/25/dont-hate-starbucks-when-it-comes-to-race-its-ok-to-ask-and-its-ok-to-answer-says-journalist-soledad-obrien/?noredirect=on&utm_term=.7dfe11fc8b0f.

Upstill, Trystan. 2018. "The New Google News: AI Meets Human Intelligence." Google blog post, May 8. https://www.blog.google/products/news/new-google-news-ai-meets-human-intelligence/.

USAToday.com. n.d. "About Us." Accessed June 1, 2019. https://marketing.usatoday.com/about.

Verge Staff. 2018. "Google Turns 20: How an Internet Search Engine Reshaped the World." The Verge, September 27. https://www.theverge.com/2018/9/5/17823490/google-20th-birthday-anniversary-history-milestones.

Volpe, Joseph. 2015. "Nonny de la Peña: The Godmother of Virtual Reality." *Engadget*, January 24. https://www.engadget.com/2015/01/24/the-godmother-of-virtual-reality-nonny-de-la-pena/.

Wallace, Benjamin. 2014. "Here, Let Ezra Explain." *New York Magazine*, February 2. http://nymag.com/news/features/ezra-klein-2014-2/.

Walters, Barbara. 2008. *Audition: A Memoir.* New York: Alfred A. Knopf.

Wang, Shan. 2018. "Google Announces a 300M Google News Initiative (Though This Isn't about Giving Out Grants Directly to Newsrooms Like It Does in Europe)."

Nieman Lab, March 20. http://www.niemanlab.org/
2018/03/google-announces-a-300m-google-news-initiative-
though-this-isnt-about-giving-out-grants-directly-to-
newsrooms-like-it-does-in-europe/.

Whyte, Kenneth. 2009. *The Uncrowned King: The
Sensational Rise of William Randolph Hearst.* Berkeley, CA:
Counterpoint.

"William Randolph Hearst." n.d. Encyclopedia.com. Accessed
September 2, 2018. http://www.encyclopedia.com/
history/encyclopedias-almanacs-transcripts-and-maps/
william-randolph-hearst.

Williams, Mary E. 2013. "There Will Never Be Another
Barbara Walters." *Salon*, May 5. https://www.salon.com/
2013/05/13/there_will_never_be_another_
barbara_walters/.

Wilner, Isiah. 2006. "The Man Time Forgot." *Vanity Fair*,
October. https://www.vanityfair.com/news/2006/10/
henry-luce-briton-hadden-rivalry.

Yu, Roger. 2016. "Arianna Huffington to Leave Huffington
Post for Wellness Startup." *USA Today*, August 11.
https://www.usatoday.com/story/money/2016/08/11/
arianna-huffington-leave-huffington-post-stress-reduction-
startup/88555782/.

Introduction

This chapter assembles detailed information that supports some of the topics raised in the first two chapters of the book. In the first section, Data, summaries of research findings related to Americans' news consumption practices and perceptions of the news media are provided. This section also highlights additional data about news deserts in the United States. Selective findings from investigations that have compiled a list of websites that host unreliable information and from research into how different nations are addressing misinformation are shared.

The second part of this chapter, Documents, presents a series of texts that further explore some of the issues discussed in the book. The section begins with some historical examples of "fake news." Government documents in this section speak to some of the contemporary concerns about news and information in the United States. Included here are excerpts from judiciary hearing testimonies and statements that address technology companies' role in content dissemination. Finally, this section provides information from organizations that are studying some of the dominant issues that challenge public trust in news and information.

Those with an internet connection can easily access news and information online from a diverse slate of sources. (Kadettmann/Dreamstime.com)

Ways Consumers Access News

The rise of online news and, more recently, social media has changed the way consumers access their news. The Pew Research Center regularly studies American news habits, looking at how often different demographics engage with news and from where they obtain their news. There has been a shift in the news access routines in the past decade. In 2008, the Pew Research Center for U.S. Politics and Policy found that 34 percent of participants read the newspaper, and 35 percent of participants listened to radio news "yesterday," while 39 percent regularly watched cable television news, 52 percent regularly watched local television news, 29 percent watched nightly network news, 22 percent watched network morning news, and 37 percent read online news three or more times a week. A decade later, television remains a popular news outlet with 37 percent of participants indicating they often get news from local television, 30 percent indicating they often watch cable news, and 25 percent indicating they often get news from network television news shows (Shearer 2018). However, the reliance on other news sites has shifted. Figure 5.1 indicates where adults were most often to obtain their news from in 2018.

The research that shows social media as a news source indicates that consumers are relying on social media more so than print newspapers. Additionally, research has found that while 20 percent of participants rely on social media as a news source "often," 27 percent of participants get news from social media "sometimes," 21 percent of participants get news from social media "hardly ever," and 32 percent never get news from social media (Matsa and Shearer 2018). The research also shows that among all social media users, 57 percent "expect" news obtained via social media to be "largely inaccurate," yet social media users indicate they enjoy the

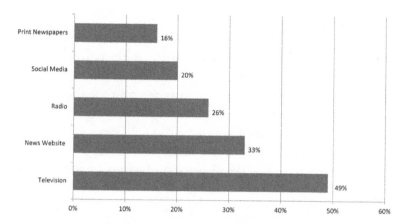

Figure 5.1 Percentages of Adults Who Note They *Often* Get News from These Sources in 2018

Source: Shearer, Elisa. 2018. "Social Media Outpaces Print Newspapers in the United States as a News Source." *Pew Research Center*, December 10. http://www.pewresearch.org/fact-tank/2018/12/10/social-media-outpaces-print-newspapers-in-the-u-s-as-a-news-source/.

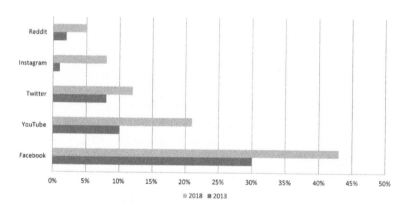

Figure 5.2 Percentages of Adults Who Obtain News from Popular Social Media Sites, 2018 versus 2013

Source: Anderson, Monica, and Andrea Caumont. 2014. "How Social Media Is Reshaping News." Pew Research Center Journalism and Media, September 14. Accessed June 19, 2018. http://www.pewresearch.org/fact-tank/2014/09/24/how-social-media-is-reshaping-news/; Matsa, Katerina E., and Elisa Shearer. 2018. "News Use across Social Media Platforms 2018." Pew Research Center, September 10. http://www.journalism.org/2018/09/10/news-use-across-social-media-platforms-2018/

convenience of getting their news from these sites. Thirty-six percent of social media users believe the news they obtain from these platforms helps them understand current events (Matsa and Shearer 2018).

Other Pew Research Center reports demonstrate the increasing popularity of social media platforms as pathways to accessing news. The percent of adults who obtain news from social media sites has increased over a period of about five years. Figure 5.2 shows that in 2018, 5 percent of adults obtained news from Reddit (versus 2 percent in 2013), 8 percent obtained news from Instagram (versus 1 percent in 2013), 12 percent obtained news from Twitter (versus 8 percent in 2013), 21 percent obtained news from YouTube (versus 10 percent in 2013), and 43 percent obtained news from Facebook (versus 30 percent in 2013).

News Deserts

The shifts in news consumption practices have had an impact on the newspaper industry. According to Penelope Muse Abernathy and the Center for Innovation and Sustainability in Local Media at the University of North Carolina (UNC) School of Media and Journalism, 171 counties in the United States do not have a local newspaper and 1,449 counties, about half of all the counties in the entire country, only have one newspaper, and this newspaper is usually a weekly paper. The increasing presence of these "news deserts" raises concerns that many citizens are not getting the news they need about their communities and regions. Table 5.1 displays how many counties in each state do not have a newspaper and how many counties in each state have only one newspaper, identifying what states are home to more news deserts than others.

Table 5.1   State Counts of Counties with No Local Newspaper or Only One
Local Newspaper

(State: No. of counties with no newspaper/No. of counties with only one
newspaper)

Alabama: 2/36	Hawaii: 1/2	Massachusetts: 0/2	New Mexico: 4/22	South Dakota: 3/33
Alaska: 14/12	Idaho: 7/29	Michigan: 5/41	New York: 1/13	Tennessee: 4/68
Arizona: 0/6	Illinois: 1/33	Minnesota: 0/8	North Carolina: 6/58	Texas: 21/134
Arkansas: 0/45	Indiana: 2/40	Mississippi: 1/64	North Dakota: 2/27	Utah: 6/17
California: 2/12	Iowa: 0/17	Missouri: 2/54	Ohio: 0/38	Vermont: 1/2
Colorado: 3/33	Kansas: 3/57	Montana: 5/35	Oklahoma: 4/31	Virginia: 6/68
Connecticut: 1/1	Kentucky: 4/91	Nebraska: 8/43	Oregon: 2/15	Washington: 1/11
Delaware: 0/0	Louisiana: 2/39	Nevada: 1/12	Pennsylvania: 2/18	West Virginia: 1/42
Florida: 5/22	Maine: 1/4	New Hampshire: 0/2	Rhode Island: 0/0	Wisconsin: 1/22
Georgia: 28/111	Maryland: 0/9	New Jersey: 0/2	South Carolina: 1/3	Wyoming: 0/8

Source: Penelope Muse Abernathy and UNC School of Media and Journalism
Center for Innovation and Sustainability in Local Media. Accessed March 13,
2019 from https://www.usnewsdeserts.com/.

Perceptions of News Media

Given that research shows lower than ideal levels of trust in
the news media among adults during an era of political polarization, different organizations are attempting to learn more
about this trend and address the issue. Because assessing people's trust in the news media is complicated, the Media Insight
Project (2018) designed an inquiry that, in part, looked at
2,019 adults' perceptions of the news media in general and of

the news media they consumed over the past year. They found that 32 percent of participants noted their level of trust in news sources they relied on increased over the past year, while 13 percent noted that their trust in these sources decreased. In comparison, when people were asked to consider their level of trust in the more general news media, 17 percent said their level of trust increased while 44 percent indicated their level of trust decreased over the past year. Thirty-nine percent of participants indicated their trust in the general news media remained the same in comparison to 54 percent of participants who indicated their trust in their preferred news source remained consistent. Figure 5.3 displays these comparisons.

The Media Insight Project study also noted distinctions between Democrats' and Republicans' perceptions on news

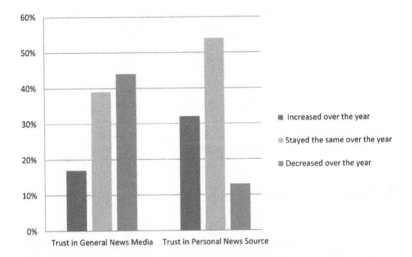

Figure 5.3   Trust in News Media (Percentages of participants (N=2,019) who report whether trust in the general news media and their own news source increased, stayed the same, or decreased over the year)

Source: Media Insight Project. 2018. *Americans and the News Media: What They Do—and Don't—Understand about Each Other.* The American Press Institute and the Associated Press-NORC Center for Public Affairs Research, June 11. Accessed March 1, 2019. https://www. americanpressinstitute.org/publications/reports/survey-research/ republicans-democrats-trust-understand-media/.

and journalists. Overall, Democrats indicate they have a more positive perception of the news media than Republicans do. Eighty-three percent of Democrats indicate they have a positive view of their preferred news sources, and 54 percent of Democrats indicate they have a positive view of individual journalists they follow. In comparison, 66 percent of Republicans indicate they view their preferred news source positively, and 36 percent of Republicans indicate they have a positive view of individual journalists they follow. Fifty-three percent of Democrats trust the news in general in contrast to 18 percent of Republicans, and 60 percent of Democrats indicate trust in journalists in general in comparison to 16 percent of Republicans. Republicans and Democrats also differ in their perceptions of what type of content makes up the news. Figure 5.4 and Figure 5.5 display how Democrats and Republicans in the Media Insight Project's survey of 2,019 adults perceive news media content.

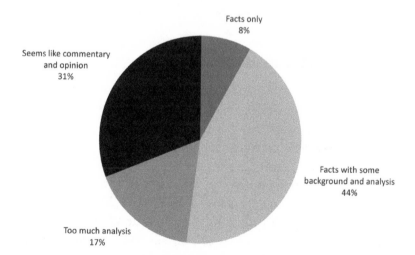

Figure 5.4 Democrats' Perceptions of the Composition of News Coverage

Source: Media Insight Project. 2018. *Americans and the News Media: What They Do—and Don't—Understand about Each Other.* The American Press Institute and the Associated Press-NORC Center for Public Affairs Research, June 11. Accessed March 1, 2019. https://www.americanpressinstitute.org/publications/reports/survey-research/republicans-democrats-trust-understand-media/.

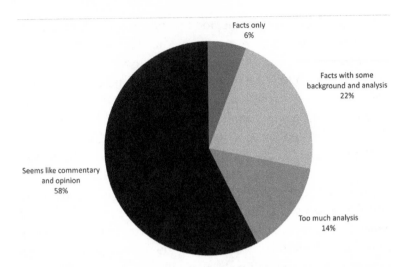

Figure 5.5   Republicans' Perceptions of the Composition of News Coverage

Source: Media Insight Project. 2018. *Americans and the News Media: What They Do—and Don't—Understand about Each Other.* The American Press Institute and the Associated Press-NORC Center for Public Affairs Research, June 11. Accessed March 1, 2019. https://www.americanpressinstitute.org/publications/reports/survey-research/republicans-democrats-trust-understand-media/.

Research on Unreliable Information

While there are certain partisan differences in perceptions of news, the rise of false information in the digital age is an international concern. In 2017, Politifact published a Fake News Almanac based on their research in identifying fake news sites, misinformation, and disinformation. They've described the types of "false or fake news" they have come across over the 330 sites they've cataloged (as of November 2017) as falling into four categories: parody or joke sites, news imposter sites, fake news sites, and sites that contain fake news (Gillin 2017). Parody sites are satirical, imposter sites are designed to look like recognizable legitimate news organizations, fake news sites are sites that are completely fictitious, and sites that contain fake news are outfits where false content is posted, sometimes by site users and sometimes by the organization editors who were unaware the story was illegitimate. Table 5.2 provides

Table 5.2 Examples of "Fake News" Websites

News Imposter Websites	Completely Fake News Websites	Websites That May Contain Fake News	Parody or Joke Websites
ABCNews.com.co	247NewsMedia.com	City-Herald.com	AsAmericanAsApplePie.org
AlabamaObserver.com	FederalistTribune.com	Conservative7.com	BostonLeader.com
CNNews3.com	The-Insider.co	DailyStormer.com	BostonTribune.com
Fox-News24.com	USANewsToday.com	FactRider.com	DailySnark.com
HoustonChronicle-TV.com	USHerald.com	FreeRepublic.com	FloridaSunPost.com
TheMiamiGazette.com	USASupreme.com	HealthyCareAndBeauty.com	Huzlers.com
Times.com.mx	USAConservativeReport.com	HigherPerspectives.com	Newslo.com
USATodayNews.me	VoxTribune.com	IndependentMinute.com	Politicalo.com
WashingtonEvening.com	WeConservative.com	NewsForMeToday.com	Politicono.com
WashingtonPost.com.co	YourNewsWire.com	UrbanImageMagazine.com	TheSeattleTribune.com

Source: Gillin, Joshua (2017). "Politifact's Guide to Fake News Websites and What They Peddle." Politifact.com, April 20. https://www.politifact.com/punditfact/article/2017/apr/20/politifacts-guide-fake-news-websites-and-what-they/.

a sampling of the fake news site data compiled by Politifact. Examining the website URLs provides insight into how some consumers, if they only glance at the website URL, might be persuaded to believe in the legitimacy of the sites. Looking at the URLs carefully also allows consumers to identify particular tricks used to suggest legitimacy. For example, the correct URL for ABC News is abcnews.go.com, CNN's website is cnn.com, and while the Florida Sun Post sounds like a newspaper title, there is no legitimate newspaper by that name.

Poynter's Daniel Funke (2018) has assembled a guide of how nations around the world are dealing with misinformation and disinformation, summarizing how countries are taking action to limit the spread and/or impact of this material. The discussion of the issue is complicated as the lines between distributing misinformation and free speech are blurry, and free press advocates are wary of too much government involvement. Additionally, not all countries have free speech protections, and some government leaders view challenges to their decisions and actions seen in the press as a type of misinformation that they use to justify punishing journalists, and/or they perpetuate misinformation themselves (Funke 2018). Table 5.3 summarizes the approaches being implemented by a sampling of nations that have taken steps to address misinformation online.

Table 5.3 Examples of Approaches Some Countries Are Taking to Address Misinformation Online

Country	Approach
Belgium	• Convened a group of journalists and scholars to examine the issue and propose solutions. • Launched a media literacy–oriented website that engages citizens in learning about and helping to stop the spread of misinformation.
Brazil	• Numerous proposed bills address the criminalization of spreading misinformation, particularly in advance of an election. However, it is unclear what any legislation will ultimately look like.
Canada	• Appointed a task force that will monitor and inform on any disinformation campaigns.

Country	Approach
	• Social media companies are being asked to do more to stop misinformation by the Canadian government, and a bill is being drafted that compels technology companies to be more transparent. • Resources have been allocated to support media literacy initiatives.
France	• Focusing on information related to elections, France has passed a law that defines "manipulation of information" and allows content meeting that definition to be removed or blocked from offending sites when requested by individuals or groups. • France's legislation also requires that platforms disclose who has purchased campaign ads or sponsored content. • A counsel was established to ensure media organizations comply with the law and do not represent interests of a foreign state.
India	• India has periodically shut down the internet to prevent the spread of misinformation on the social platform WhatsApp, given the content on the platform has allegedly been linked to the spread of violence. • The state government of West Bengal is pursuing legislation that would punish those who spread false information and maintains a database of "fake news" stories.
Sweden	• Sweden's government plans to strongly promote and advance factual content to counter disinformation campaigns. The government will call attention to any disinformation campaigns that emerge and highlight their attempts at manipulation.
United Kingdom	• After a parliamentary report that was commissioned to study the issue, the United Kingdom is considering the report's recommendations that include studying the spread of misinformation and requiring that current media regulations be applied to online news. • In light of the acknowledgment that Russia may have spread misinformation about Brexit, a National Security Communications Unit is charged with stopping the spread of disinformation.
United States	• As part of governmental information gathering, the U.S. government compelled representatives from Facebook, Google, and Twitter to testify after the 2016 presidential election about the spread of disinformation. Additionally, a few members of Congress have asked for an assessment of "deep fake" technology threats from the intelligence community. • A bill is being proposed that will require technology companies to keep copies of all the advertising on their site and document who paid for them. • Media literacy initiatives have been increased in California.

Source: Funke, Daniel. 2018. "A Guide to Anti-Misinformation Actions around the World." Poynter. Last updated April 2018. Accessed March 15, 2019. https://www.poynter.org/ifcn/anti-misinformation-actions/.

Media Ownership Rules

Document 5.1. FCC Changes in Broadcast Ownership Rules (2017)

On November 20, 2017, the Federal Communications Commission (FCC) updated the ownership rules that govern newspaper, television, and radio ownership. The new rules, which took effect in February 2018, eliminate some cross-ownership restrictions and relax some ownership caps. Those who oppose the changes argue that they will lead to more media consolidation, while those who support them agree with the FCC's assessment that the previous rules were hindering competition in the new digital marketplace. Selections from the FCC fact sheet—published before the official adoption of the rules—highlight some of the ownership rule changes.

Newspaper/Broadcast Cross-Ownership Rule

The current rule prohibits common ownership of a full-power broadcast station (AM, FM, or TV) and a daily newspaper if the station's contour (defined separately by type of station) completely encompasses the newspaper's city of publication and the station and newspapers are in the same relevant Nielsen market, when defined. This prohibition does not apply if the newspaper or broadcast station is failed or failing.

> Action: Eliminates Cross-Ownership Rules. The Order eliminates the antiquated rule prohibiting newspaper-broadcast cross-ownership and the rule restricting radio-television cross-ownership (discussed further below). These two rules are outdated considering the explosive growth of the number and variety of sources of local news and information in the modern marketplace.

Radio/Television Cross-Ownership Rule

The current rule prohibits an entity from owning more than two television stations and one radio station in the same market, unless the market meets certain size criteria. Specifically, if at least 10 independently owned media voices would remain in the market post-merger, an entity may own up to two television stations and four radio stations. If at least 20 independently owned media voices would remain in the market post-merger, an entity may own either: (1) two television stations and six radio stations, or (2) one television station and seven radio stations. In all instances, entities also must comply with the local radio and local television ownership limits.

Action: Eliminate the rule. Separate Local Radio Ownership and Local Television Ownership Rules continue to restrict the number of radio stations and television stations a single entity can own in a market.

Local Television Ownership Rule According to the current rule, an entity may own up to two television stations in the same market if: (1) the digital noise limited service contours (NLSCs) of the stations do not overlap; or (2) at least one of the stations is not ranked among the top-four stations in the market and at least eight independently owned television stations would remain in the market following the combination.

Action: Eliminates Eight Voices Test. The Order eliminates the requirement that at least eight independently owned television stations must remain in the market following the combination of two television stations in a market. This test was unsupported by the record or any reasoned basis. Eliminating the requirement will allow broadcasters, particularly in small and mid-sized markets, to realize the benefits of common ownership and better serve their local communities.

Action: Modifies Top-Four Prohibition. The Order also modifies the prohibition against common ownership of two top-four rated stations in a local market. While retaining the underlying prohibition, the Order adopts an option for applicants to seek case-by-case review of a transaction in order to account for circumstances in which strict application of the Top-Four Prohibition may be unwarranted.

***

Local Radio Ownership Rule

Under the current rule, the total number of radio stations that may be commonly owned in a local radio market is tiered, depending on the total number of full-power commercial and noncommercial radio stations in the market. For example, in markets with 45 or more radio stations, an entity can own no more than 8 commercial radio stations, no more than 5 of which may be in the same service (AM or FM).

> Action: No change to the rule. Adopts a narrow presumption in favor of a waiver of the rule in certain circumstances involving the New York City and Washington, DC markets.

***

Source: "FCC FACT SHEET: Review of the Commission's Broadcast Ownership Rules, Joint Sales Agreements, and Shared Services Agreements, and Comment Sought on an Incubator Program." Accessed from "Update on Ownership Rules." https://docs.fcc.gov/public/attachments/DOC-347796A2.pdf.

Considering Unreliable Information

What is broadly referred to as "fake news" has always been part of the information landscape. Included here are portions of three examples that showcase different versions of unreliable information from the past three centuries.

Document 5.2. The Great Moon Hoax (1835)

An often-cited early example of fake news, a six-part series of articles that ran in the New York Sun *now referred to as The Great Moon Hoax of 1835 chronicles the development of an incredible telescope that leads to findings of vegetation and animals on the moon. While the real astronomer Sir John Hershel was credited with these discoveries, the actual author of the series was Richard Adams Locke who claimed to have published it as satire that addressed religion and science but fooled the public nonetheless (Zielinski 2015). The following selection describes a beach that was "discovered" on the moon.*

A beach of brilliant white sand, girt with wild castellated rocks, apparently of green marble, varied at chasms, occurring every two or three hundred feet, with grotesque blocks of chalk or gypsum, and feathered and festooned at the summit with the clustering foliage of unknown trees, moved along the bright wall of our apartment until we were speechless with admiration. The water, we obtained a view of it, was nearly as blue as that of the deep ocean, and broke in large white billows upon the strand. The action of very high tides was quite manifest upon the face of the cliffs for more than a hundred miles; yet diversified as the scenery was during this and a much greater distance, we perceived no trace of animal existence, notwithstanding we could command at will a perspective or a foreground view of the whole. Mr. Holmes, indeed, pronounced some white objects of a circular form, which we saw at some distance in the interior of a cavern, to be bona fide specimens of a large cornu ammonis; but to me they appeared merely large pebbles, which had been chafed and rolled there by the tides.

Source: "The Great Moon Hoax of 1835" (text). Excerpted from the *New York Sun*, Wednesday, August 26, 1835. The Museum of Hoaxes. Accessed March 15, 2019. http://hoaxes. org/text/display/the_great_moon_hoax_of_1835_text/.

Document 5.3. Louis Seibold's Fabricated Interview with President Wilson (1920)

Louis Seibold won a Pulitzer Prize for an interview with Woodrow Wilson that was published in the New York World. *However, Wilson had suffered a stroke in October 1919 and never fully recovered before his death in 1924. Wilson's incapacity was not immediately known by the public; his wife assumed some of his duties, and some refer to this deception as "one of the greatest cover ups in the annals of the American Presidency" (Glass 2018). The "interview" Seibold published in 1920 was fabricated with the help of Wilson's wife, Edith, and presidential aide Joe Tumulty (Glass 2018). The following is an excerpt of Seibold's work.*

Later on, when the President had dictated more than twenty letters, ranging in volume from three lines to four or five hundred words, he turned his attention to the disposition of documents that had already been reduced to typed writing and affixed his signature. At a distance of six feet, I could see that the President wrote firmly and without difficulty, and left on the document before him the same copper-plate signature that can be found on more official instruments probably than were ever signed by any other man living today. He affixed his signature with meticulous care and without the slightest trace of embarrassment. Once in a while the President collected a laugh out of the documents that passed in review, Mr. Tumulty to Mrs. Wilson, Mrs. Wilson to the President. There was one telegram that caused the President to knit his brows, purse his lips and then ejaculate: "I wonder what he wants."

The telegram was from a gentleman in the West who requested the President to give him some advice concerning a matter of which the President had no information.

"I wonder what he wants, Tumulty," said the President. "I mean, I wonder what kind of advice he wants. Here is something about which he probably knows everything there is to know, but regarding which I am absolutely in the dark. Perhaps you had better wire him and ask him to stipulate exactly what kind of advice he wants. I have several kinds."

Source: Seibold, Louis. 1920. "Woodrow Wilson's Recovery." *New York World,* June 18. In Cunliffe, J. W., and Gerhard Lomer. 1923. *Writing of Today: Models of Journalistic Prose.* 3rd ed. New York: The Century Co., 105–109.

Document 5.4. Call for U.S. Government Disclosure of Video News Release Use (2005)

In 2005, congressional hearings discussed prepackaged news stories, sometimes referred to as video news releases (VNRs), or in 2005, "fake news." At issue are concerns that the viewing public may be unaware that what they are seeing is not content produced by a journalist. The following is an excerpt of Senator Frank Lautenberg's call for legislation to require that government authorship of VNRs be disclosed.

Over the past year, the American people have learned of numerous incidents in which the Administration produced fake news stories that concealed the Government's role. And we have also learned of journalists who were paid off to write favorable articles about Administration policies. The best known example of journalism for hire was the columnist and radio commentator, Armstrong Williams, who was paid to write and say favorable things about the No Child Left Behind law.

And cases of journalism for hire continue to be exposed. Just this week, we learned that the Department of Agriculture had paid a writer to produce favorable articles, which were then placed in publications. The people who read the article had no way of knowing that these news stories, so-called, were bought and paid for by the Government.

When President Bush learned about the Armstrong Williams case, he said it was wrong and he correctly said that the

Administration policies should be able to stand on their own merits without need to bribe journalists. And we commend him for that.

When it comes to another form, however, of Government propaganda, the Administration has been unwilling to shut it down. That other form of propaganda is the production and distribution of fake video news reports that conceal the Government's role. One notorious example of such prepackaged news stories are the news stories paid for by the Department of Health and Human Services that promoted the new Medicare drug law. Not only did this supposed news report contain misleading and slanted information, but it was signed off as "this is Karen Ryan reporting from Washington," but Karen Ryan was not the reporter. She is a public relations consultant that was contracted to voice over that fake news report. And the fake news segment gave no indication that it was actually a Government production.

Source: Senate Hearing 109–1091—S. 967 "Pre-Packaged News Stories." Hearing before the Committee on Commerce, Science and Transportation, U.S. Senate. May 12, 2005. https://www.govinfo.gov/content/pkg/CHRG-109shrg61937/pdf/CHRG-109shrg61937.pdf.

Current Discussions of News and Information

Document 5.5. Overview of Social Media Use by Russian Operatives (2018)

A contemporary turning point in discussions of misinformation and disinformation campaigns during the twenty-first century was the discovery that Russia distributed disinformation via American social media. In a summary titled "Exposing Russia's Efforts to Sow Discord Online: The Internet Research Agency and Advertisements," the U.S. House of Representatives Permanent Select Committee on Intelligence provided an overview of what is known about the use of social media by Russian operatives who were attempting to disrupt civic life in the United States. Linked online from the published summary are examples of tweets, advertisements, and other materials that were disseminated on social media platforms. The following are excerpts from the committee's overview.

On February 16, 2018 Special Counsel Robert S. Mueller III indicted 13 Russian individuals and three Russian organizations for engaging in operations to interfere with U.S. political and electoral processes, including the 2016 presidential election. This was a significant step forward in exposing a surreptitious social media campaign and holding accountable those responsible for this attack. The indictment spells out in exhaustive detail the breadth and systematic nature of this conspiracy, dating back to 2014, as well as the multiple ways in which Russian actors misused online platforms to carry out their clandestine operations.

Throughout the indictment, Mueller lays out important facts about the activities of the Internet Research Agency (IRA)—the notorious Russian "troll" farm—and its operatives:

"Defendants, posing as U.S. persons and creating false U.S. personas, operated social media pages and groups designed to attract U.S. audiences. These groups and pages, which addressed divisive U.S. political and social issues, falsely claimed to be controlled by U.S. activists when, in fact, they were controlled by Defendants. Defendants also used the stolen identities of real U.S. persons to post on ORGANIZATION-controlled social media accounts. Over time, these social media accounts became Defendants' means to reach significant numbers of Americans for purposes of interfering with the U.S. political system, including the presidential election of 2016."

***

Additionally, in their October 2016 joint attribution statement, the Department of Homeland Security and the Office of the Director of National Intelligence laid out the Intelligence Community's assessment that senior Russian government officials had directed a hacking-and-dumping campaign to interfere in the November 2016 U.S. election. In its subsequent Intelligence Community Assessment (ICA) in January 2017, the Intelligence Community further documented Moscow's interference in our election and its efforts to assist Donald Trump's campaign and harm Hillary Clinton's.

***

The House Intelligence Committee Minority has worked to expose the Kremlin's exploitation of social media networks since the ICA was first published, highlighting this issue for the American public during an open hearing with social media companies in November 2017. The Committee Minority also released a list of Twitter accounts associated with the Internet Research Agency and a representative sampling of Facebook ads paid for by the group.

Throughout our investigation, the Committee Minority has sought to make available to the public advertisements, accounts and information related to the IRA because of our strong belief that sunlight is the best disinfectant against any future attempts to weaken our democracy or interfere in our free and fair elections process. Moreover, Congress does not have the technical expertise to fully analyze this data—that lies in outside groups such as news publications and academic researchers. We hope that the publication of these materials will facilitate this important work.

Facebook data:

As part of the Committee's open hearing with social media companies in November 2017, the Minority used a number of advertisements as exhibits, and made others available as part of a small representative sampling. During the hearing, Committee Members noted the breadth of activity by the IRA on Facebook:

- 3,393 advertisements purchased (a total 3,519 advertisements total were released after more were identified by the company);
- More than 11.4 million American users exposed to those advertisements;
- 470 IRA-created Facebook pages;
- 80,000 pieces of organic content created by those pages; and
- Exposure of organic content to more than 126 million Americans.

Twitter data:

During the Committee's November 2017 open hearing, the Minority introduced into the record 2,752 Twitter accounts that Twitter identified as connected to the Internet Research Agency (IRA), the Kremlin-linked "troll farm." These accounts were designed to impersonate U.S. news entities, political parties, and groups focused on social and political issues. During the hearing, the Minority also revealed a selection of Twitter advertisements paid for by Russian news outlet RT, which the January 2017 Intelligence Community Assessment labeled as "the Kremlin's principal international propaganda outlet."

According to data provided to the Committee by Twitter, a snapshot of relevant Twitter activity in the period between September 1 and November 15, 2016 reveals:

- More than 36,000 Russian-linked bot accounts tweeted about the U.S. election
- Approximately 288 million impressions of Russian bot tweets; and
- More than 130,000 tweets by accounts linked to the IRA.

Source: U.S. House of Representatives Permanent Select Committee on Intelligence. "Exposing Russia's Efforts to Sow Discord Online: The Internet Research Agency and Advertisements." Accessed January 11, 2019. https://intelligence.house .gov/social-media-content/.

Document 5.6. News Media Alliance's David Chavern's Statement on Technology Companies and Journalism (2018)

The U.S. government has also engaged in a series of investigations that look at the tremendous reach of social media and technology platforms in light of their impact on journalism and their role in advancing, monitoring, and removing content on their platforms. During one judiciary hearing, David Chavern, the CEO and president of the News Media Alliance, a nonprofit trade group that represents news organizations, described how he believes the technology companies' practices impact journalism. A portion of his statement follows.

Too often in today's information-driven environment, news is included in the broad term of digital content. It is actually much more important than that. While low-quality entertainment or posts by your friends might be disappointing, inaccurate information about the world can be immediately destructive. Civil society depends on the availability of real, accurate news.

The internet represents an extraordinary opportunity for broader understanding and education. We have never been more interconnected or had easier access to information or quicker communication. However, as currently structured, the digital ecosystem gives tremendous viewpoint control and economic power to a very small number of companies. That control and power must come with new responsibilities.

Historically, newspapers controlled the distribution of their product. They invested in the journalism and then printed it in a form that could literally be handed to their readers directly. No other party decided who got access to the information or on what terms. The distribution of online news is now dominated by the major technology platforms. They decide what news is delivered and to whom, and they control the economics of digital publishing. The First Amendment prohibits the government from regulating the press, but it does not prohibit Facebook and Google from acting as de facto regulators of the news business.

Neither Google nor Facebook are or have ever been neutral pipes. To the contrary, their businesses depend on their ability to make nuanced decisions through sophisticated algorithms about how and when content is delivered. The term algorithm itself makes these decisions seem scientific and neutral. The fact is that, while their decision process may be highly automated, both companies make extensive editorial decisions about relevance, newsworthiness, and other criteria.

The business models of Facebook and Google are complex and varied. However, we do know that they are both immense advertising platforms that sell people's time and attention. Their secret algorithms, and they are secret, are used to cultivate that time and attention, and we have seen many examples of the types of content favored by these systems, namely clickbait and anything that can generate outrage, disgust, passion.

The systems also favor giving users information very similar to what they had previously consumed, thereby generating intense filter bubbles undermining common understanding of issues and challenges.

All of these things are antithetical, actually, to a healthy news business and a healthy democracy. Good journalism is factual, verified, and takes into account multiple points of view. It takes a lot of time and investment. Most particularly, it requires someone to take responsibility for what is published.

Whether or not one agrees with a particular piece of journalism, my members at least put their names on the product and stand behind it. Readers know where to send their complaints. The same cannot be said about the sea of bad information that is delivered by platforms in paid priority over my members' quality information.

Source: Serial No. 115–156. "Filtering Practices of Social Media Platforms." Hearing before the Committee on the Judiciary House of Representatives. April 26, 2018. https://www.govinfo.gov/app/details/CHRG-115hhrg32930/CHRG-115hhrg32930.

Document 5.7. Judiciary Hearing on Social Media and Content Filtering Practices (2018)

On July 17, 2018, Monika Bickert, the head of global policy management at Facebook; Juniper Downs, the global head of public policy and government relations at YouTube; and Nick Pickles, the senior strategist of public policy at Twitter, gave testimony in a judiciary hearing titled "Facebook, Google and Twitter: Examining the Content Filtering Practices of Social Media Giants." The following are excerpts from the hearing.

From Chairman Bob Goodlatte's opening statement: Indeed, given the scale of Facebook and other social media platforms, a large portion of their content filtering is performed by algorithms without the need of human assistance. And Facebook is largely free to moderate content on its platform as it sees fit. This is in part because, over 20 years ago, Congress exempted online platforms from liability for harms occurring over their services.

In 1996, the internet was just taking shape. Congress intended to protect it to spur its growth. It worked because the vibrant internet of today is no doubt a result of Congress' foresight in part.

But the internet of today is almost nothing like the internet of 1996. Today we see that the most successful ideas have blossomed into some of the largest companies on Earth. These companies dominate their markets, and perhaps rightfully so, given the quality of their products.

However, this begs another question. Are these companies using their market power to push the envelope on filtering decisions to favor the content the companies prefer. Congress must evaluate our laws to ensure that they are achieving their intended purpose. The online environment is becoming more polarized, not less. And there are concerns that discourse is being squelched, not facilitated.

From Representative Jamie Raskin's opening statement: It might instead be helpful to know what these companies are doing to weed out the prevalence of false information, fake news spread by hostile foreign powers and by others in order to poison our political discourse and divide our people. It might also be useful to know how social media companies enforce community standards that target racist, bigoted, or other inappropriate content and whether their enforcement practices need more refinement and focus.

From Monika Bickert's opening statement, explaining steps Facebook is taking in addressing content on their platform: First, we recently published a new version of our community standards, which includes the details of how our reviewers, our content reviewers, apply our policies governing what is and what is not allowed on Facebook. We've also launched an appeals process to enable people to contest our content decisions. We believe this will also enhance the quality of our automated filtering.

We have engaged former Senator Jon Kyl to look at the issue of potential bias against conservative voices. Laura Murphy, a national civil liberties and civil rights leader, is also getting feedback directly from civil rights groups about bias and related topics.

As part of Facebook's broader efforts to ensure that time on our platform is well spent, we're also taking steps to reduce the spread of false news. False news is an issue that negatively impacts the quality of discourse on both right and left, and we are committed to reducing it. We are working to prioritize news that is trustworthy, informative, and locally relevant. We are partnering with third-party fact-checking organizations to limit the distribution of stories that have been flagged as misleading, sensational, or spammy.

From Juniper Downs's opening statement in her discussion of Google Search: We strive to make information from the web available to all of our users, but not all speech is protected. Once we are in notice of content that may violate local law, we evaluate it and block it for the relevant jurisdictions. For many issues, such as defamation or hate speech, our legal obligations may vary as different jurisdictions deal with these complex issues differently. In the case of all legal removals, we share information about government requests for removal in our transparency report.

Where we've developed our own content policies, we enforce them in a politically neutral way. Giving preference to content of one political ideology over another would fundamentally conflict with our goal of providing services that work for everyone. Search aims to provide all users with useful and relevant results based on the text of their query.

From Nick Pickles's opening statement in his discussion of Twitter: We strive to protect expression, including views that some of our users may find objectionable or with which they vehemently disagree. We do not believe that censorship will solve societal challenges, nor that removing content will resolve disagreements. Threats of violence, abuse of conduct, and harassment are an attack on free expression intended to silence the voice of others, thereby robbing Twitter of valuable perspectives and threaten the free expression that we seek to foster.

Accordingly, the Twitter rules prohibit this and other types of behavior on our platform. Our rules are not based on ideology or particular sets of beliefs. Instead, the Twitter rules are based on behavior. Accounts that violate our rules can be subject to a range of enforcement actions, including temporary and, in some cases, permanent suspension. We are increasing the transparency of these decisions so that users better understand our rules and why we are taking action.

This hearing addressed a range of issues. In this section of testimony, the technology company representatives are being asked about Alex Jones and his use of social media to advance his conspiracy theories. After this hearing, in the summer of 2018, Jones's InfoWars was removed from Facebook and YouTube. However, his InfoWars videos are still able to be located on the platforms (Breland 2019).

Mr. DEUTCH. I represent Parkland, Florida, and in this discussion of social media the first thing that comes to mind to me is the savage attacks on the student survivors of Stoneman Douglas. One of the most virulent strains of these attacks was that the students didn't survive a school shooting, that they were crisis actors, that they were planted by some mysterious cabal to finally get Congress to do something about gun violence. And in the weeks after the shooting, Alex Jones' YouTube channel posted a video that was seen by 2.3 million subscribers alleging that these were merely—that these were actors and not real students who had experienced the most horrific thing anybody one could possibly imagine. The video violated You-Tube's rule against bullying, and it was removed. An article posted to Slate.com describes this as a strike against the channel. Ms. Downs, how many strikes does a channel get?

Ms. DOWNS. Typically, a channel gets three strikes, and then we terminate the channel.

Mr. DEUTCH. So the reason I ask is, Alex Jones obviously is one of the conspiracy theorists whose brand is bullying. He wants similar attacks against the families whose 6- and 7-year-old kids were slaughtered at Sandy Hook, and he's not the only one. Truthers have spread these lies claiming that Sandy Hook never happened at all. A Slate article references a study by Jonathan Albright, director of the Tow Center for Digital Journalism at Columbia who found 9,000 videos on You-Tube with titles that are—and I quote, a mixture of shocking vile and promotional themes that include rape game jokes, shock reality, social experiments, celebrity pedophilia, false flag rants, and terror-related conspiracy theories dating back to the Oklahoma City attacks in 1995. Ms. Downs, does Google think that this is a problem, and what is the solution that you're coming up with to address it?

Ms. DOWNS. Thank you for the question. So, as you noted, when Alex Jones posted the video you described saying that the survivors at the Parkland massacre were crisis actors, that violated other harassment policy. We have a specific policy that says if you say a well-documented violent attack

didn't happen and you use the name or image of
survivors or victims of that attack, that is a malicious attack, and it violates our policy. In terms
of conspiracy theory content generally, our goal
is to promote authoritative content to our users.
So we have two principles that guide the way
here. That's the first one, as we want to provide
users with authoritative, trustworthy and—

Mr. DEUTCH. I'm sorry to cut you off. I only have a min-
ute and a half, and I don't really need to hear
what you're trying to provide. I want to know
how you're dealing with all these conspiracy
theorists on your platform.

Ms. DOWNS. So the first way is by demoting low-quality content and promoting more authoritative content.
And the second is by providing more transparency for users. So we're introducing boxes that
provide factual information at the top of results
that have shown themselves to turn up a lot
of information that is counterfactual, such as
searching for the Earth is flat on YouTube, where
you see a lot of videos claiming—

Mr. DEUTCH. Okay. Your response is to put a box saying,
"Nope, the Earth is not flat"?

Ms. DOWNS. Correct.

Mr. DEUTCH. I have a question, Ms. Bickert, for you. You
recently decided not to ban Infowars. Can you
explain that decision? And do you use a strikes
model like YouTube?

Ms. BICKERT. Congressman, we do use a strikes model.
What that means is, if a page or a profile or a
group is posting content and some of that violates our policies, we always remove the violating post at a certain point, and it depends—it

depends on the nature of the content that is violating our policies. At a certain point, we would also remove the page or the profile or the group at issue.

Mr. DEUTCH. So the question is, how many strikes does a conspiracy theorist who attacks grieving parents and student survivors of mass shootings get? How many strikes are they entitled to before they can no longer post those kinds of horrific attacks?

Ms. BICKERT. I want to be very clear that allegations that survivors of a tragedy like Parkland are crisis actors, that violates our policy and we removed that content. And we would remove and continue to remove any violations from the Infowars page. If they posted sufficient content that it violated our threshold, the page would come down. That threshold varies depending on the severity of different types of violations.

Source: Serial No. 115–164. "Facebook, Google and Twitter: Examining the Content Filtering Practices of Social Media Giants." Hearing before the Committee on the Judiciary House of Representatives. July 17, 2018. https://www.govinfo.gov/app/details/CHRG-115hhrg33418/CHRG-115hhrg33418.

Addressing "Deepfake" Videos

Document 5.8. Excerpts of the Malicious Deep Fake Prohibition Act of 2018

State and government law makers are also looking into the potential problem of "deepfake" videos, considering what legislation might be effective in preventing the destructive use of these videos. Laws or policies that strive to criminalize deepfake videos or their spread are controversial and may not garner support because they need to appropriately target the creators and platform distributors in ways that are fair and do not hamper free speech (Waddell 2019). In December 2018, Senator Ben Sasse introduced a bill titled the Malicious Deep Fake Prohibition Act of 2018, legislation he intends to reintroduce in 2019 (Waddell 2019). The bill proposes that creators of deepfake videos with illegal intentions or those who knowingly distribute deepfake videos are subject to fines or imprisonment.

Offense.—

It shall be unlawful to, using any means or facility of interstate or foreign commerce—

"(1) create, with the intent to distribute, a deep fake with the intent that the distribution of the deep fake would facilitate criminal or tortious conduct under Federal, State, local, or Tribal law; or

"(2) distribute an audiovisual record with—

"(A) actual knowledge that the audiovisual record is a deep fake; and

"(B) the intent that the distribution of the audiovisual record would facilitate criminal or tortious conduct under Federal, State, local, or Tribal law.

Penalty.—

Any person who violates subsection (b) shall be—

"(1) fined under this title, imprisoned for not more than 2 years, or both; or

"(2) fined under this title, imprisoned for not more than 10 years, or both, in the case of a violation in which the creation, reproduction, or distribution of the deep fake could be reasonably expected to—

"(A) affect the conduct of any administrative, legislative, or judicial proceeding of a Federal,

State, local, or Tribal government agency, including the administration of an election or the conduct of foreign relations; or

"(B) facilitate violence.

Source: S3805: Malicious Deep Fake Prohibition Act of 2018. Introduced December 21, 2018. https://www.govinfo.gov/app/details/BILLS-115s3805is/summary.

Organizational Initiatives

First Draft News is a leading organization working toward addressing issues of trust and problematic information. First Draft's Claire Wardle (2017) developed a typology to visualize her suggestion that "there are seven distinct types of problematic content that sit within our information ecosystem. They sit on a scale, one that loosely measures the intent to deceive." This typology is seen in Figure 5.6 "7 Types of Mis- and Disinformation." Figure 5.7, "Misinformation Matrix," also created by Wardle, breaks down potential motivations for advancing each type of problematic information. These visuals may help people make sense of the complexity of information they encounter that may not be reliable.

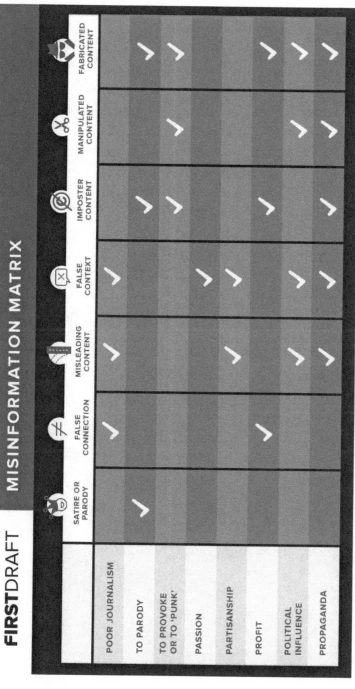

Figure 5.6 7 Types of Mis- and Disinformation

Source: Claire Wardle. First Draft at firstdraftnews.org. Used with permission.

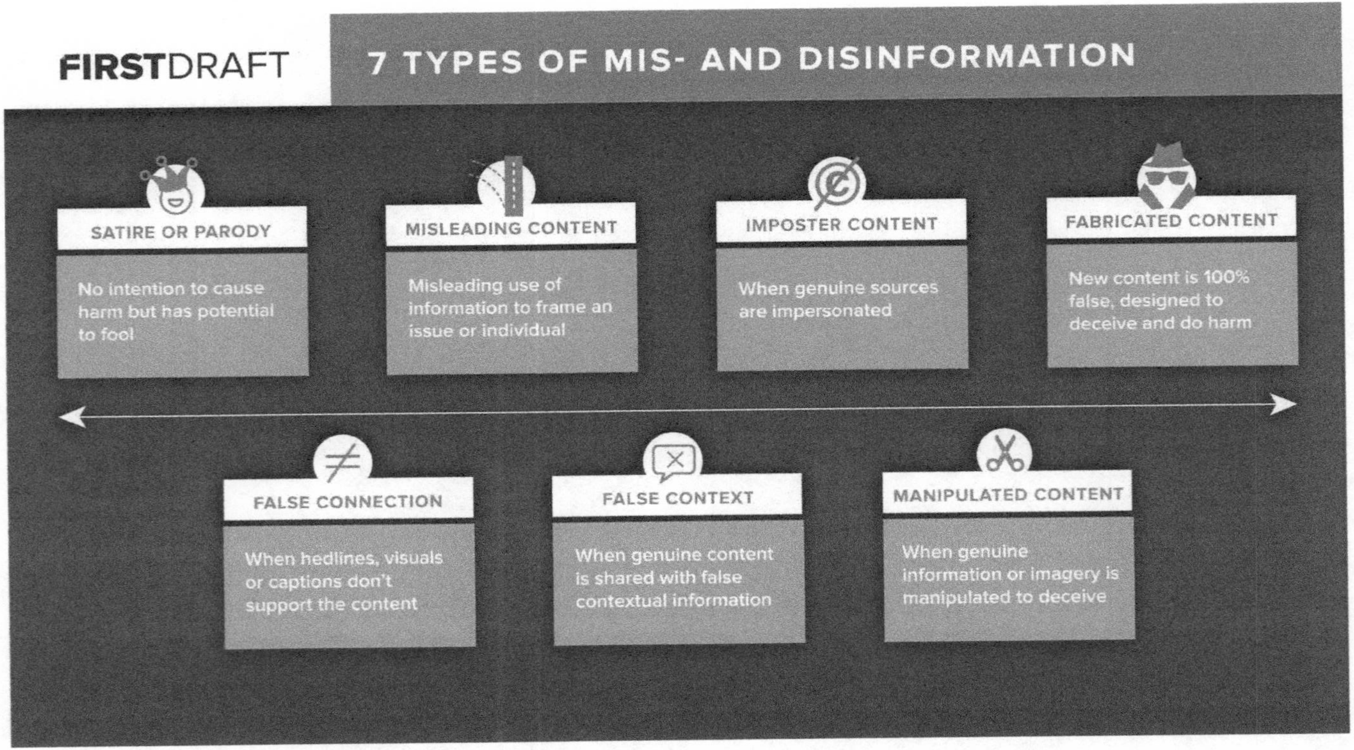

FIRSTDRAFT   **7 TYPES OF MIS- AND DISINFORMATION**

SATIRE OR PARODY
No intention to cause harm but has potential to fool

MISLEADING CONTENT
Misleading use of information to frame an issue or individual

IMPOSTER CONTENT
When genuine sources are impersonated

FABRICATED CONTENT
New content is 100% false, designed to deceive and do harm

FALSE CONNECTION
When headlines, visuals or captions don't support the content

FALSE CONTEXT
When genuine content is shared with false contextual information

MANIPULATED CONTENT
When genuine information or imagery is manipulated to deceive

Figure 5.7 Misinformation Matrix
Source: Claire Wardle. First Draft at firstdraftnews.org. Used with permission.

Document 5.9. Recommendations from the Knight Commission on Trust, Media and Democracy (2019)

The Knight Commission on Trust, Media and Democracy's report titled Crisis in Democracy: Reviewing Trust in America *(2019) summarizes a year of research whereby a "nonpartisan commission of 27 leaders in government, media, business, non-profits, education and the arts examined the collapse in trust in the democratic institutions of the media, journalism and the information ecosystem, and developed new thinking and solutions around rebuilding trust." The findings produced ten recommendations in categories of journalism, technology, and citizenship that speak to a number of identified values.*

Recommendations:

JOURNALISM VALUES: The Commission calls for all news media to rededicate themselves to the ideals of the profession: to provide citizens with the information they need to be free and self governing, to hold the powerful accountable, and to pursue the truth.

1. Practice radical transparency. The media should develop industrywide, voluntary standards on how to disclose the ways they collect, report and disseminate the news. The Commission calls for a convening of news leaders across competitive boundaries to work together to develop and adopt common standards and best practices that promote transparency. These include: labeling news, opinion and fact-based commentary; best practices on corrections, fact-checking, anonymous sources and tracking disinformation; and avoiding advertising formats that blur the line between content and commerce. They should also develop strategies to better engage with the public and reflect the interests of their communities.

2. Expand financial support for news. There are some promising new models for funding for-profit journalism. But

market solutions alone are insufficient to provide the quality of journalism that citizens need and deserve, especially news about local communities. Philanthropy should increase its support for journalism in the public interest. The Commission focuses on the development of new nonprofit models to achieve sustainability and to serve journalistic missions. It calls for the creation of one or more national venture philanthropy entities dedicated to funding new and existing nonprofit organizations across the country.

3. Use technology to combat disinformation. To remain relevant, the media must learn to use advanced technology in all aspects of their businesses. Some of the larger entities are leading this effort, but many more need to catch up. In particular, the Commission urges media and technology companies to improve technologies to determine and then address disinformation. The media should also expose their audiences to diverse viewpoints, understanding the tendency of new media environments to create and amplify "filter bubbles" in which people tend to view only material that already supports their opinions.

4. Diversify news organizations. News organizations should adopt recruitment, hiring and retention practices that increase diversity of staff, and even of owners. Newsrooms should develop mentoring and training programs that can help enlist, retain and promote more women and journalists of color at all levels. And they need to include other underrepresented groups, such as underrepresented geographical and political groups, so that the reporting they produce reflects the entire community. The Commission also challenges all news organizations to develop and publish metrics for hiring and employment in newsrooms.

TECHNOLOGY VALUES: The internet has vastly expanded the ability to access information and communicate with others around the world. Yet this new technology has also made people vulnerable to abuse of personal data, disinformation, hate speech, harassment, trolling, foreign manipulation and more. The Commission affirms the importance of free expression, an open internet and inclusion, understanding that there are no quick solutions, or single-shot inoculations against future threats to American democracy. But leaders and new media entities must act responsibly and serve democratic principles.

5. Online services must take responsibility for protecting their users. In other areas of American life, professionals and businesses such as doctors and accountants that have access to personal data about customers commonly have a "fiduciary duty" to protect their interests. To complement privacy legislation and enforcement, the Commission supports proposals that technology companies and online services become "information fiduciaries." As fiduciaries they must act in a trustworthy manner by ensuring security of user data, keeping it confidential and not using it for their own benefit in ways that compromise the interests of the user.

6. Online services should track and disclose sources of information. Online platforms should develop technology and standards to disclose to their users where the information they see comes from—identifying the author and publisher of articles, for example. In addition, the Commission encourages the development of an automated tracking system that would enable analysis on the original source of a story, as well as how it spread to the public. The Commission also recommends that the sponsors of all digital advertising be clearly identified. This requirement should apply particularly to "native advertising," which looks similar to independently produced editorial content but is paid for by a third party. Finally, the Commission recommends disclosure of information regarding the targeting of political ads intended to affect attitudes toward a political issue.

7. Empower people to make technology work for them. The Commission recommends that researchers develop ways to measure healthy dialogue online. These include creating metrics to help analyze balanced, democratic discourse. It recommends that internet platforms provide people with information about how algorithms work that determine which information they see, as well as opportunities to customize them. It also recommends enabling people to move their data from one social network to another. And it proposes a multi-stakeholder forum for technology, journalism and consumer interests to work out solutions to a variety of issues that arise in this space.

CITIZENSHIP VALUES: Citizens need knowledge as well as the opportunity and a sense of responsibility to participate fully in public debate and other democratic activities. Yet many lack the basic skills to do so. Every citizen should have a basic understanding of the Constitution and our system of government. Citizens also need opportunities to engage in productive dialogue about local civic matters with others who hold opposing political viewpoints.

8. Provide students of all ages with basic civic education and the skills to navigate online safely and responsibly. Too many Americans lack an understanding of basic elements of their government and governing principles. Before they graduate from high school, all students should be able to pass the U.S. citizenship exam or a civic knowledge test. Furthermore, individuals who lack digital literacy skills are less able to assess the reliability of information sources in order to tell fact from fiction. They are easier to harass, mislead or defraud online. They can find it harder to gain knowledge, pursue education or careers, stay healthy, protect their rights and help their communities improve.

State and local educational authorities need a plan to provide their citizens with the skills to access, analyze, evaluate, create and act on digital information based on new standards for civic and 21st century literacies. Prior to participating in social media, every child should have a basic understanding of digital media and how to use them safely. Before reaching the legal voting age of 18, individuals should be digitally as well as civically literate, able to find and use information necessary to be knowledgeable voters. These goals should apply to everyone, no matter their income, where they live or what their background.

9. Reach across political divides. The Commission recommends that communities develop programs hosted by trusted local institutions to convene dialogue among citizens. These exchanges should address important questions ranging from local issues to relevant constitutional questions. Public libraries are one obvious place for such discussions. The Commission also recommends the development of public awareness campaigns to encourage people to participate in civic institutions.

10. Encourage a commitment to a year of national service. As politics has become increasingly tribalized, citizens have lost a shared American narrative and a sense of citizenship. To address this, the time has come to revitalize efforts to encourage a year of voluntary national service. The Commission identifies four primary areas in which national service could help renew trust in our democratic institutions and particularly in the press: general civic service; teaching traditional and digital literacy; engaging in public service journalism, particularly at the local level; and serving in libraries. Efforts can be inspired by existing programs, such as the Service Year Alliance, AmeriCorps and Report for America.

Source: Knight Commission on Trust, Media and Democracy. 2019. *Crisis in Democracy: Renewing Trust in America.* February. Washington, DC: The Aspen Institute. Used with permission.

Bibliography

Breland, Ali. 2019. "Despite Ban Infowars Conspiracy Videos Are Easy to Find on Facebook and YouTube." *Mother Jones*, January 23. https://www.motherjones.com/politics/2019/01/alex-jones-facebook-youtube-ban/.

Glass, Andrew. 2018. "Woodrow Wilson Suffers Debilitating Stroke, October 2, 1919." Politico, October 2. https://www.politico.com/story/2018/10/02/this-day-in-politics-oct-2-1919-853186.

Matsa, Katerina E., and Elisa Shearer. 2018. "News across Social Media Platforms 2018." Pew Research Center, September 10. https://www.journalism.org/2018/09/10/news-use-across-social-media-platforms-2018/.

Media Insight Project. 2018. *Americans and the News Media: What They Do—and Don't—Understand about Each Other.* The American Press Institute and the Associated Press-NORC Center for Public Affairs Research, June 11. Accessed March 1, 2019. https://www.americanpressinstitute.org/publications/reports/survey-research/americans-and-the-news-media/.

Pew Research Center for U.S. Politics and Policy. 2008. "Key News Audiences Now Blend Online and Traditional Sources." Pew Research Center, August 17. http://www.people-press.org/2008/08/17/key-news-audiences-now-blend-online-and-traditional-sources/.

Waddell, Kaveh. 2019. "Lawmakers Plunge into 'Deepfake' War." Axios, January 31. https://www.axios.com/deepfake-laws-fb5de200-1bfe-4aaf-9c93-19c0ba16d744.html.

Wardle, Claire. 2017. "Fake News. It's Complicated." First Draft, February 16. https://firstdraftnews.org/fake-news-complicated/.

Zielinski, Sarah. 2015. "The Great Moon Hoax Was Simply a Sign of Its Time." Smithsonian.com, July 2. https://www.smithsonianmag.com/smithsonian-institution/great-moon-hoax-was-simply-sign-its-time-180955761/.

We the People *of the*

insure domestic Tranquility, provide for the common defence, p
and our Posterity, do ordain and establish this Constitution for

THE FIRST
AMENDMENT

Congress shall ma
respecting an esta
religion, or prohib
exercise thereof; o
the freedom of spe
or of the pre
or the right of the
peaceably to assen
petition the Gover
redress of grievanc

Introduction

This chapter provides lists of additional resources for those wishing to explore and learn more about specific topics related to those discussed in this book. The chapter begins with brief annotations of books and articles that further address areas of journalism, media, and "fake news" in the United States. The books and articles are organized into two sections. The first section compiles sources that address historical content, while the second section contains a list of sources that address more contemporary topics. A list of relevant research and nonprofit organizations follows; their useful websites present information on current professional initiatives and contemporary research inquiries. Many of these organizations post reports, articles, insightful blogs, relevant links, and other resources. A list of scholarly journals that publish recent research on topics related to journalism and news audiences follows. This chapter then shares additional web resources of possible interest, including digital news sites, TED talks, and podcasts. A descriptive list of tools and organizations to help users evaluate information is supplied. Finally, the chapter concludes with two short reference lists—one of mainstream legacy news organizations that

---

Many news literacy and media literacy programs empower consumers to critically evaluate information. Here, a teacher with the Newseum's education department gives a class on "fighting fake news" to high school students in Washington, DC. (Bill O'Leary/The Washington Post via Getty Images)

are popular in the United States and the other of commonly used news agencies in the country.

Books and Articles/Historical Resources

Daly, Christopher. 2012. *Covering America: A Narrative History of a Nation's Journalism.* Amherst: University of Massachusetts Press.

>In a narrative style, Daly tells the story of the development of journalism from the early days of American history through the digital era. He divides journalism history into five periods: the politicization of news, the commercialization of news, the professionalization of news, the conglomeration of news, and the digitization of news. Though a scholarly book, this is a readable account that includes many interesting anecdotes.

Doss, Erika, ed. 2001. *Looking at Life Magazine.* Washington, DC: Smithsonian Institution Press.

>Arguing *Life* magazine "shaped and influenced ideas about class, ethnicity, gender and race in America, and throughout the world," this edited volume explores the popular publication through a series of essays written by scholars. Essays explore such topics as *Life*'s readership, its representations of men and women, its discussion of the civil rights movement, and its coverage of the atomic age.

Douglas, Susan. 2004. *Listening In: Radio and the American Imagination.* Minneapolis: University of Minnesota Press.

>By providing a cultural history of radio, Douglas describes how radio became part of American life. Specific chapters address the development of broadcast journalism and talk radio, and her discussion of different modes of listening provides a template for thinking about both radio programming and podcasting in the twenty-first century.

Halberstam, David. 1979. *The Powers That Be.* Champaign: University of Illinois Press.

In this now classic work, journalist and author David Halberstam details the history of print and electronic media while pointing out the powerful forces that shaped their development and, in turn, resulted in media outlets that shaped public opinion. This lengthy book contains detailed accounts of such news companies as the *Los Angeles Times*, CBS, and *Time* magazine.

Hillstrom, Laurie C. 2010. *Defining Moments: The Muckrakers and the Progressive Era.* Detroit, MI: Omnigraphics, Inc.

Hillstrom traces the history of the muckraker movement in journalism and explains how it parallels aspects of the Progressive Era of U.S. history. The book details ways muckrakers used investigative journalism to report on and expose corruption and business practices that led to significant problems in the country such as poor and unsafe working conditions, poverty and homelessness, and political corruption. Connections are made between the muckraking tradition and current investigative journalism. Included in this text are a series of biographies of key figures and excerpts from primary sources that serve as examples of the content summarized and discussed.

McMillian, John. 2011. *Smoking Typewriters: The Sixties Underground Press and the Rise of Alternative Media in America.* New York: Oxford University Press.

In this book, McMillian contextualizes the development of the underground press in the culture and counterculture of the 1960s. In doing so, he discusses key underground press leaders, writers, and newspapers, detailing events and decisions that informed this radical press movement and the wider culture's reaction to it. The final sections of the book reflect on contemporary trends and discuss the alternative press in light of the failing print industry and the rise of the internet.

Miller, Sally M., ed. 1987. *The Ethnic Press in the United States: A Historical Analysis and Handbook.* Westport, CT: Greenwood Press.
This book presents twenty-seven essays that address various aspects of different ethnic presses that were in operation in the United States as newspapers became integrated into the culture. The compilation of essays is representative of geographically diverse immigrant populations' newspapers. Examples include essays on the Russian press, the Arabic-language press, the German press, the Mexican American press, and the Chinese American Press.

Mott, Frank L. 1962. *American Journalism: A History, 1690–1960.* New York: The Macmillan Company.
Mott provides a thorough account of American journalism history. The book includes copies of primary sources that illustrate how news evolved. Mott traces the development of the newspaper and the beginnings of radio and television, providing histories of key figures and movements that contributed to the development of American news reporting and its reception.

Peterson, Theodore. 1964. *Magazines in the Twentieth Century.* 2nd ed. Urbana: University of Illinois Press.
Peterson describes how the magazine industry struggled, survived, and innovated during the twentieth century. This scholarly publication presents numerous facts and figures helpful to those looking to understand the specifics of the history of the magazine industry during the first part of the twentieth century.

Ponce de Leon, Charles. 2015. *That's the Way It Is: A History of Television News in America.* Chicago: University of Chicago Press.

This well-researched book is about the history of television news, beginning in the late 1940s as the genre began to establish itself and ending in the twenty-first century when many television news stations are producing content for their websites. Network news, cable news, public television news, and satirical news are discussed in the shifting landscape of news production. By summarizing the trajectory of newscast choices made to serve the public and to achieve high ratings, Ponce de Leon traces the evolving tensions present in the news business through the years.

Roberts, Gene, and Hank Klibanoff. 2006. *The Race Beat: The Press, the Civil Rights Struggle, and the Awakening of a Nation.* New York: Alfred Knopf.

Demonstrating the impact reporting can have on public opinion and action, this book describes the way the press came to report on issues of racial segregation and the civil rights movement. After providing background about the Negro press, Roberts and Klibanoff detail the ways black and white reporters and news organizations moved into covering racial injustice after the end of World War II through the civil rights movement, showing how the press played a role in capturing national support for better equality.

Schudson, Michael. 1978. *Discovering the News: A Social History of Newspapers.* New York: Basic Books.

Schudson provides a history of newspapers that is anchored in the social and cultural context of the period. He additionally discusses the evolution of journalistic reporting styles, particularly the idea of objectivity.

Shapiro, Bruce, ed. 2003. *Shaking the Foundations: 20 Years of Investigative Journalism in America.* New York: Thunder's Mouth Press.

Shapiro compiles a sample of original investigative journalism reports from 1795 to the end of the twentieth century, highlighting aspects of the breadth and depth of this reporting over the years with brief annotations. Shapiro's selection begins with Benjamin Franking Bache's 1795 account of President George Washington's use of public money for personal use and ends with a story by William Greider published in 1993 on the devastating toy factory fire that killed and injured hundreds in Bangkok. The thirty-eight selections include a diverse set of stories that focus on disastrous conditions, government practices, and business dealings.

Stephens, Mitchell. 1998. *A History of News: From the Drum to the Satellite*. New York: Viking Penguin, Inc.

In his book, Stephens provides a synthesized history of news, beginning with the spoken word and ending with the use of technology in newsgathering and news production that was being used at the end of the twentieth century. The book is organized by sections—spoken news, written news, printed news, newspapers, reporting, and electronic news. Each section consists of several chapters that explore elements of the human need for, and interest in, news. Stephens argues a "long view of news" provides the context needed to understand both journalism's history and contemporary issues. Stephens's interdisciplinary discussion of this topic is informed by philosophy, technological developments, cultural studies, and primary documents. Multiple, diverse examples from many countries are used to both explore and contextualize how news and information have been produced, disseminated, and consumed in the United States and throughout the world.

Wagman, Robert J. 1991. *The First Amendment Book*. New York: Pharos Books.

This book overviews the history of the First Amendment. It clearly explains the legal terms, court cases, and societal debates that have informed the First Amendment's application, interpretation, and practice over the first two hundred years since the passage of the Bill of Rights in 1791.

Whitt, Jan. 2008. *Women in American Journalism: A New History*. Urbana: University of Illinois Press.
Whitt tells the story of many talented female journalists overlooked in a journalism history that often centers on the accomplishments of their male counterparts. In doing so, she highlights aspects of how female journalists were treated as writers while also spotlighting the work of those who completed groundbreaking investigative work, wrote for society pages, took a literary approach to reporting, and contributed to alternative publications.

Winfield, Betty H., ed. 2008. *Journalism 1908: Birth of a Profession*. Columbia: University of Missouri Press.
Anchoring their discussions in the year 1908, this collection of essays from media scholars explores a turning point in journalism history from a variety of perspectives. Essays include discussions of advertising, sports reporting, women and journalism, and the immigrant press.

Books and Articles/Contemporary History and Topics

Abramson, Jill. 2019. *Merchants of Truth: The Business of News and the Fight for Facts*. New York: Simon and Shuster.
Former *New York Times* executive editor Jill Abramson examines trajectories of the *New York Times*, the *Washington Post*, BuzzFeed, and Vice Media as they navigate the challenging journalism landscape of the twenty-first century. Abramson details the struggles, and successes, of the four news companies as a way of telling the story of how news reporting has been disrupted by the emergence of free internet content. Her inside view and professional knowledge complement her research.

Allan, Stuart. 2006. *Online News: Journalism and the Internet.* Maidenhead, England: Open University Press.
In this examination of the evolution of journalism as a result of the internet, Allan examines the rise of blogs, participatory journalism, citizen engagement, and digital news websites. Examples of reporting from the terrorist attacks on September 11, 2001, the war in Iraq, and Hurricane Katrina are used to illustrate his perspectives and explanations.

Amarasingam, Amarnath, ed. 2011. *The Stewart/Colbert Effect: Essays on the Real Impacts of Fake News.* Jefferson, NC: McFarland & Company, Inc.
This edited volume of scholarly essays examines elements of two popular news satire programs once dubbed "fake news," *The Daily Show* and *The Colbert Report.* The ten essays examine empirical and theoretical approaches used to examine the potential impact these influential shows had on the culture.

Anderson, C.W., Leonard Downie, and Michael Schudson. 2016. *The News Media: What Everyone Needs to Know.* New York: Oxford University Press.
This addition to Oxford's What Everyone Needs to Know series examines the past, present, and future state of the news industry through a series of questions and answers. Readers can locate a question they are interested in via the table of contents and read the response. Questions in the "present" and "future" sections provide a primer on common contemporary news issues.

Atkins, Larry. 2016. *Skewed: A Critical Thinkers Guide to Media Bias.* Amherst, NY: Prometheus Books.
While providing a history of the evolution of journalism in the United States, Atkins points out that advocacy has always been a part of journalism practice. The author aims to educate the reader on how to separate news constructions that support a particular point of view from factual

reporting in his discussion of print media, talk radio, cable news, blogs, and websites.

Ball, James. 2017. *Post-Truth: How Bullshit Conquered the World*. London: Biteback Publishing Ltd.
Journalist James Ball provides a candid look at how false and misleading information operates as a factor in the current information sphere, at times influencing perceptions and actions of citizens. Chapters examine the election of President Trump and discussions of Brexit through this lens, and Ball also details how "bullshit" is spread by politicians, old media, new media, and consumers. He advances an argument as to why false information is believed and offers suggestions for addressing the problem.

Barclay, Donald. 2018. *Fake News, Propaganda, and Plain Old Lies: How to Find Trustworthy Information in the Digital Age*. Lanham, MD: Rowman & Littlefield.
Written by a librarian, this book provides readers with strategies for evaluating information that are based on principles of information literacy. In so doing, the author discusses the need for credible information and explains how less than credible information can be produced and disseminated with contemporary technology. A chapter on "fake news" explores the new version of this old issue. Barclay discusses how the current information-saturated climate requires consumers to be vigilant when evaluating sources. Readers are prompted to think about how propaganda techniques, deceptive practices, and statistics can be used to convey unreliable information. The author also provides guidance for evaluating scholarly sources.

Bulger, Monica, and Patrick Davison. 2018. "The Promises, Challenges, and Futures of Media Literacy." Data & Society Research Institute, February. https://datasociety.net/pubs/oh/DataAndSociety_Media_Literacy_2018.pdf.

Pointing out the media literacy is not a "panacea" for the problems of "fake news," Bulger and Davison explore the potential benefits and failures of media education, pose questions about the practice, and offer suggestions for future media literacy initiatives.

Chapman, Jane, and Nick Nuttall. 2011. *Journalism Today: A Themed History*. Malden, MA: Wiley-Blackwell.
This title documents and discusses the historical context that informs some of the twenty-first century's contemporary issues in journalism that emerge from the oversaturation of information, citizen participation in news gathering and sharing, concentration of media ownership, and the relationship between news and democracy. The authors' explorations of four themes—journalism and democracy; technology, work, and business; ethics; and audience and its impact on journalism—are informed by elements of journalism history. Helpful sidebars elaborate on the content discussed in the chapters and may inspire further research.

Chesney, Robert, and Danielle Citron. 2019. "Deepfakes and the New Disinformation War." *Foreign Affairs* 98, no. 1: 147–155.
This article presents a readable overview of deepfakes and how they may be used in problematic ways. The authors argue that deepfakes will make the disinformation "war" more difficult to address.

Gitlin, Martin, ed. 2019. *Politics and Journalism in a Post-Truth World*. New York: Greenhaven Publishing.
A series of essays in this edited book by notable scholars and writers explore some of the contemporary issues facing news coverage of politics. Topics include media trust, journalism and politician privacy, bias, and the 24-hour news cycle.

Gladstone, Brooke. 2011. *The Influencing Machine*. New York: W.W. Norton and Company.

This book overviews elements of journalism history while offering a critique of contemporary news. In a fun graphic novel format, journalist and *On the Media* host Brooke Gladstone and artist Josh Neufeld engage readers in thinking about concepts such as objectivity, bias, and news construction through a discussion of numerous specific examples.

Graves, Lucas. 2016. *Deciding What's True: The Rise of Political Fact Checking in American Journalism.* New York: Columbia University Press.

Graves explores the culture of fact-checking in this three-part book. Part one looks at the landscape of fact-checking, part two examines the work of fact-checking, and part three considers the effects of fact-checking. Graves's research is informed by conversations with those working in fact-checking organizations, his documentation of the history of fact-checking work, and discussions about the production of knowledge.

Howcroft, Elizabeth. 2018. "How Faking Videos Became Easy and Why That's So Scary." Bloomberg, September 10. https://www.bloomberg.com/news/articles/2018-09-10/ how-faking-videos-became-easy-and-why-that-s-so-scary-quicktake; Bloomberg. 2018. "It's Getting Harder to Spot a Deep Fake Video." Bloomberg.com, September 26. https://www.bloomberg.com/news/videos/2018-09-26/ it-s-getting-harder-to-spot-a-deep-fake-video-video.

This brief Bloomberg article provides a clear and concise Q&A about deepfake videos. The article ends with a "reference shelf"—links to four additional resources that provide more context on the topic. The Bloomberg video provides an understandable explanation of how the technology works and looks.

Hunter, Andrea. 2015. "Crowdfunding Independent and Freelance Journalism: Negotiating Journalistic Norms of

Autonomy and Objectivity." *New Media & Society* 17, no. 2: 272–288. doi:10.1177/1461444814558915.

As the news industry tries to find sustainable business models, one avenue journalists are pursuing is to ask for citizen donations to support the news. This study reports on interviews with twenty-one journalists in the United States and Canada who use crowdfunding to support their work. The author documents how the journalists discuss autonomy and objectivity as they acknowledge their funding sources.

Jones, Alex S. 2009. *Losing the News*. New York: Oxford University Press.

Jones, the director of Harvard University's Shorenstein Center on the Press, Politics and Public Policy from 2000 to 2015, offers his assessment of the changing news industry in this work. The book is part history, part contemporary analysis, and part personal reflection on the challenges facing the news industry at the beginning of the twenty-first century. Jones argues that while partisanship exists, the real problem facing the news industry is the decline in "iron core" reporting and support for the journalists who produce it.

Kennedy, Dan. 2018. *The Return of the Moguls*. Lebanon, NH: ForeEdge.

After overviewing some historical background that summarizes the state of the newspaper industry, Kennedy tells the story of three wealthy individuals—Jeff Bezos, John Henry, and Aaron Kushner—and their attempts to generate successful subscription-based business models for the *Washington Post*, the *Boston Globe*, and the *Orange County Register*. The case study approach provides the reader with the story of each publication and what decisions were made to try to create a financially viable newspaper.

King, Elliot. 2010. *Free for All: The Internet's Transformation of Journalism*. Evanston, IL: Northwestern University Press.

In this book, King provides a history of journalism as it has been enabled by technology. While focusing on how the development of computer platforms and the internet prompted changes in journalism, King provides examples of how developing internet technologies, consumer interaction, new forms of communication such as blogging, and issues of credibility shaped the way online news developed.

King, Gary, Benjamin Schneer, and Ariel White. 2017. "How the News Media Activate Public Expression and Influence National Agendas." *Science Magazine* 358: 776–780.

This experimental research examines whether public exposure to news stories prompts people to participate in democratic politics. The study noted that exposure to news media causes Americans to engage in components of the political process.

Kovach, Bill, and Tom Rosenstiel. 2010. *Blur: How to Know What's True in the Age of Information Overload.* New York: Bloomsbury.

In *Blur*, journalism experts Bill Kovach and Tom Rosenstiel guide readers through identifying the aspects of journalistic practice that result in reliable and verifiable information. The authors explore how the "information culture" is changing in light of new technology and provide meaningful information citizens need to increase their news literacy skills and evaluate news-oriented material.

Larson, Stephanie G. 2006. *Media & Minorities: The Politics of Race in News and Entertainment.* Lanham, MD: Rowman & Littlefield.

In this scholarly title, Larson examines how African Americans, Hispanic Americans, Native Americans, and Asian Americans are represented in news and entertainment. Two of the three sections of the book deal primarily with news coverage.

Maheshwari, Sapna. 2016. "How Fake News Goes Viral: A Case Study." *New York Times*, November 20. https://www.nytimes.com/2016/11/20/business/media/how-fake-news-spreads.html.

> This article demonstrates how a citizen's inaccurate tweet can be shared and retweeted relatively quickly in a digital environment where information spreads quickly. The brief case study can help readers understand how unreliable information can be amplified.

McChesney, Robert, and John Nichols. 2010. *The Death and Life of American Journalism*. Philadelphia, PA: Nation Books.

> Longtime media reform advocates McChesney and Nichols argue for the establishment of a public news media system that is publicly funded and operates free of corporate and government influence. This book details ways public money could and should be used to pay for such a system, arguing that the public need for reliable news is central to a functioning democracy.

McChesney, Robert, and Victor Pickard, eds. 2011. *Will the Last Reporter Please Turn Out the Lights?* New York: The New Press.

> This edited volume of thirty-two essays addresses various aspects of the so-called crisis in journalism. Commentators and scholars address such topics as news media economics, news objectivity, the decline in newspapers, and newsroom diversity.

McDonald, Natalie H. 2019. "Popping the Filter Bubble: How Newspapers Are Navigating through Social Media Bots, Trolls and Misinformation to Bring Readers the Truth." *Editor & Publisher* 152, no. 2: 46–50.

> This article explores how media organizations are managing the challenges of social media while also using it to leverage their own reporting in successful ways.

McDonald notes the strategies news organizations are using to combat misinformation and monitor responses to their own content on social media to gauge what works and what does not.

Morrison, Sara, and Eryn Carlson. 2018. "Reinventing Local News." *Neiman Reports*, April 18. https://niemanreports.org/articles/reinventing-local-tv-news/.

This *Neiman Report* examines how the local television news industry is engaging in new initiatives to attract younger audiences. Different innovative projects are discussed, including a partnership between the University of North Carolina and local media, and the Reinventing Local News project at Northeastern University.

Mudge, Amy R., and Randal Shaheen. 2017. "Native Advertising, Influencers and Endorsements: Where Is the Line between Integrated Content and Deceptively Formatted Advertising?" *Journal of Internet Law* 21, no. 5: 1–16.

This article summarizes definitions of native advertising, influencers, and promotional messaging and discusses these techniques in light of Federal Trade Commission policy and approaches. The authors also discuss how these types of advertising practices can be deceptive.

Owen, Taylor, Fergus Pitt, Raney Aronson-Rath, and James Milward. 2015. *Virtual Reality Journalism*. The Tow Center for Digital Journalism. Accessed March 1, 2019. https://www.cjr.org/tow_center_reports/virtual_reality_journalism.php.

This report traces the history of virtual reality and considers its use in journalistic practice. By discussing the outcomes of a case study research effort between the Tow Center for Digital Journalism and PBS's *Frontline*, the authors detail aspects of virtual reality and journalistic practice that need to be considered as the technology is developed for news reporting.

Pavlik, John. 2019. *Journalism in the Age of Virtual Reality*. New York: Columbia University Press.

In his discussion of what he calls experiential news, Pavlik explains how new technologies offer new ways of telling and experiencing news stories. This book explores new ways of storytelling that include the use of virtual reality and drones while also presenting a series of ethical issues that should be considered and standards that should be adopted.

Phillips, Lisa. 2006. *Public Radio: Behind the Voices*. New York: CDS Books.

In this book, Phillips offers over forty biographical profiles of public radio reporters, commentators, and program hosts, including Robert Segal, Michele Norris, Ira Glass, Brooke Gladstone, Scott Simon, Steve Inskeep, and Nina Totenberg. Her profiles are informed by research and in-depth interviews.

Powers, Matthew. 2018. *NGOs as Newsmakers*. New York: Columbia University Press.

Because news organizations no longer cover international news to the extent they once did, nongovernmental organizations (NGOs) utilize their own reporters, videographers, and photographers to make their own news. Powers explores the dynamics of this practice.

Rampton, Sheldon, and John Stauber. 2001. *Trust Us, We're Experts*. New York: Jeremy P. Tarcher/Putnam; Stauber, John, and Sheldon Rampton. 1995. *Toxic Sludge Is Good for You: Lies, Damn Lies and the Public Relations Industry*. Monroe, ME: Common Courage Press.

These two books provide details into how the public relations industry influences news coverage and advances misleading messaging on such topics as environmental issues, food safety, and scientific research findings. Through numerous examples, the authors detail how the public relations industry can operate in ways that are unethical to alter information narratives, stifle articulated concerns, and mislead the public.

Rosenberg, Howard, and Charles Feldman. 2008. *No Time to Think: The Menace of Media Speed and the 24-hour News Cycle.* New York: Continuum International Publishing Group.

Using examples from news coverage and interviews with several notable journalists and news experts, Rosenberg and Feldman offer a critique of the 24-hour news cycle that began with CNN and continues with online news. Though published in 2008, many of the issues raised by the authors that emerge from a speed-driven news environment are relevant today.

Russell, Adrienne. 2011. *Networked: A Contemporary History of News in Transition.* Malden, MA: Polity Press.

Focusing on the years from 1990 to 2010, Russell provides a history of "networked journalism." She discusses a cultural shift from newspapers' dominance to the reliance on online news that resulted in different types of reporting, commenting, and responding by professional journalists and citizens. Russell discusses participatory journalism, personalized news, social media, and news parody from an academic perspective that includes interviews with professionals in the field and examples of digital news projects.

Schmidt, Christine. 2018. "So What Is That, er, Trusted News Integrity Trust Project All About? A Guide to the Many (Similarly Named) New Efforts Fighting for Journalism." Nieman Lab, April 5. http://www.niemanlab.org/2018/04/ so-what-is-that-er-trusted-news-integrity-trust-project-all- about-a-guide-to-the-many-similarly-named-new-efforts- fighting-for-journalism/.

This article provides brief summaries of several journalism industry trust initiatives that emerged after the 2016 presidential election, including Trusting News, the Trust

Project, the News Integrity Initiative, NewsGuard, and several others. Helpful descriptions disclose the groups' goals, funders, and projects.

Schudson, Michael. 2018. *Why Journalism Still Matters.* Cambridge, England: Polity Press.
This collection of essays written by journalism expert Michael Schudson encourages readers to think about contemporary professional journalism from numerous vantage points. Pointing out that "we should not be too high minded in talking about journalism," Schudson explores some of the complexities of the democratic role of the profession.

Seife, Charles. 2014. *Virtual Unreality.* New York: Viking.
While acknowledging the many positives the digital age offers the culture, Seife details the problematic possibilities of digital information given its ease of creation and dissemination. He argues that the virtual world and the real world can no longer be separated and offers numerous examples, often with witty commentary, of how hoaxes, internet scams, algorithms, and sock puppets are used to manipulate the public. Seife also discusses how the digital environment has shifted the definition of what news is and has allowed for the amplification of voices and content that can be incorrect, hateful, or overly provocative.

Sherman, Gabriel. 2014. *The Loudest Voice in the Room: How the Brilliant, Bombastic Roger Ailes Built Fox News—And Divided a Country.* New York: Random House.
When Rupert Murdoch started Fox News in 1996, he hired Roger Ailes as the channel's CEO and chairperson. This book provides some biographical information about Ailes and documents the steps he took and choices he made to develop Fox News into the powerful, partisan network it is today. He also discusses how Ailes used Fox News as a way of supporting a particular political agenda. In addition to other research, Sherman interviewed 614

people who worked with Ailes to tell this story but was unable to secure Ailes's cooperation.

Siapera, Eugenia, and Andreas Veglis, eds. 2012. *The Handbook of Global Online Journalism*. Malden, MA: Wiley-Blackwell.
Essays about journalism fill this comprehensive, international examination of how the internet has influenced journalism. Contributions are written by a diverse group of scholars and journalism professionals. The essays address such topics as news business models, crowdsourcing, and news media accountability. Examples from specific countries are detailed.

Singer, P. W., and Emerson Brooking. 2018. *LikeWar: The Weaponization of Social Media*. New York: Houghton Mifflin.
Focusing on social media, Singer and Brooking detail how digital spaces have been used, and are anticipated to be used, to manipulate information. With a security focus, the book explores how social media has changed, and continues to change, international politics and war.

Sorgatz, Rex. 2018. *The Encyclopedia of Misinformation*. New York: Abrams Image.
Relevant to the current cultural moment where terms such as "fake news" and "post truth" are dominant, this book compiles and defines an expansive historic and contemporary list of terms, hoaxes, propaganda, and conspiracies that have contributed to the distribution of misinformation in our society. The almost three hundred encyclopedia entries ranging from "alternative facts" to the made-up word that became the name of the state Idaho to the fake movie critic David Manning provide for a broad understanding of the place deception plays in our culture. Sorgatz's informal tone and the book's accessible layout make for fun reading.

Suarez, Eduardo. 2018. "The Present Crisis of Western Democracy Is a Crisis of Journalism." *Nieman Reports*, September 10. https://niemanreports.org/articles/the-present-crisis-of-western-democracy-is-a-crisis-of-journalism/.

In synthesizing some of the influential columnist Walter Lippmann's ideas about journalism with contemporary concerns, Suarez demonstrates how Lippmann's perspectives on disinformation, anonymous sources, and reporting versus opinion writing are relevant today.

Sumpter, David. 2018. *Outnumbered: From Facebook and Google to Fake News and Filter Bubbles—The Algorithms That Control Our Lives*. London: Bloomsbury Sigma.

Written by an applied mathematics professor, this book explains how algorithms work from a mathematical perspective, assisting readers in understanding this element of online operations. Perhaps of particular interest are the two chapters that discuss echo chambers and filter bubbles (Chapter 11) and "fake news" (Chapter 13). While explaining how algorithms function in digital spaces, Sumpter questions whether filter bubbles and the spread of fake news have as powerful of an impact as some suppose.

Usher, Nikki. 2016. *Interactive Journalism*. Urbana: University of Illinois Press.

In this book, Usher considers how interactive journalism—reporting that might take the form of immersive storytelling, data visualization, explanatory graphics or interactive features—has become part of journalism's evolution. Historical and theoretical foundations of interactive journalism are discussed. Usher also addresses the work and perspectives of those working in this part of the field.

Ward, Stephen. 2018. *Ethical Journalism in a Populist Age*. Lanham, MD: Rowman & Littlefield.

Anchoring his discussion in the current age of "fake news," partisanship, and "alternative facts," media ethicist Stephen Ward argues that democracy and journalism are in trouble. Ward presents ideas about how journalists should complete their work in ways that require them to be "democratically engaged" in reporting. In offering specific guidelines to journalist practitioners and scholars, Ward addresses some contemporary issues in national and international news reporting.

Wineburg, Sam, Sarah McGrew, Joel Breakstone, and Teresa Ortega. 2016. "Evaluating Information: The Cornerstone of Civic Online Reasoning." Stanford Digital Repository. Accessed January 11, 2019. https://purl.stanford.edu/fv751yt5934.
This comprehensive study of students' responses to information demonstrates how young people across multiple grade levels think about, evaluate, and describe information. Reading through the sample student responses to the information presented to them in the study provides insight into how well students are able to critically analyze and question content. The authors found that across multiple grade levels, critical analysis skills are lacking.

Women's Media Center. 2018. *The Status of Women of Color in the U.S. Media 2018.* Accessed January 11, 2019. http://www.womensmediacenter.com/assets/site/reports/the-status-of-women-of-color-in-the-u-s-media-2018-full-report/Women-of-Color-Report-FINAL-WEB.pdf.
This report compiles the most recent available data from news industry organizations to present a demographic picture of news professionals, showing that women and women of color hold few positions in comparison to their white, male counterparts. The report also summarizes thoughtful interviews with several journalists who comment on relevant issues related to news coverage and diversity.

Research Organizations and Nonprofits

American Press Institute

https://www.americanpressinstitute.org/

As a nonprofit educational organization associated with the News Media Alliance, the American Press Institute offers articles, a newsletter, tools, and other resources for professionals, students, and interested parties on areas of news publishing, digital news, and journalism. Comprehensive reports from the Media Insight Project, a research initiative of the American Press Institute and Associated Press-NORC Center for Public Affairs Research, are available to users.

Berkman Klein Center for Internet and Society at Harvard University

https://cyber.harvard.edu/

This organization researches and explores, via multiple scholarly approaches, the internet. It shares and discusses elements of its work through numerous workshops, conferences, videos, podcasts, and publications. The center also creates its own projects, tools, and platforms that support its focus.

Columbia Journalism Review

https://www.cjr.org/

The *Columbia Journalism Review* (or *CJR*) is a leading magazine for journalists and others published by Columbia University's Graduate School of Journalism. The website houses numerous articles on aspects of journalism practice and the current state of the news media as well as its weekly podcast. The magazine is also available in print form. The *CJR* website also posts reports from Columbia's Tow Center for Digital Journalism on this landing page: https://www.cjr.org/tow-center.

Data & Society

https://datasociety.net/

> This research institute examines issues that emerge "at the intersection of technology and society." The institute produces reports on topics ranging from artificial intelligence to data privacy to online disinformation. The "output" component of the website provides links to forms of the institute members' work—from "explainers" to videos to academic journal articles.

The Expanding News Desert

Penelope Muse Abernathy, Knight Chair in Journalism and Digital Media Economies

https://www.usnewsdeserts.com/

> This website, produced by Center for Innovation and Sustainability in Local Media in the School of Media and Journalism at the University of North Carolina at Chapel Hill, houses an interactive map that details the absence or presence of local newspapers across each state in the country. Users can also select a state to find out detailed information about state county demographics, types of newspapers available, newspaper circulation, and online news organizations that cover news in the state. The comprehensive reports that inform this information, *The Rise of the New Media Baron and the Emerging Threat of News Deserts* (2016), *Thwarting the Emergence of News Deserts* (2017), and *The Expanding News Desert* (2018), are available on the site.

First Draft News

https://firstdraftnews.org/

> First Draft is an organization that supports journalists around the world who are aiming to increase trust in the news media and combat problematic information. Summaries of their research and tools and articles journalists and news consumers may find helpful are available on the website.

Institute for Nonprofit News

https://inn.org/

This nonprofit organization, focused on supporting nonprofit news organizations whose work supports the public interest, was founded in 2009. Although the website is tailored for member organizations, one can find links to "Best nonprofit news" reports on the home page.

Journalist's Resource at the Shorenstein Center on Media, Politics and Public Policy

https://journalistsresource.org

This web resource curates and summarizes scholarly research on popular news topics. The site hosts a searchable database, or users can browse by topic. Though called "journalist's resource," the scholarly information that is compiled by topic is useful for anyone interested in learning more about general news topics (i.e., health care, drug policy, climate change) and issues related to news media, social media, digital media, and campaign media.

Knight Foundation Reports

https://www.knightfoundation.org/reports

A funder of journalism and other initiatives, the Knight Foundation has also supported research efforts that have led to the publication of research reports on such topics as media trust, twitter campaigns, and local television news. Complete reports are available on the foundation website.

News Media Alliance

https://www.newsmediaalliance.org/

This nonprofit trade organization represents almost two thousand news organizations in the United States. Numerous articles about aspects of the contemporary news business and resources for professionals and students are found on their website.

Nieman Foundation

https://nieman.harvard.edu/

Harvard University's Neiman Foundation is an organization that supports the development of high-quality journalism through its fellowship programs, publications, and programming. It supports online reporting through Nieman Lab, an industry magazine titled *Nieman Reports*, and Nieman Storyboard, which focuses on narrative nonfiction storytelling. Numerous articles and reports about aspects of news and information are available on the Nieman Lab (http://www.niemanlab.org/) and *Nieman Reports* (https://niemanreports.org/) websites, while Nieman Storyboard features quality examples of narrative journalism.

The Pew Research Center for Internet & Technology

https://www.pewinternet.org/

This section of the nonpartisan Pew Research Center completes and publishes research about such topics as the internet, mobile devices, social media, algorithms, and artificial intelligence.

The Pew Research Center for Journalism & Media

http://www.journalism.org/

This section of the nonpartisan Pew Research Center completes and publishes research about journalism and media, including research about media use, public perceptions of news, social media, the economics of the news industry, and trends in journalism.

The Poynter Institute

https://www.poynter.org/

As a school for journalists, Poynter makes many resources available for those researching aspects of journalism practice and contemporary issues in the field. The "Media

News" section of the website features numerous articles that address aspects of reporting, fact-checking, ethics, and the news business. The website also features information about the organization's International Fact Checking Network.

Reuters Institute for the Study of Journalism

https://reutersinstitute.politics.ox.ac.uk/

Located at the University of Oxford, this institute advances the study of journalism through education, research, and support of practicing journalists. Available on the research section of the website are many research reports, working papers, academic articles, and fact sheets that address aspects of the contemporary, international journalism landscape.

The Shorenstein Center on Media, Politics and Public Policy

https://shorensteincenter.org/about-us/

Located at Harvard University's Kennedy School, this organization looks at how the press, politics, and public policy intersect. Areas of focus include news quality, technology and social change, and digital journalism. The center hosts many events and makes available current research papers on its website.

Society of Professional Journalists

https://www.spj.org/

This organization provides resources for journalists, students, and journalism educators. It publishes the quarterly journalism magazine *Quill*, where topics in journalism are discussed.

University of Southern California Annenberg School for Communication and Journalism Research

https://annenberg.usc.edu/research

This landing page at the University of Southern California Annenberg School for Communication and Journalism research links to the many research centers and programs the university houses. Research centers and programs that include the Center for Health Journalism, Center for Public Relations, and the Knight Digital Media Center provide a variety of resources.

Relevant Scholarly Journals

Available via many library databases, articles in these journals publish research on various aspects of news and information in the culture.

International Journal of Press/Politics
Journal of Broadcasting and Electronic Media
Journal of Social Media and Society
Journalism
Journalism and Mass Communications Educator
Journalism and Mass Communications Quarterly
Journalism Practice
Media, Culture & Society
New Media & Society
Newspaper Research Journal
Social Media & Society

Additional Web Resources, Videos, and Podcasts

Abridge News
https://abridgenews.com/

This news site describes its goal as one that "tackles news echo chambers." The site presents a current topic to users in a summary format that relies on factual information. An "opinion spectrum" of perspectives for each topic is provided where readers can read summaries of opinions from the left, mid left, mid right, and right that are published in mainstream and other media. Readers are invited to submit their own views on the topic as well.

American Archive of Public Broadcasting

http://americanarchive.org/

This archival initiative is the result of a partnership between the Library of Congress and WGBH, a public station in Boston, Massachusetts. The goal of the project is to preserve and archive significant amounts of public media for use by the public. The organization reports that currently over seven thousand public radio programs and public television programs have been digitized and are available to stream.

Bourg, Anya, and James Jacoby. 2018. "The Facebook Dilemma, Parts One and Two." *Frontline*. PBS. Boston: WGBH, October 29; October 30. https://www.pbs.org/wgbh/frontline/film/facebook-dilemma/.

This two-part investigative *Frontline* documentary is essential viewing for those interested in understanding how the social media company Facebook evolved to become a central piece of the digital landscape. The program clearly explains how the business model works to provide customized newsfeeds and provides examples of how the site's algorithms contribute to the promotion of misinformation. Additionally, the program demonstrates how Facebook was, and can be, used to promote disinformation campaigns launched by other countries.

BuzzMachine

https://buzzmachine.com/

BuzzMachine is a blog by Jeff Jarvis, a professor at the Tow-Knight Center for Entrepreneurial Journalism at the City University of New York's Graduate School of Journalism. Jarvis blogs about media, journalism, and politics; his expertise is informed by his experiences as a journalist, blogger, editor, media consultant, and president of Advance.net, the online division of Advance Publications. Recent posts include discussions of media education, people's use of social media, and internet regulation.

Conboy, Martin, Scott Eldridge, Jairo Luco-Ocando, and John Steel. n.d. "Media and Journalism: Covering World News." TED Studies. https://www.ted.com/read/ted-studies/media-and-journalism.

TED Studies, a division of TED, pulls together curated collections of videos on particular topics and presents them in a context that includes an introductory essay and analysis. This selection presents TED talks and analysis that address issues pertaining to global news coverage.

de la Peña, Noni. 2015. "The Future of News? Virtual Reality." TED Talk. https://www.ted.com/talks/nonny_de_la_pena_the_future_of_news_virtual_reality?language=en.

In this TED talk, the virtual reality pioneer Noni de la Peña overviews how she believes virtual reality can be effectively used in news reporting. She discusses her vision of how news audiences can gain a different understanding of news stories by being immersed in the storytelling via a virtual platform.

Digiday

https://digiday.com/

This site is focused on reporting on how the marketing and media industries are being disrupted by, and adapting to, the evolving online climate. Articles and podcasts address big technology, journalism, unreliable information, and promotional content.

FiveThirtyEight

https://fivethirtyeight.com/

Initially founded by Nate Silver as a blog, this site uses statistical analysis to offer insight into topics in politics, sports, science, health, economics, and culture. Now owned by ABC News, the site also features videos and podcasts.

The FlipSide

https://www.theflipside.io/

Those who read and/or subscribe to this site's newsletter are presented with a summary of aggregated content that represents political news from the left and right perspectives.

"How to Pop Our Filter Bubbles." TED playlist. https://www .ted.com/playlists/470/how_to_pop_our_filter_bubbles.

This curated list of TED talks addresses nine various perspectives on filter bubbles and echo chambers with speakers collectively arguing that citizens who resist the ease of only paying attention to information in their usual social media or social circle will be better informed. The featured talks include Eli Pariser's "Beware of Online Filter Bubbles," Markham Nolan's "How to Separate Fact and Fiction Online," Sally Kohn's "Let's Try Emotional Correctness," and Kevin Slavin's "How Algorithms Shape Our World."

"Investigating Power."

https://investigatingpower.org/.

This multimedia website produced by journalist Charles Lewis highlights examples of investigative journalism that had an impact on American culture. The site spotlights reporters' roles in such topics as civil rights, corporate power, and the War on Terror. Individual journalists are profiled, and content is shared using video, timelines, and text.

MediaBuzz

https://video.foxnews.com/playlist/on-air-mediabuzz/

Media critic Howard Kurtz discusses news media coverage on a variety of topics on this weekly Fox News program and podcast. Panelists and journalists are invited to weigh in and provide perspective.

On the Media

https://www.wnycstudios.org/shows/otm

From the NPR station WNYC, this show describes itself as "a weekly investigation into how the media shapes our world view." Brooke Gladstone and Bob Garfield host this radio program where they examine how the news media addresses current events through analysis of media coverage and interviews with experts. The program is also available as a podcast.

Press Think

http://pressthink.org/

New York University professor Jay Rosen is the author and editor of this blog, launched in 2003 as a project of the Arthur L. Carter Journalism Institute at the New York University. The blog focuses on new directions in journalism and features numerous entries ranging from essays to interviews that all center on aspects of journalism in the digital age.

Reading the Pictures

https://www.readingthepictures.org/

This site discusses and analyzes the pictures and images used in news reporting. Because photographs have persuasive power, the site advocates for citizens to increase their visual literacy skills. To assist with this, Reading the Pictures aims to "study the content and context of key images to reveal bias, narrative, stereotypes and personality."

Recode

https://www.recode.net/

Founded by Kara Swisher and Walt Mossberg, Recode is a news website dedicated to reporting on technology and media. The site also hosts podcasts where editors and writers discuss contemporary issues related to big technology. Several articles and podcasts discuss the relationship between technology companies and news and information.

Reliable Sources

https://www.cnn.com/shows/reliable-sources

Reliable Sources is a CNN talk show and accompanying podcast hosted by Brian Stelter. Each week, Stelter offers a critique of the news media, often engaging in conversation with journalists and experts.

Silverman, Craig. 2016. "This Analysis Shows How Viral Fake News Election News Outperformed Real News on Facebook." BuzzFeed News, November 16. https://www.buzzfeednews.com/article/craigsilverman/viral-fake-election-news-outperformed-real-news-on-facebook.

This article summarizes collected data that show the prevalence of fake news on Facebook during the three months prior to the 2016 presidential election. The analysis suggests an increase in engagement with "fake news" over "real news" among users during this time period.

Spaceship Media

https://spaceshipmedia.org/

Describing itself as "journalism to bridge divides," this organization, founded in 2016, aims to engage people from different vantage points in conversation about provocative issues in ways that increase understanding. Participants engage in what is called "dialogue journalism" where journalists ask questions, encourage listening among others, and supply factual reporting in an effort to decrease news polarization.

Tufekci, Zeynep. 2017. "We are Building a Dystopia Just to Make People Click on Ads." TEDGlobal. https://www .ted.com/talks/zeynep_tufekci_we_re_building_a_dysto pia_just_to_make_people_click_on_ads.

In this talk, Zeynep explains how algorithms work to keep users online and craft information spaces that potentially impact their view of the world. She raises concerns about algorithms, big tech, and surveillance and argues that the system needs to change.

Wardle, Claire. 2016. "Timeline: Key Moments in the Fake News Debate." First Draft News, November 30. https:// firstdraftnews.org/key-moments-fake-news-debate/.

This slideshow takes users through a chronological series of linked articles that elaborate on different aspects of "fake news" and the 2016 presidential election. Scrolling through the article titles provides readers with an understanding of how aspects of the conversation about problematic information evolved after the election, while the articles themselves provide substantial discussion.

"Who Owns the Media?" Freepress.net. https://www.freepress.net/issues/media-control/media-consolidation/who-owns-media.

Freepress.net maintains downloadable spreadsheets of what companies own what media outlets in the United States. The data collected include company holdings, revenue estimates, and descriptions.

Wired Magazine's News in Crisis Series https://www.wired.com/tag/news-in-crisis/

This section of *Wired*'s online website compiles a series of articles dealing with the current state of journalism as it pertains to the challenges the news industry is facing.

Tools and Organizations That Help People Develop Skills to Critically Assess Information

Accuracy in Media (AIM)

https://www.aim.org/

On the political right, this news media watchdog group highlights news coverage they see as biased.

AllSides

https://www.allsides.com

One of this site's goals is to show users multiple perspectives on the same news story in an attempt to highlight how different sources, aligned with left-, center-, or right-leaning political positions, discuss the same issue. The site encourages consideration of different points of view to combat polarization and decrease the proliferation of filter bubbles.

Botometer

https://botometer.iuni.iu.edu/#!/

When logged into their Twitter account, users can use this service to evaluate how likely another Twitter account is to be a bot.

Caulfield, Mike. 2017. *Web Literacy for Student Fact-Checkers*. Creative Commons Attribution 4.0 International License. https://webliteracy.pressbooks.com/.

This is an easy-to-use e-book for students and others who are looking for practical tips in evaluating information online. With examples and activities, Caulfield takes readers through what he calls the "four moves" of evaluating information: "check for previous work, go upstream to the source, read laterally, and circle back" to assess content on the web.

Center for Media and Democracy's PR Watch

https://www.prwatch.org/

This progressive watchdog organization investigates and reports on use of corporate and government public relations spin in media messaging.

Center for Media and Information Literacy

https://centermil.org/

Based out of Temple University, this center researches and engages with national and international media literacy initiatives.

Center for Media Literacy

http://www.medialit.org/

This is an organization promoting and supporting the development of media literacy skills.

Digital Resource Center from the Center for News Literacy

https://digitalresource.center/splashpage

Available on this site are news literacy resources for grade school teachers, students, and college instructors.

Edutopia's "5-Minute Film Festival: Nine Videos on News Literacy."

https://www.edutopia.org/blog/film-festival-news-media-literacy

This collection of short, instructive videos provides information and instruction on ways consumers can critically consider information.

Evaluating Internet Health Information Tutorial from Medlineplus.gov

https://medlineplus.gov/webeval/webeval.html

Medlineplus.gov is produced by the U.S. National Library of Medicine. Its "Evaluating Internet Health Information" tutorial provides instruction for users on how to evaluate information on health that they may see online. Medlineplus.gov itself is also a searchable health resource.

FactCheck.org

https://www.factcheck.org/

Established in 2003, this organization from the Annenberg Public Policy Center at the University of Pennsylvania works to fact-check statements made by public figures. The site has a section that addresses science-based claims, a feature that allows users to submit a fact-checking question, and a resource guide that assists readers in identifying false news. Its fake news page lists false information circulating on social media.

Fact Checker, led by Glenn Kessler at the *Washington Post*

https://www.washingtonpost.com/news/fact-checker

This service uses a Pinocchio rating system to evaluate the truthfulness of statements made by public figures or interest groups. As with similar sites, analysis is supported by documented facts.

Fairness and Accuracy in Reporting (FAIR)

https://fair.org/

On the political left, this news media watchdog group highlights news coverage they see as biased.

Google Reverse Image Search

https://images.google.com/

After navigating to images.google.com, users can drag an image into the search bar or paste an image URL into the search bar to determine where online that image or very similar images are found. Alternatively, when using Google's Chrome browser, users can "right click" on the image and "search Google for image" to locate the same results. Users can then look critically at the results to determine the credibility of the image based on where it appears, how it is being used, and whether or not it is attributed to a reliable source.

Hoax-Slayer

https://www.hoax-slayer.net/

This comprehensive blog, founded in 2003 and operated by Brett Christensen in Australia, aims to debunk hoaxes, internet scams, and spam. It attempts to increase users' information literacy skills by providing tips on how people can protect themselves from scams and spam.

Making Sense of the News: News Literacy Lessons for Digital Citizens

https://www.coursera.org/learn/news-literacy

This free six-module class is offered through Coursera from the University of Hong Kong and Stony Brook University's Center for News Literacy. Students who wish to earn a certificate for course completion are required to pay a fee.

Media Bias/Fact Check

https://mediabiasfactcheck.com

Established in 2015, this nonpartisan website attempts to determine how biased news sources are by employing a methodology that examines a news source's use of facts, key words, and choice of stories. The organization also fact-checks major news stories.

Media Education Lab

https://mediaeducationlab.com/

> Located at the University of Rhode Island, this center promotes media literacy and provides resources for educators, researchers, and learners.

National Association for Media Education (NAMLE)

https://namle.net/

> NAMLE is a national organization focused on media literacy.

NewseumED

https://newseumed.org/medialiteracy

> The education division of the Newseum provides free media literacy resources.

NewsFeed Defenders Game from iCivics

https://www.icivics.org/games/newsfeed-defenders

> In this online game, players join a fictional social media site and use their skills to determine what information is reliable. It requires players to consider journalism standards to try to identify deceptive online information practices.

News Literacy Research from Stony Brook

https://www.centerfornewsliteracy.org/research/

> This landing page from Stony Brook University's Center for News Literacy links to published research and articles on news literacy and media literacy.

PolitiFact

https://www.politifact.com/

> Initially started as a project of the *Tampa Bay Times* in 2007, PolitiFact is now owned by the Poynter Institute of Media Studies. It uses a truth-o-meter ratings system to evaluate political information and a flip-o-meter ratings system to

evaluate politicians' consistency on their stated viewpoints. The organization also has a Facebook fact-checking section.

Propaganda Critic

https://propagandacritic.com/

This website provides a comprehensive and contemporary view of propaganda by defining the term's core principles, key techniques, and historical and current applications. Propaganda case studies, advice on critically evaluating information, and terms associated with the digital landscape are explored with the goal of educating the user on how to identify, analyze, and evaluate persuasive texts. The site addresses such concepts as fake news, fake audiences, media bias, and cognitive bias and provides links to additional information.

Rinehart, Aimee. 2018. "Free Online Course on Identifying Misinformation." First Draft News, March 19. https://firstdraftnews.org/free-online-course-on-identifying-misinformation/.

This article summarizes the content of an online course in verifying information users come across online and links to where users can register and take the course for free. The class is one-hour long and was developed by Claire Wardle of First Draft News.

Snopes

https://www.snopes.com/

Snopes began in 1994 as a service that evaluated the veracity of popular rumors and urban legends. It has since expanded its fact-checking reach to include mainstream topics and is a popular online fact-checking site.

Verification Junkie

http://verificationjunkie.com/

Maintained by journalist Josh Sterns, this site provides a "growing directory of apps, tools, sites, and strategies for verifying, fact checking, and assessing the validity of social media and user generated content."

Wardle, Claire. 2018. "Information Disorder: The Definitional Toolbox." First Draft News, July 6. https://firstdraftnews. org/infodisorder-definitional-toolbox/.

This tool box contains three sections. First, a downloadable glossary defines words associated with false and misleading information. Second, an overview of the information disorder landscape is provided. Third, information disorder explanatory graphics help users visualize the issue.

Popular "Legacy" News Media

The popular legacy news organizations on these short lists also often produce such multimedia material as video for the web, radio programming, podcasts, and blogs.

High Circulating Newspapers

Boston Globe: https://www.bostonglobe.com/

Chicago Tribune: https://www.chicagotribune.com/

Los Angeles Times: https://www.latimes.com/

Newsday: https://www.newsday.com/

New York Times: https://www.nytimes.com/

New York Post: https://nypost.com/

Star Tribune: http://www.startribune.com/

USA Today: https://www.usatoday.com/

Wall Street Journal: https://www.wsj.com/

Washington Post: https://www.washingtonpost.com/

Broadcast/Cablecast News Organizations
ABC News: https://abcnews.go.com/
CBS News: https://www.cbsnews.com/
CNN: https://www.cnn.com/
Fox News: https://www.foxnews.com/
MSNBC: https://www.msnbc.com/
NBC News: https://www.nbcnews.com/

Public News Organizations
American Public Media: https://www.americanpublicmedia.org/
National Public Radio: https://www.npr.org/
PBS *NewsHour*: https://www.pbs.org/newshour/
Public Radio International: https://www.pri.org/
The Corporation for Public Broadcasting's List of Public
    Media Organizations: https://www.cpb.org/stations/
    pborganizations

Common News Agencies in the United States

*News agencies, or newswire services, provide news reports for use
by their subscribers. The news byline reveals whether the story is
from a news agency. Agencies publish some news on their websites.*

The Associated Press (AP news site: https://www
    .apnews.com/)
Bloomberg (Bloomberg news site: https://www
    .bloomberg.com/)
Reuters (Reuters news site: https://www.reuters.com/)
Storyful (a social media newswire where content is verified):
    https://storyful.com/
United Press International (UPI news site: https://www
    .upi.com/)

This chronology provides a broad overview of the evolution of news in the United States, noting some of the key turning points that became influential factors in the news industry's growth and development. The chronology can be used as a referential starting point to consider how various technological developments, news organizations, reporting styles, journalists, and, eventually, consumers informed the way news and information was produced, distributed, accessed, and consumed.

1638 The first printing press is set up in the colonies in Cambridge, Massachusetts. Because colonists were busy establishing life in the New World, newspapers did not become a part of their culture for decades.

1690 The first American newspaper, *Publick Occurrences Both Forreign and Domestick*, is published but only lasts one issue.

1704 The first continuously published newspaper in America, the *Boston News-Letter*, is published.

1735 A court ruling in a case against John Peter Zenger, accused of libel, results in the freedom for newspapers to publish criticism of government leaders if such criticism has merit. This decision set a press precedent.

An issue that all news organizations, including the newspaper industry, continue to grapple with is finding a business model that will generate enough revenue to support quality reporting. (Oleg Dudko/Dreamstime.com)

1741   The first colonial magazines are published but are not successful.

1765   The political period of American colonial journalism begins when some newspapers advance arguments against British government rule and policies. Newspapers supported the views of the British government or the views of patriots—those who ultimately advocated and gathered support for the American Revolution. Historians marked the end of this political period in journalism with end of the Revolutionary War in 1783.

1791   The Bill of Rights is passed on December 15, containing the first ten amendments to the U.S. Constitution. The First Amendment guaranteed the freedom of speech and the freedom of the press as central to the U.S. democracy.

1827   *Freedom's Journal*, the first African American newspaper in America, is published. The paper countered some ideas in the mainstream press and addressed issues related to slavery and black rights.

1828   The *Cherokee Phoenix*, the first Native American newspaper, is published. The tribe used this paper as a means of educating and uniting tribal members as they faced pressures to move west.

1833   Benjamin Day publishes the first penny paper, the *Sun*, establishing the beginning of the penny press. Sold on the street for one cent, this new type of newspaper was embraced by readers for its attention-grabbing stories that extended beyond the political reporting of the time.

1841   The *New York Tribune*, a high-quality paper under the editorial direction of Horace Greeley, begins. The paper published powerful editorials that may have shaped public opinions on social issues of the time.

1846   The Associated Press is established as a news agency, an organization that reports on the news and distributes it to cooperating news outlets.

1855 The *New York Herald*, founded by James Bennett, begins. The paper expanded news coverage to include reports on city life, high society, sports, finance, and the arts, establishing a new template for newspaper reporting.

In the early to mid-nineteenth century, magazine publishing establishes itself, and publications discuss a variety of social issues. Popular magazines included *Godey's Ladies Book*, *Harper's Weekly*, and the *Saturday Evening Post*.

1861–1865 Reporting on the Civil War includes photographs that depict scenes from the battlefields, visually conveying horrible aspects of war.

1890s Sensational reporting called "yellow journalism" fuels competition between newspapers for readers, most notably between Joseph Pulitzer's *New York World* and William Randolph Hearst's *Morning Journal*.

1896 The *New York Times*, which had begun publication in 1851, is purchased by Adolph Ochs, who advanced an information model of news reporting that stands in contrast to yellow journalism. Ochs aimed to make the *New York Times* the country's "paper of record."

1903 *McClure's Magazine* publishes three investigative stories that become famous in the "muckraking era" of journalism; the era lasts from the end of the nineteenth century until about 1914 and is known for journalistic reporting on problematic aspects of society. Prominent muckrakers included Ida Tarbell, Ray Baker, Upton Sinclair, and Lincoln Steffens. Muckrakers during this time period advocated for social reform, a central characteristic of what is called the Progressive Era in American history.

1906 Radio transmissions begin. Radio experimenters and hobbyists broadcast to small groups of listeners.

1907 Corresponding with a welcoming immigration policy, the ethnic press sees a rise in the number of publications. Diverse newspapers provided valuable information to different demographic groups.

1908   The University of Missouri establishes the first School of Journalism, taking a key step toward professionalizing reporting standards.

1911   Joseph Pulitzer dies and leaves $2 million to Columbia University to establish a graduate school of journalism. He also earmarked money to establish the Pulitzer Prizes, a series of awards that recognize journalistic and artistic achievements.

1922   The famous journalist and columnist Walter Lippmann publishes *Public Opinion*, which became well known as a critique of news reporting and democracy.

1923   *Time Magazine* is published by creators Harry Luce and Brit Hadden. The success of this weekly newsmagazine inspired competitors *U.S. News* (later called *U.S. News and World Report*) and *Newsweek* to emerge in 1933.

1925   The *New Yorker*, founded by Harold Ross with the goal of developing a new standard of journalistic reporting, begins publication.

1926   Both the National Broadcasting Company (NBC) and the Columbia Broadcasting System (CBS) create a network of radio stations.

1927   The Radio Act of 1927 is passed as a legislative response to the proliferation of radio stations and interest in the new medium. Commercial radio develops.

1936   *Life* magazine debuts and establishes pictorial journalism as a means of reporting and conveying information.

1940s   The public listens to news about World War II on the radio. Broadcast journalism is developed as a form of news. Edward R. Murrow reports on the war from Europe. Radio news begins to impact the newspaper industry.

1941   CBS begins broadcasting two short television newscasts a day. Although commercial broadcasting had begun, few Americans owned television sets.

1943 The American Broadcasting Company (ABC) is established.

1950s The network era of television news begins as televisions become a staple in American households. The network nightly newscast, and the authoritative role of the television anchor, became part of the culture.

1950s–1960s The press covers aspects of the civil rights movement and racial inequality, perhaps influencing public support of the eventual Civil Rights Act.

1960s As the United States becomes more involved with the war in Vietnam, upsetting footage of this "first television war" is shared on news programs. Print publications publish photographs and stories as well. News media coverage begins to influence public opinion about the war.

Print publications, called the underground press, challenge mainstream news reporting and aspects of the country's social, political, and economic status quo.

A new genre of reporting called "new journalism" emerges whereby elements of fictional storytelling, such as personal voice, scene description, and the use of conversation, are used in fact-based nonfiction reporting. Writers associated with the development of this form included Tom Wolfe and Joan Didion. The genre is later referred to as literary journalism.

1963 Katharine Graham takes over the *Washington Post* after her husband's suicide. There were not many female leaders in the news business. Graham ultimately shepherded the paper into a successful enterprise.

After the assassination of President Kennedy, the country was brought together as they watched television coverage of the aftermath and funeral.

1967 The Public Broadcasting Act is passed, establishing public broadcasting on radio and television in the United States.

The Public Broadcasting Service (PBS) is founded in 1969 and begins distributing programs to public television stations.

1968   The popular weekly newsmagazine program *60 Minutes* begins on CBS, establishing a new genre of news programming. The debuts of NBC's *Dateline* and ABC's *20/20* soon followed.

1970   National Public Radio is established. Its newsmagazine program *All Things Considered* begins in 1971. *Morning Edition* debuts in 1979.

1971   The *New York Times* publishes the first installment of the Pentagon Papers. The courts prevented them from publishing more installments. Despite this judicial action against the *Times*, the *Washington Post* decides to publish further installments. Among other things, these government documents showed an acknowledgment that the war in Vietnam is unwinnable.

1972   The establishment of gonzo journalism, a subjective and personal reporting style, begins with the publication of Hunter Thompson's *Fear and Loathing in Las Vegas: A Savage Journey to the Heart of the American Dream*. Thompson's book writing and article contributions to such magazines as *Rolling Stone* and *Harper's* magazine, as well as his rejection of authority and personal embrace of alcohol and other drugs, established him as an iconic counterculture writer.

1972–1973   *Washington Post* reporters Robert Woodward and Carl Bernstein publish a series of stories that expose connections between President Nixon's administration and break-ins at the Democratic National Headquarters, located at the Watergate Hotel. The Watergate scandal resulted in Nixon's resignation.

1980   CNN (Cable News Network), created by Ted Turner, debuts as the first twenty-four-hour news station.

1982   *USA Today* is published for the first time by Gannett, the largest newspaper chain in the country. Founder Al Neuharth designed *USA Today* to be a visually oriented paper that adheres to a consistent structure each day and includes short stories that are easy to read as well as photos, charts, and graphics that are visually appealing.

1985   Rupert Murdoch creates the Fox Television Network, the first broadcast television network to emerge in decades.

1986   *A Current Affair* debuts, launching the development of tabloid television in a newscast format.

1988   Political talk radio host Rush Limbaugh begins his nationally syndicated program.

1990   CNN begins around-the-clock coverage of the conflict in the Persian Gulf, becoming a news source for government officials.

1990s   The World Wide Web becomes available to the public via the internet. Within a few years, institutions begin networking their computers. By the mid-1990s, graphic web browsers are being used. People and organizations create their own websites, link to other sites, and use platforms such as Yahoo!, Amazon.com, and Google.

1994   The information fact-checker Snopes begins operations. More fact-checking organizations launched in the twenty-first century, discussing statements made by leaders and information spread via the media.

1995   *Salon*, an online-only magazine, debuts. Another online magazine, *Slate*, debuted in 1996. These publications developed the form of the online magazine.

The Drudge Report is launched in an email newsletter form. It moved to the web in 1997. In 1998, it published information about President Clinton's relationship with an intern, eclipsing more traditional media.

Craigslist is started as an email distribution list. It soon moved to the web and eventually resulted in disrupting the classified advertising revenue newspapers rely on, contributing to their economic struggles in light of the public's move to internet news sources.

1996   Rupert Murdoch and his company News Corp establish Fox News as an around-the-clock cable channel. Murdoch hired Roger Ailes to run the network. Ailes developed Fox News into a successful enterprise that prioritizes conservative-oriented programming.

MSNBC, a collaboration between Microsoft and NBC News, launches a website and 24-hour news channel.

The Telecommunications Act of 1996 is passed, lifting media ownership limits and contributing to the eventual establishment of media consolidation as a key characteristic of the media landscape.

1999   Jon Stewart takes over hosting Comedy Central's *The Daily Show* and transforms the program into political satire. It became a popular and influential late night program that some consider as a news source.

Really Simple Syndication, or RSS, feeds allow news aggregators to collect stories from sources on the World Wide Web.

Blogger software becomes available, and the blog emerges as a widespread source of information. As this type of writing became popular, bloggers began to advance news stories and participate in news production, prompting debates about bloggers and journalism.

2000   Talking Points Memo debuts, establishing itself as one of the first digital native political news organizations.

2001   After the terrorist attacks on September 11, news organizations share resources and television news reports without commercial interruption for several days. All forms of news media are relied on during this time.

2002   Google News launches. The service began by aggregating news reports from the web to present users with a selections of stories. Google News increased traffic to a number of news sites, shifting previously held ideas about news distribution.

Bloggers call attention to Senator Trent Lott's racial comments, amplifying a story the mainstream media initially did not cover. Bloggers are credited with keeping this news story alive.

2004 *The Colbert Report* debuts on Comedy Central, satirizing television political punditry. In his critique, Colbert coined the term "truthiness" to refer to ideas that feel true or that some believe should be true regardless of existing evidence or logic.

Digg begins as a social news site that invites people to vote for stories they like.

Bloggers demonstrate the power of their voices in the journalism sphere when they challenge the accuracy of a CBS news report about George W. Bush's service in the National Guard, prompting longtime anchor Dan Rather's resignation.

2005 YouTube begins. This social media video sharing site was purchased by Google in 2006.

2005 Apple allows for podcasts to be downloaded from iTunes, resulting in the form's increasing popularity.

The Huffington Post is launched. A key feature of the news aggregator site is a group blog where thousands of contributors post written pieces. Over the years, the site expanded its content, staff, and original reporting; developed international sites; and produced additional digital content. The controversial practice of not paying its blogging contributors is often referenced.

2006 Twitter, a microblogging site, begins. Twitter became a site for breaking news, a platform for multiple types of users, and a site of activism.

Facebook, the social networking site that began at Harvard in 2004, becomes available to anyone with an email address. It launches News Feed. Algorithmically driven, News Feed provides users with a running list of news stories.

2007 Apple's iPhone is released. Though access to the internet was previously available on some phones prior to this, the iPhone, and smartphones that followed, prompted journalists and citizens to gather, report on, and distribute news.

Breitbart News begins. The provocative organization established itself as one that counters perceived media bias that favors the left.

The power of crowdsourcing, when the public participates in an investigation and shares information, is demonstrated via an initiative started by Talking Points Memo and Talking Points Memo Muckraker. The crowdsourced investigation revealed a pattern of U.S. attorneys being fired.

2009 The *Rocky Mountain News*, a daily newspaper operating out of Colorado since 1859, closes. A *Columbia Journalism Review* piece documented how the news industry has been impacted by the digital revolution, citing cuts in local news reporting in particular. The report highlighted how news coverage of town and city public life, state news, national news, and international news is decreasing. Additional reports over the years documented the struggles of all sizes of newspapers and the emergence of news deserts across the country.

2010 The Arab Spring begins. Social media use by citizens in the Middle East and Northern Africa alerted the world of protests and government actions. News organizations relied on these Facebook posts, tweets, and YouTube videos in their reporting. This is an often-cited example of how social media allows for anyone to report on, advance awareness of, and call attention to events and issues.

2013 Amazon's founder Jeff Bezos purchases the *Washington Post*, investing in the struggling paper and contributing to its viable transformation. Many newspapers continue to struggle, however, as staff layoffs and paper consolidations persist.

2016 The U.S. Department of Labor notes that for the first time there are more jobs in internet publishing and broadcasting than there are at newspapers.

Although false news and unreliable information is not a new thing, digital technology has made it easy for anyone to generate and quickly spread misinformation and disinformation.

Discussions of "fake news" peaked when it became clear that "fake news" shared on social media sites was part of the 2016 presidential election campaign. Some of the false information was the result of a Russian disinformation campaign designed to influence the presidential election. False information is also spread by bots on social media.

2018   As discontent with the presence of misinformation, disinformation, and conspiracy theories on technology platforms' increases, Google, YouTube, and Facebook attempt to prevent the spread of this content via several initiatives. Concerns were raised that these companies have too much power over the spread of information.

Jordan Peele releases a video that demonstrates deepfake technology, attempting to raise awareness that this technology is developing quickly.

Verizon, the current owner of the Huffington Post, ends the practice of publishing unpaid contributing bloggers in order to better vet the information that appears on the site.

YouTube and Facebook continually remove problematic content from their platforms. Facebook and Twitter acknowledge and remove misinformation and disinformation seemingly connected to disrupting the nation's midterm elections.

2019   Numerous news organization layoffs and restructuring demonstrate the economic struggles the news industry continues to face. Innovative news partnerships and reporting approaches are explored by some news organizations as they try to determine the successful next stages in the evolution of the news industry.

Technology companies Facebook and Google engage in a variety of initiatives that are designed to support and prioritize quality journalism. Facebook faces ongoing criticism for its inability to thwart problematic uses of its platform and is under investigation for its use of private customer data.

This glossary provides a list of key terms commonly used in the context of discussing aspects of journalism and news media in the United States.

advocacy journalism   a style of journalism that, while relying on facts, advances a particular perspective that is transparently disclosed.

agenda setting function   a mass media theory that suggests when news media focus on particular topics, they "set the agenda" for what people and society are thinking about.

algorithm   A set of rules, or formula, developed to complete a task. Computer algorithms are used by social media companies to prioritize and filter information that is shown to individuals.

artificial intelligence (AI)   higher-level computer programs that have the ability to use machine learning to complete tasks that typically required the use of human abilities or "intelligence." These "smart" computer programs are developed to "think" like humans.

augmented reality   when a perspective or view, often seen through a smartphone or device, is altered by the overlay of additional images or other superimposed content.

blogs   online, content-driven posts that share information about a topic, often including links to other information on the web. Blogs usually present the most recent entry first.

botnet   a network of bots, often operated by a certain person or group.

bots   computer programs that can complete various tasks, including engaging on social media. The word "bot" is derived from "robot."

broadcasting   the transmission of content using radio waves or television signals.

broadcast network   when groups of radio or television stations are linked to share programming.

broadsides   an early form of news colonists in the New World used. News and notices were printed on single pieces of paper.

citizen journalism   a practice where citizens who are not professional journalists report and share news and information, often over the internet.

deepfakes/deepfake videos   fabricated media where artificial intelligence is used to achieve the look and sound of authenticity. Deepfakes utilize previously recorded audio and video of individuals in ways that generate new, false media texts.

digital native news   news or news organizations that only ever have been available online.

disinformation   false information, often created to disrupt or cause harm to others or organizations, that is deliberately spread by those knowing it is untrue.

echo chamber   in a news context, this term refers to a space where users engage with content that is primarily reflective of their own points of view, thus potentially reinforcing these held beliefs while limiting exposure to alternative perspectives.

editorial   an opinion piece about news content written by news editors, writers, or publishers of the news organization.

editorial content   in journalism, content that is independently produced by news reporters and editors, like articles and photographs, that is not advertising or commissioned by advertisers.

explanatory journalism   a type of journalism that explains the complexities of a particular subject or news story.

fake news   in general, this broad term refers to information that is not reliable, false, or problematic. However, many dismiss this term as problematic because the application of it is broadly and imprecisely used.

Federal Communications Commission (FCC)   the U.S. governmental agency that oversees and regulates radio, broadcast and cable television, satellite, and the internet.

filter bubble   in responding to online searches, filter bubbles present information to users that is reflective of their held points of view because internet search results are generated by algorithms informed by previous internet use.

gatekeeper   in traditional media, the person or persons who filter and select information that is distributed through media forms.

interpretive journalism   a style of journalism that situates factual reporting in context, providing information around how the facts or events are relevant.

inverted pyramid reporting or journalism   a style of journalism that features the most important, or essential, components of the story at the beginning of the report.

investigative journalism   a style of journalism relying on various research strategies to uncover societal problems, corruption, or abuses of power.

journalism   the process of gathering, presenting, and assessing news and information for an audience. The outcome of this process (e.g., the news article) is also called journalism.

legacy media   a term that refers to the news organizations who were dominant in the news industry before the rise of the internet.

literary journalism   once called "the new journalism" by Tom Wolfe, a style of journalism where elements of fictional storytelling, such as personal voice, scene description, and the use of conversation, are used in fact-based nonfiction reporting.

media consolidation   the term that refers to the increasing media holdings among a handful of large media companies; a structure where fewer media companies own increasingly more media outlets.

media convergence   when media content is merged over multiple platforms—for example, newspapers are available in print and online forms. Media convergence can also refer to cross-platform business models whereby one corporation owns and/or operates various media entities.

misinformation   information that is false but may be shared by those believing that it is true.

muckraking   a style of investigative journalism that peaked in the early 1900s. Muckraking journalists wrote well-researched stories about societal problems.

native advertising   paid-for content that is created to blend into the spaces where it appears.

net neutrality   the principle that the same internet speed is available to every website, regardless of who owns and runs the website.

network era   a period of time in television history, from the early 1950s until the mid-1980s, when the three television networks, CBS, NBC, and ABC, dominated television.

news   reports of topics, issues, or events via various media forms by journalists and others.

news agency   an organization that shares news reports with members.

news aggregator   a software program or web application that aggregates, or collects, online content and presents it in one place.

news desert   a local or regional area where access to comprehensive local news is limited.

news polarization   the term that refers to the practice of news consumers only engaging with news that reflects their self-interests and beliefs.

objectivity in journalism   an approach to news reporting where journalists attempt to adhere to standards of neutrality when reporting on events, topics, or issues.

oligopoly   an industry where only a few companies control the majority of the market. In the United States, only a few media companies control the majority of the industry, resulting in a structural media oligopoly.

op-ed   referring to "opposite the editorial" page, these commentary or opinion pieces are usually written by people not associated with a newspaper's editorial staff.

participatory culture   this term refers to the ability of the public to create and distribute content in the culture rather than just being consumers of culture.

penny press   newspapers sold on the street for a penny each. The invention of the cylinder press allowed for the mass printing of newspapers, prompting a shift in the way newspapers were sold.

propaganda   information that is distributed in an attempt to influence people's points of view, opinions, and/or actions.

public broadcasting   noncommercial radio and television alternatives to their commercial counterparts. Public broadcasters attempt to serve the public interest by providing content that informs or entertains without prioritizing profit making.

sock puppet   an online account that falsely suggests that it represents a person or organization. Sock puppets may be used to spread disinformation.

verify   to determine whether information is authentic. Verification of online information is an essential component of reporting in the digital age.

virtual reality   simulated environments generated by computer technology that are experienced through the use of such equipment as screen-fitted helmets.

yellow journalism   a term referring to sensational news reporting that was derived from a comic book character dressed in yellow that ran in newspapers featuring such reporting.

Note: Page numbers in *italics* refer to figures; page numbers in **bold** refer to tables.

analytics, 147, 150, 151
anchormen, 192–193
Android, 225
animation, 63
Annenberg Public Policy
    Center, 116
Apple, 68, 101–102, 341
    iPhone, 341
Applegate, Edd, 3
Arabs, Western news coverage
    of, 157–159
Arab Spring, 227, 342
Aral, Sinan, 110
artificial intelligence (AI), 69,
    110, 226
Asian American Twitter, 229
Aspen Institute, 211
Aspen Journalism, 117
Associated Press, 10, 14, 78,
    107, 334
AT&T, 68, 150
audiences
    ideologically diverse, 73
    shifts in, 44–48
augmented reality (AR), 48
automation, 108, 166

bad news bias, 83
Bagdikian, Ben, 37
Baier, Bret, 224
Baker, James, 218
Baker, Ray, 335
Baldwin, Alex, 200
Ball, James, 93
Bannon, Steve, 231–232
Barbara Walters Specials, 195

Barnum, P.T., 154
Beck, Glen, 31, 222
Bee, Samantha, 34, 169, 221
Begin, Menachem, 192, 195
Benet, Siobhan, 211
Bennett, James, 9
Bennett, W. Lance, 3
Bergstein, Brian, 117–118
Berlin Wall, 25
Bernstein, Carl, 18, 198, 338
Beyerstein, Lindsay, 115
Bezos, Jeff, 119, 342
Bharat, Krishna, 225
bias, 73, 80–84
Bickert, Monika, 272,
    273–274
Biden, Joseph, 95
big data, 100, 150
big media, 36, 38, 68
Bill of Rights, 7–8, 334
Black in America, 213
Black Twitter, 229
Blair, Jayson, 101
blogs and bloggers, 44–46,
    67, 84, 90, 144, 151,
    341, 343
    on Breitbart News,
    230–231
    Ezra Klein, 215–216
    and the Huffington Post,
    200–201
    live blogging, 46
    software for, 340
Bly, Nellie, 12
Borel, Brooke, 91
Boston Globe, 119

About the Author

Amy M. Damico, PhD, is a professor at the School of Communication and the faculty advisor to the Endicott Scholars Honors Program at Endicott College in Beverly, Massachusetts. She teaches a variety of classes in the areas of mass communication and media and cultural studies. Her previous books are *21st-Century TV Dramas: Exploring the New Golden Age* and *September 11 in Popular Culture: A Guide*, both collaborations with Sara Quay. She has also authored articles and essays in the subject areas of popular culture, media literacy, and teaching and learning.